GREATNESS AND DECLINE

McGill-Queen's Transatlantic Studies

Series editors: Alan Dobson, Robert Hendershot, and Steve Marsh

The McGill-Queen's Transatlantic Studies series, in partnership with the Transatlantic Studies Association, provides a focal point for scholarship examining and interrogating the rich cultural, political, social, and economic connections between nations, organizations, and networks that border the Atlantic Ocean. The series combines traditional disciplinary studies with innovative interdisciplinary work, stimulating debate about and engagement with a field of transatlantic studies broadly defined to capture a breadth and richness of scholarship. Books in the series focus on but are not limited to the twentieth and twenty-first centuries, normally falling within the subfields of history, economics, politics and international relations, literature, and cultural studies.

GREATNESS AND DECLINE

National Identity
and
British
Foreign Policy

SRDJAN VUCETIC

MCGILL-QUEEN'S UNIVERSITY PRESS

Montreal & Kingston | London | Chicago

© McGill-Queen's University Press 2021

ISBN 978-0-2280-0586-5 (cloth)
ISBN 978-0-2280-0587-2 (paper)
ISBN 978-0-2280-0639-8 (ePDF)
ISBN 978-0-2280-0640-4 (ePUB)

Legal deposit first quarter 2021
Bibliothèque nationale du Québec

Printed in Canada on acid-free paper that is 100% ancient forest free
(100% post-consumer recycled), processed chlorine free

This book has been published with the help of a grant from the Canadian
Federation for the Humanities and Social Sciences, through the Awards
to Scholarly Publications Program, using funds provided by the Social
Sciences and Humanities Research Council of Canada.

We acknowledge the support of the Canada Council for the Arts.

Nous remercions le Conseil des arts du Canada de son soutien.

Library and Archives Canada Cataloguing in Publication

Title: Greatness and decline : national identity and British foreign policy /
    Srdjan Vucetic.
Names: Vucetic, Srdjan, 1976- author.
Series: McGill-Queen's transatlantic studies ; 3.
Description: Series statement: McGill-Queen's transatlantic studies ; 3 |
    Includes bibliographical references and index.
Identifiers: Canadiana (print) 20200338560 | Canadiana (ebook)
    20200338749 | ISBN 9780228005865 (hardcover) | ISBN 9780228005872
    (softcover) | ISBN 9780228006398 (PDF) | ISBN 9780228006404 (EPUB)
Subjects: LCSH: Great Britain—Foreign relations. | LCSH: National char-
    acteristics, British. | LCSH: Nationalism—Great Britain.
Classification: LCC DA45 .V83 2021 | DDC 327.41—dc23

This book was designed and typeset by studio oneonone in 11/14 Minion.

Contents

Figures and Tables

Figures

Tables

Preface

Describing Britain as a diminishing actor on the international stage is a cliché. And, like most clichés, it captures an essential reality. Losing an empire, but seeking quasi-imperial roles – clinging hubristically first to sterling as a master currency then to a network of far-flung bases – outstripped the state's fiscal grasp, necessitating retrenchment. The role of "junior partner" to the United States slowed this process down, and postimperial Britain was able to wield disproportionate influence within successive iterations of the American-led order. But this arrangement came at a price, most notably in Europe, where it hobbled several opportunities for British governments to seize a leadership role. Brexit, in the same view, is a strategic blunder for the kingdom, especially now that the American order is fragmenting.

Blaming the British political establishment for Britain's maladjustments in the post-1945 world is also a cliché, one supported by no shortage of conventional academic wisdom. Foreign policy elites – whether in Westminster, Whitehall, the military, the city, or the media – have in fact persisted in affirming and boosting the notion that the kingdom must continue to project power globally, across a range of issues. However, this notion has always been delusional and deluding, a product of an obsession with greatness that belonged only to those disconnected, if not sequestered, from the rest of British society.

This book offers a different perspective. Instead of framing British foreign policy orientations exclusively in terms of elite beliefs, I situate them in everyday discourses of national identity circulating in society as a whole. I do so because I believe in the critical importance of the discursive and cultural contexts within which politics takes place. Indeed, when we divide "the British" into a ruling elite with agency and an apolitical mass public without it, we risk losing critical insight into how society shapes the range of possible foreign policies that decision makers consider, debate, and adapt.

Following this framework, I chronicle the evolution of British identity across colonial, Cold War, and post-Cold War contexts – that is, across a half a century of change from Clement Attlee's "New Jerusalem" to Tony Blair's "New Labour." I find some remarkable continuities. Playing a global power role was consistently one of the most important ways people understood what it meant to be British. In the baseline year for the study, 1950, being British meant being part of a political community that aspired to remain in the international top tier. Five decades later, after countless political, social, and cultural transformations at home and many sombre reassessments of Britain's place in the world, British society still routinely viewed British leadership – and by muscle, not just by example – as necessary for global order. I also observe that, in all years under study, everyday discourses of Britishness tended to normalize the need for an oversized military so that Britain could help the United States when the shooting started. British exceptionalism was similarly persistent, the outstanding case in point being the evergreen claim that "we" are not "just" another European country. A British voter could be for "Europe" or against it but only on the prior assumption that "it" was "over there."

The conventional wisdom therefore needs a corrective. Britain's tenaciously global foreign policy after 1945 was never simply a function of the nation's ruling class acting on the basis of elite obsessions or after some sort of bipartisan consensus. Rather, this policy developed from popular, everyday, and gradually evolving ideas about "us," "them," and "Others" generated within a broader British and, more specifically, English society. I demonstrate this empirically by analyzing debates revolving around two dozen British foreign and defence policy events, from Attlee's war in Korea to Blair's in Iraq.

Like most books, this one has several points of origin. I had already found allure in all things British when I was an early adolescent, probably by over-consuming BBC comedy on TV Sarajevo. By the time I got to university, first in Canada and then in the United States, I had developed an abiding interest in the British Empire and in how it had shaped the course of modern history across the globe. This led me to my first book, *The Anglosphere* (2011), in which I contend that a proper understanding of the origins of the contemporary international system requires closer attention to the influence of Anglo-Saxon supremacism on the so-called Anglo-American hegemonic transition and, subsequently, on the constitution of what we now call the Five Eyes community – Australia, Britain, Canada, New Zealand, and the United States. In *Greatness and Decline* I work with some of the same concepts I use in *The Anglosphere*, but this time I also take full advantage of Making Identity Count (MIC), a project to assemble the first constructivist database of national identities to be used in international relations and in social sciences and humanities more generally.

There are many to thank. My family, as always, was an immeasurable source of love and support. Melanie Mitchell and Kazim Rizvi provided superb research assistance. Kalathmika Natarajan helped me collect the sources used in chapter 2, while David Orr and Kristen M. Olver helped me code those used in chapters 4 and 5, respectively. Alyssa Maraj Grahame did most of the coding work in chapter 6, while also graciously furnishing a fine methodological commentary that served to crystallize parts of the introduction. For reading over the entire first draft, I owe special thanks to the two anonymous reviewers, Catherine Baker, Paul Beaumont, and Erin Seatter, who also helped me with meticulous editing and indexing. Karlo Basta, Oliver Daddow, James Gaskarth, and Bryan Mabee kindly gave their time and expertise as I tried to clarify my preliminary findings and ideas-in-progress. Meanwhile, presentations at the International Studies Association convention in Toronto and the British International Studies Association convention in London, plus those at my two beloved intellectual homes, the University of Ottawa and Ohio State (my PhD alma mater), all led to helpful scholarly exchanges. In particular, I thank Jarrod Hayes, Victoria Honeyman, Juliet Kaarbo, Robbie Shilliam, Jelena Subotić, James Strong, David McCourt, Jennifer Mitzen, Andrew Mycock, Dorothy Noyes, Eric Van Rythoven, and Ben Wellings.

Thanks also go to the good people of McGill-Queen's University
Press: the UK acquisitons editor Richard Baggaley, K. Joanne Richardson, Kathleen Fraser, other staff members who were involved in the production, the two anonymous reviewers, plus the series editors Alan
Dobson, Steve Marsh, and Robert Hendershot. Editors of many academic publications now expect all authors to fully engage with the work
of scholars based in the countries about which they are writing. Not an
issue here, though I feel I should offer an apology in advance, especially
to the historians: your knowledge production is so vast and rich that my
attempts to synthesize it for the purpose of evaluating international relations theories is bound to disappoint some of you.

Funding for some of the research for *Greatness and Decline* came from
the Social Sciences and Humanities Research Council of Canada, grant
number 435-2017-0004, and from Singapore's Ministry of Education
Research Fund Tier-1, grant number R -108-000-085-112. My fellow MIC
co-coordinators, Bentley Allan and Ted Hopf, gave me encouragement
from the very beginning. Ted continues to inspire us all. Without his
camaraderie, I would not have written this book.

GREATNESS AND DECLINE

Introduction

"At the very point of junction." "At the top table." "Punching above our weight." "Pivotal power." "Significant global power." "Global hub." "Global Britain." "Major global player." "Great global player." "True global player." These are some of the official and officious designations of British foreign policy in the post-Second World War period. Dreamed up by policy-makers and commentators of different eras, party politics, and ideologies to describe and proscribe the ambitions of the United Kingdom (UK) in the world, these phrases also index a long-standing policy "problem": *how* to pursue a robust global power policy in the face of relative decline, meaning the visible erosion of the state's international position.

But so elusive were the solutions that this became a problem to be managed, not solved, as in an oft-repeated saw: "In the 1950s we in Britain managed decline; in the 1960s we mismanaged decline; and in the 1970s we declined to manage" (Brown 2004). The problem persists into the twenty-first century. "We still struggle to adjust to our reality," declared the *Guardian* in a hard-hitting 25 January 2010 editorial: "The UK's World Role: Great Britain's Greatness Fixation," which argued that an exceptionalist desire to be "the leading nation, not just one of them," was bipartisan and thus hard to eradicate. "But this way hubris lies." The warning came at a time when the then Conservative-led government embarked on "austerity" – supposedly an effort to "prune" state spending in response to the global financial crisis of 2008, but in fact yet another iteration of "neoliberalization." Then, in the midst of this and many other destabilizing events and processes around the world, came "Brexit," the UK's much-bungled, and still ongoing, exit from the European Union (EU). A new round of sneers and taunts came in. "There are two kinds of European nations," said one continental politician in 2017: "There are small nations and there are countries that have not yet realized they are small nations." Brexit, said another, is "the real end of the British Empire."[1]

Although crude and rude, such statements contain an element of truth. Yes, the UK remains the fifth or sixth largest economy in the world, a top trading nation, a top cultural power, and a top military power – one fielding *both* nuclear weapons *and* a functional blue-water navy – with a permanent seat on the United Nations (UN) Security Council. Yet, rather than reasserting its "confident role" as a "global power," as per the Conservative "Brexiter" lexicon circa 2018,[2] the UK is *also* facing major constraints on economic growth, government borrowing, diplomatic influence, and national unity. The ongoing COVID-19 pandemic – disease caused by a novel coronavirus – exacerbates this predicament by orders of magnitude, not least because of the incompetent, even callous initial response of the government of Boris Johnson.

Britain's global power role fixation is a puzzle that has fascinated not only generations of scholars, historians above all (Darwin 2009, 13–17), but also political geographers (Taylor 2016 [1990], xi) and sociologists (Go 2011, 21–2). In this book, I approach it from the standpoint of international relations (IR) theory (McCourt 2014a, 3–6; see also Hill 2018; Freedman and Clarke 1991). I begin my theorizing with the basic constructivist notion that national identity informs and shapes the matrices of legitimate foreign policy. I then proceed to interpret a selection of events that are at the centre of both British policies and international politics in the post-Second World War period. Britain's bid to "be everywhere, do everything," I argue, was never simply a function of the ruling elite's obsessions; rather, it emerged from British and (mostly) English society as a whole and, more specifically, from the deep-rooted, routine, and (mostly) unreflective discourses through which "Britain" became a presence in the everyday lives of its citizens, elites and masses alike. To again put it rudely and crudely: whatever the circumstances of the kingdom's relative decline, "the British" configured themselves as a special edition of humankind. And therein lies a key reason that leaders advocating for foreign policy retrenchment could only question the *means* of global power projection, not global power projection as such.

The Third Superpower

In 1943, when American IR scholar William T.R. Fox coined the term "superpower" to describe states able to wield significant and exceptionally mobile military power independently from other states, he emphatically had the UK in mind as well. This, he later explained, was an error, albeit one that many of his peers committed that decade (Fox 1980, 417, 420).

This should not be all that surprising. Emerging victorious from the most widespread and deadliest conflict in history, Britain held to an empire so vast and so complex that John Darwin (1991) rightly calls it "a British system of world power." Even after India and four more Asian colonies gained independence between 1947 and 1948 – "an unavoidable and unique development that demanded compensation elsewhere" (Harrison 2009, 7–8) – the British Empire was still the world's largest and easily the preeminent power in Africa, the Middle East, the Mediterranean, and, thanks to the giant British Army of the Rhine, in Western Europe. Countless places in the Asia-Pacific and the Caribbean flew the Union Jack, too; some of them, like Kure in Japan, for the very first time (Perkins 2003).

Thanks to the multifaceted nature of imperial power, "decolonization" in fact enabled redeployment and redistribution of metropolitan influence – a phenomenon variously dubbed "neo-colonization," "empire by other means," "second colonial occupation," or "the Third British Empire."[3] As detailed by Sarah Stockwell (2018), for instance, assorted "development" programs provided thousands of British officials with well-paying jobs overseas well into the post-empire era.

Britain's high international status was recognized not only by the "old" and "new" Commonwealths – the old refers to the ex-colonies of white settlement where the British Crown and British power enjoyed most respect – but also by the other fifty or so states and empires, including, crucially, the two superpowers. An eloquent testimony to this fact is the Potsdam Conference of 1945, where UK prime ministers Winston Churchill and Clement Attlee sat at the "Big Three" table with Soviet leader Joseph Stalin and United States (US) president Harry Truman. The same goes for Soviet calls, in the winter of 1946–47, for an

Anglo-Soviet condominium that would divide Europe into two.[4] Others admired Britain precisely for rejecting such overtures.

Ample recognition also came in the international institutional context. British diplomats made an outsized contribution to the establishment of the Bretton Woods system and the United Nations. They would have also helped build the European Coal and Steel Community had the UK government chosen to join it like it joined the Brussels Pact and the Organization for European Economic Co-operation in 1948 or the Council of Europe and the North Atlantic Treaty Organization (NATO) in 1949 (Barker 1983, 112–20; Adamthwaite 1985; Blackwell 1993).

Next, the UK controlled almost a third of Western Europe's industrial output and almost a quarter of the world's manufacturing exports. British leadership in science and technology was even more formidable, as David Edgerton (2005, 2018b) has shown: just look at per-capita numbers of scientists, engineers, and Nobel prizes or at the UK's accomplishments in jet aviation – the world's first jet-liner, for example – or in nuclear research and development, including the swift progress to the first atomic bomb test in 1952.

Last but not least, the world's financial arrangements were mostly made in the city of London (Strange 1971; Schenk 2010; Cain and Hopkins 2016; Fichtner 2017; Green 2020). Related, nearly half of the world's trade was denominated in pound sterling, which, despite its problems, still counted as a credible "master currency" and therefore as a "prestige symbol of the first order" (Dobson 1995, 164; see also Shonfield 1958, 103–4). Put all these facts together, and you, too, might see the Britain of the late 1940s as one of the Big Three, a nation that was, "as never before, trying to act as a superpower" (Reynolds 2000, 2).

The key word, of course, is "trying," for that same Britain had larger debts than any other nation in history. Worse, this was only a symptom of a structural weakness that the war and the coming superpower era laid bare: "It was unlikely that a nation with only two per cent of the world's population could control over a fifth of its land surface, maintain half of its warships and account for 40 per cent of its trade in manufactured goods for very long" (Reynolds 2000, 33). Once the fabled hegemon of hegemons – in IR theory, hegemony refers to leadership of an international order – the British Empire was now inexorably contracting, however savvy the optics management of the Empire-to-Commonwealth transition at the time.

In materialist, objectivist IR, a great power is said to be in decline when it sheds capabilities, especially economic capabilities, relative to other great powers for at least five consecutive years. From this perspective, a "Brexit" from the top-tier league occurred sometime before the mid-1950s.[5] In contrast, above all, British "declinologists" tend to view decline as a relational and intersubjective reality – a set of interpretations and meanings that actors invent to make sense of the objective world.[6] Building on the latter ontology, I propose to trace Britain's decline and declinism via discourses of British identity, a.k.a. "Britishness" – structured practices of communication on how "we" understand "us," "them," and "Others." In a treasury memorandum penned for the new Labour government on 13 August 1945, John Maynard Keynes voiced his concerns about the risk of bankruptcy or, as he described it, "a financial Dunkirk." If this came to pass, Britain would have to come home right away: "Abroad it would require a sudden and humiliating withdrawal from our onerous responsibilities with great loss of prestige and an acceptance for the time being of the position of a second-class Power, rather like the present position of France" (Keynes 1945).

Fretting over "loss of prestige" vis-à-vis "them," the US and Soviet superpowers, and "Others," such as France, was indeed commonplace in Whitehall after the war. In the end, Her Majesty's Treasury managed to survive – in large part thanks to a steady influx of US dollars, including those associated with Marshall Plan aid. But so did the kingdom's claim to global power. In 1946–47, Foreign Secretary Ernest Bevin, the Foreign Office, and chiefs of staff famously defeated Attlee's proposals for reducing Britain's commitment-capability gaps (Bew 2016, 421–4). The prime minister was not arguing for a wholescale abandonment of the great power status that his Victorian and Edwardian predecessors had practised so well but, rather, for a withdrawal from the Middle East. Yet his opponents would have none of it, likening the proposed policy to "Munich," "the abdication of our position as a world power" (Darwin 2009, 536), and a transformation of Britain into "another Belgium" (Louis 2006, 23).

Hyperbolic comparisons with Belgium – "a country invented by the English to annoy the French," as an old jibe goes – were not new to identity discourses of Britain's ruling class even then. In 1908, then ex-viceroy of India Lord Curzon saw England sinking from the position of "the arbiter" to that of "a sort of glorified Belgium" (Danchev 1998, 164). What is puzzling is that this trope never went out of fashion – not after 1945, not after 1956, not after 1973, not after 1990, not after Brexit. "Not just another Belgium" was in fact akin to a strategy.

Just Another?!

Let us start with the so-called postwar, a.k.a. Bevinite, consensus.[7] Ernest Bevin certainly deserves to have his name immortalized in this way for he ensured that Labour stayed the course on foreign policy. "Russia is Socialist, we are partly Socialist, America may believe in private enter-prise. The great task of Great Britain is to weld these forces together to keep the peace," he declared at the 1946 Labour Party conference, pan-dering to the party's left wing (Schneer 1984, 204). The following year at the International Trade Organization negotiations in Geneva, he painted a similar picture for the American diplomats as well. Rather than "just another European country," Bevin argued, Britain was an imperial power that "could make a contribution to European recovery second only to that of the United States" (Hogan 1987, 46–9). None of this was cheap talk for behind these pronouncements there actually was a plan he called a "Third Force" – an all-but-Churchillian vision of Britain as the leader of a global bloc made up of the Empire and Western Europe, including France and its colonies.[8]

The Bevinite consensus had other country referents. A decade after the Attlee-Bevin debate, Chancellor of the Exchequer Harold Macmillan told a US diplomat that "Britain would become another Netherlands" if it failed to confront Egyptian president Gamal Abdel Nasser over the Suez Canal (quoted in McCourt 2014a, 70). Shortly afterwards he gave his first broadcast as prime minister:

> Every now and again since the war I have heard people say: "Isn't Britain only a second or third-class power now? Isn't it on the way out?" What nonsense! In my lifetime I have heard the same old tale

about our being a second rate power, and I have lived to see the answer ... Britain has been great, is great and will stay great, provided we close our ranks and get on with the job. (Quoted in Wallace 1970, 207–8)

"Getting on with the job" spectacularly backfired in this case, yet Macmillan kept countering any talk of decline – first in the context of his "Winds of Change" shift towards Africa, then even more strongly vis-à-vis the European Economic Community (eec), a.k.a. the Common Market: "Would entry confirm the image of Britain as merely another *European* state, no longer capable of playing a major role upon the larger stage of *world* politics?" (Sprout and Sprout 1963, 680, emphasis in original).

Similar questions abounded in many subsequent affairs, from Harold Wilson's devaluation of the pound and withdrawal from "East of Suez" – are we not "a sort of poor man's Sweden" now? (Mangold 2001, 120) – to the run-up to the Falklands War under Margaret Thatcher. Next came her famous Bruges Speech of 1988, in which she railed against "a European superstate," and after which some Eurosceptics began to refer to the eec as "Belgium."

Fast forward through the end of the Cold War to Tony Blair's back to East of Suez era and we see yet more continuity. In the same year that the aforementioned *Guardian* editorial declared that "our national interest should be to play our important role as a true, trusted and committed European partner on the world stage," Sir Malcolm Rifkind, the man who served as both foreign secretary and defence secretary in the 1990s, wrote this: "The question for the UK and its Conservative led Government is whether it wishes to retain a global approach, or resign itself to the lesser status. Is it still prepared to act like France, or is it content to have influence comparable with that of Spain?" (Rifkind 2010). The question was once again rhetorical: no party or faction advocated a reduction in foreign policy ambitions to "the level of a Spain" (Christopher Hill, quoted in Gaskarth 2013, 126). In fact, if we are to judge from the interwar musings of figures such as Oswald Mosley, the longevity of "Spain" is second only to "Belgium" (Rubin 2010, 345–7).

Scratch any number of imperial-era shifts in Britain's geostrategic position – 1938, 1922, 1914, even 1873 – and you will no doubt find plenty of evidence of Britain's leaders obsessing about their country's greatness. Conversely, review discourses UK prime ministers left behind and you will find but two prime ministers who came close to entertaining the idea of abandoning pretensions to global leadership: Edward Heath, a Tory prime minister from 1970 to 1974 best known for his working-class origins, idiosyncratic views, and declaring a record five states of emergency, and Harry Perkins, the fictional protagonist of *A Very British Coup*, a 1982 novel by Labour left politician Chris Mullin.[9]

The Brexit era follows the same trend. "The feeling that Britain is not just another country and can never be 'another Switzerland,'" explains a British foreign policy textbook published in 2017, is still a constant (Sanders and Houghton 2017, 7). In 2018, Lord Richards, former chief of defence staff, spoke about a risk of the UK becoming "militarily and strategically insignificant" (Lester 2018) – or, in the words of Conservative backbencher Tony Baldry uttered earlier, a "Belgium with nukes" (McCourt 2014b, 165). (Baldry coined the phrase in 2010 in reaction to the National Security Strategy and the Strategic Defence and Security Review, the twin cost-cutting exercise that prompted the reaction from Rifkind quoted above.) At the risk of exaggeration, but with an eye on the rhetoric of the cabinet of the current prime minister, Boris Johnson, I would venture so far as to say that "Belgium" might continue to constitutionalize the British sense of exceptionalism even in a fragmented UK – that is, in a hypothetical future situation in which Scottish independence (and/or Irish unification) radically transforms the polity's constitutional settlement (and its military power).

Select comparisons with France, a fellow European major power likewise bursting with exceptionalism, uncover further foreign policy puzzles. Much like their UK counterparts after the war, authorities in the Élysée and the Quai d'Orsay sought to manage a crumbling empire while pursuing world power – a fact aptly illustrated by the Anglo-French invasion of Suez, for instance. Yet "Western unity" and "Cold War neutrality" meant different things in London and Paris, respectively. A decade after Suez, for example, French president Charles de Gaulle moved to first denounce Bretton Woods and call for a "return to gold" and then detach French forces from NATO's integrated command. Why was this never an option in London? Simply put, British and French decision makers made different decisions when faced with similar structural pressures, whether in relation to debt, to decolonization, or to the US-Soviet face-off.[10]

Britain's zigzags vis-à-vis "Europe" are part of the same puzzle. As the British world-system all but disintegrated by the 1960s, entry into the Common Market became a new strategic goal – or rather, as most British leaders believed at the time, a new means for pursuing the old goal. This U-turn was never completed. Rather than championing or co-championing European federalism like their counterparts in Paris, UK governments remained committed to a "limited liability" policy, thus reinforcing a membership status that scholars have called "reluctant," "awkward," "aloof," "semi detached," and "on the sidelines" (for overviews, see Daddow 2004; Ellison 2007; and Smith 2017). Moreover, as Christopher Hill (2019, 28, 34–5) observes, UK officials and politicians routinely underestimated the Europeans, based on an erroneous belief that the UK could always either exploit Franco-German tensions or be warmly welcomed as a *tertium quid* of the European project.

Contrast all this with the "reverential" attitudes towards the Anglo-American (a.k.a. UK-US) "special relationship" – a term some have argued is an Orwellian euphemism for a plot designed to turn Britain into America's "unsinkable aircraft carrier."[11] Considering just how ruthlessly the US exploited the power asymmetry in this relationship, this view is not necessarily wrong. Recall, for example, that it was President Truman who, weeks after the Potsdam Conference, moved to terminate lend-lease aid, thus sparking the very first of the three major sterling crises that rocked the country before 1951. And yet, the special relationship carried on, with UK governments usually acting not as Greeks to America's Romans, as Macmillan famously wished it, but as "the warrior satellite" (Barnett 1972, 592): a spear-carrying Sidon to America's Carthage (Danchev 1998, 161).

Surely some UK politicians questioned these foreign policy parameters at some point? *Some* did. Far on the political right we have Enoch Powell, the man best known for white supremacist speechifying in the 1960s. As Camilla Schofield (2013) details, his other obsession at that time was what he called a "non-Commonwealth policy." Britain's overseas commitments, he wrote in the *Times* of 1 April 1964, "combine the maximum chance of involvement, embarrassment, expense, and humiliation, with the maximum effect" (quoted in Schofield 2013, 173).[12]

On the other side of the spectrum we have Labour left figures such as the long-forgotten Fenner Brockway, Konni Zilliacus, and C.A.R. Crosland, or the semi-forgotten early Robin Cook, the iconic Tony Benn, and Jeremy Corbyn, the party's Brexit-era leader. These politicians distinguished themselves as "mavericks" for many reasons, one of which was their willingness to imagine alternative foreign policy sensibilities for the country. In this, they occasionally found common ground with hardcore communists and members of the far-left Socialist Workers' Party, not to mention supporters of the New Left and the Campaign for Nuclear Disarmament. Yet even as they contemplated politics beyond the interests of the British state, neutrality, or pro-gender norms in foreign policy, most if not all of these "radical" leftists themselves struggled to imagine their country as just another Sweden. Instead, as Jodi Burkett (2013) has shown, they made claims of moral exceptionalism and exemplarity much as did liberals and conservatives.[13] One of the most striking statements of this sensibility was made in 1948 and comes from none other than Aneurin (Nye) Bevan, the human engine behind the National Health Service (NHS): "The eyes of the world are turning to Great Britain. We now have the moral leadership of the world, and before many years are over we shall have people coming here as to a modern Mecca, learning from us in the twentieth century as they learned from us in the seventeenth century.[14]" Bevan remained convinced of British greatness even after the Suez fiasco: "this county is a depository of probably more concentrated experience and skill then any other in the world" (Harrison 2009, 96, 543–4).

The fact there seem to be only a few, if any, ready examples of UK politicians accepting their country even as merely distinctive rather than as self-evidently unique and superior compels us to ponder the role of a ruling elite harbouring "delusions of grandeur" (Shonfield 1958, 97; see also, inter alia, Barnett 1972; Marcussen et al. 1999; Haseler 2007, 2012; O'Toole 2019). This hypothesis has gone through a number of memorable articulations over the years. In a book published right after the victory in the Falklands, Anthony Verrier (1983, 321) pathologized the kingdom's foreign policy orientation with reference to the Alice in Wonderland syndrome, a perceptual disorder of the size of the patient's own body or its position in space that one English psychiatrist identified in 1955. And, in 1998, Alex Danchev (1998, 164) revisited Curzon's 1908 prophecy thus: "Britain is Belgium, though the British do not know it yet."

Analyses that connect the nature and causes of the formal foreign policy action of post-1945 UK governments to delusional or illusory frames of references circulating in the Westminster, Whitehall, Fleet Street, and city corridors of power come in many forms. One could, for instance, accept that elite actors were to various degrees delusional, or at least illusion-prone, and then proceed to argue that they managed the country's relative decline relatively well, including in foreign policy, or perhaps especially in foreign policy.[15] One could also contend that the UK's illusion of power was only a second-order effect of assorted postwar and post-imperial adjustments made to meet the needs of finance and commerce – that is, of the owners of capital and property.[16]

Such nuanced approaches are vital but I think still incomplete. My argument here is that Britain's search for global leadership was always an expression not so much of bipartisan consensus, ruling-class interests, elite culture, or the "official mind" but of everyday self-understandings circulating in British society as a whole.[17] Most important among those was British, and specifically English, exceptionalism – the idea that "we" are not just another part of Europe but are different from, and superior to, it: a kingdom so great that it must look out to a wider world. For all the complexity, heterogeneity, and contestation of meanings that twentieth-century Britons attached to their nation, this sense of greatness remained ever-present, even if only tacitly – sort of the like prefix "Great" in "Great Britain." Greatness, in other words, was akin to a totem pole, the product of a vertically shared, deep-seated agreement between assorted elites and sub-elites, on the one hand, and the broader mass consumer public, on the other.

My aim in this book is simple. I want to provide a theoretically and methodologically grounded argument about the relationship between national identity and foreign policy against a backdrop of political, social, and cultural transformations in postwar, post-imperial British society and beyond. In so doing, I make an effort to build upon the insights of other scholars who have grappled with these themes and to redirect scholarly attention to an area I regard as fruitful for further research.

Do Anglo-Saxons Have All the Best Tunes?

Historically, IR scholars have tended to view states' foreign policies as a function of rational calculus based on objective self-interests. Some focused on the interests of national leaders powerful enough to bend the arch of history to their will. Others started with the interest of domestic and transnational groups and coalitions. Yet others foregrounded national interest as conditioned by systemic constraints and opportunities, such as the regional and international distributions of material power existing in objective reality. Beginning in the 1990s, however, the concept of self-interest has given considerable way to identity and nearby "constructivist concepts." The preface of *Losing an Empire, Finding a Role*, a British foreign policy textbook, indexes this change. In the first edition, published in 1990, David Sanders privileged "economic interests and realist balances of power"; in the second edition, published in 2017, Sanders teamed up with David Patrick Houghton to explain "complexity" and "new developments," including "new developments in IR theory": "The debate about EU membership which raged in 2016 in the run-up to the referendum illustrated the importance of national identity, domestic politics, and psychological perceptions of reality, not simply objective interests (however defined)."[18]

There is much to be said about the importance of each of these factors – variables, if you prefer – in the making and shaping of British foreign policy. In the same year that *Losing an Empire, Finding a Role* first appeared, William Wallace gave a speech at the Royal Institute of International Affairs, now better known as Chatham House, subsequently published in the institute's flagship journal, in which he, too, reflected on State Secretary Dean Acheson's famous quip. Wallace, then the institute's director of studies, agreed that Britain needed to define a new role for itself, particularly now that the Cold War was over, suggesting in the end that being "a link between Europe and the rest of the developed world" would do the trick. The problem, however, was that this new role was incommensurate with the prevailing "national identity" – that is, with "concepts of our position in the world, from which flow presuppositions about which other nations are our natural allies or enemies, which share our values and which do not." Regardless of the crisis du jour and whatever the party in power, Wallace observed, Britain's policy and political elite appeared to be divided between "Anglo-Saxon" and "European" identities and identifications, but with the former having "all the best tunes." Acting as a bridge between Europe and the rest of the (developed) world was a good idea, but it did not come naturally to the British, he argued, because of, among other things, "the myth of English exceptionalism – a free country confronting an unfree European continent."[19]

Wallace, who would later go on to become Liberal Democrat peer Lord Wallace of Saltaire, was certainly not the only elite voice calling for a reorientation towards a European identity in the 1990s (Gaskarth 2014, 52). More important, his original analysis and subsequent publications on the same theme appear to have stood the test of time. At the time of this writing, Anglo-Saxons are Brexite(e)rs who cheer the nation's departure from the EU as the beginning of the great new phase in British engagement with what Churchill called the open sea.[20] Europeans, then, encompass "Remoaners" ("Bremoaners"), who fret about an isolated and irresolute Britain, buffeted by geopolitical forces beyond its control.

More important, Wallace's article presages the rise of constructivist and interpretivist developments in IR theory.[21] Like, for example, Roxanne Lynn Doty's (1996b) analysis of the construction of British sovereignty after empire published a few years later, Wallace's analysis eschews a static view of "Britain." Both authors similarly approach Britishness as a compound identity, meaning one containing not only multiple subselves – that of the British-Irish state as a single unit plus those of its constituent regions, with their particular national contents and contestations in tow – but also empire (Doty 1996b, 130) and/or its transnational afterlife (Wallace 1991, 70). Finally, both authors advocate a discursive approach. We cannot understand the evolving relationship between Englishness and Britishness, Wallace (1991, 79n38) suggests, without paying close attention to "coded phrases [that] carry depths of conscious and unconscious meaning."[22]

"Unconscious meaning" brings us to Contemporary Cultural Studies and Everyday Nationalism, two large and interdisciplinary literatures spurred by critical interrogations of modern British society by, respectively, Stuart Hall and Michael Billig. There, analysis begins with concepts such as Antonio Gramsci's *senso comune*, Raymond Williams's "structure of feeling," and Pierre Bourdieu's *habitus* and *doxa* – all social-theoretic reminders of the simple fact that most people carry out their social lives by following the assemblage of truisms accepted within a particular society.[23] From these perspectives, "Britain" is not an aggregate of citizens who share common values or a common culture so much as a social and political construct that is performed, often unselfconsciously and unreflexively, through quotidian goings on.

For Hall (1981), who builds on Gramsci, hegemony is a system of rule that operates in and through the universalization and internalization of particular beliefs linked to particular social forces.[24] So, to understand nationalism, racism, or related hegemonies, we must regard elites and masses as co-producers of this system, without the former simply manipulating the latter and without people being aware of their nationalism or racism.[25] And national identity is constructed specifically through the stories that are told about "the nation" (Hall 1996b, 613).

Billig (1995) and other scholars of everyday nationalism are also focused on things people say, especially pronouns, demonstratives, locatives, possessive adjectives, adverbs, and tense, that point to the time, place, or situation in which a speaker is speaking. "*Our* confident role as a global power." "*This* empire *was* liberal." "*They* play by different rules."[26] Known as deixis in linguistics, these "small words" – Wallace's "coded phrases" – speak volumes about the banality of nationalism, which means that they are precisely the type of "coded phrases" that Wallace suggested contain key information about Britishness.

Consider Wallace's (1991, 78) view of the relationship between identity and foreign policy: "States cannot survive without a sense of identity, an image of what marks their government and their citizens from their neighbors, of what special contribution they have to make to civilization and international order. Foreign policy is partly a reflection of that search for identity." This evokes late 1980s poststructuralist IR: state identity is not a "thing" and not simply "there" but, rather, constantly evolving or "becoming," including in and through foreign policy. We also see parallels with ontological security theory (OST), which is of more recent vintage in IR.[27] Why seek Brexit at all costs? Why gamble with a referendum on EU membership in the first place, even after securing so many "opt-outs" on key parts of EU legislation? Why commit to a four-boat Trident missile fleet and/or to continuous at-sea deterrence? Why invest in *two* aircraft "super-carriers," while the Royal Navy has but seventy-five commissioned ships left in total and also while training across all three branches of the armed forces is being mercilessly cut? Why tolerate such a one-sided partnership with the US – including with respect to the technology and facilities that enable the operational capabilities of not only Trident but also your biggest ships and finest aircraft? Or, looking back to the twentieth century, why fight tooth and nail to protect sterling as the master currency and the antiquated system of imperial preference? Why support decolonization and then keep troops deployed east of Suez, halfway around the world from the home base? In purely materialist, objectivist terms, all of these policies – policies that Labour and Conservative parties largely shared or still share – might appear exceedingly costly and even illogical. Not so from the perspective of ontological security, or confidence in knowing who you are when going on in the world. Analyzing why the retrenchment from Asia took so long, Phillip Darby, writing in 1973, made a pointed observation: "the protection of India was part of an ingrained pattern of thought. It was above politics" (quoted in Self 2010, 166; see also Rees 2001, 38). If state survival is a function of predictability and order in an otherwise unpredictable world, then we should not be surprised to see the UK craving routines and relationships that feed its appetite for self-importance even to the point of compromising its own material, physical security.

Significant complementarities exist with Ted Hopf's (2002; Hopf 2013) "societal constructivism" as well. Foreign policy decision makers, Hopf argues, draw on national identity categories – classifications attached to the nation and members of the nation – to construct meanings, constitute action, coordinate their activities, and make claims in political life.

While such practices are strategic, positional, fragmented, and deeply contextual, they also tend to be situated in particular discursive formations, or discourses, through which people articulate their experience of living in, and belonging to, nations. Written, spoken, or "simply" performed, discourses are shot through with power: Some are hegemonic or dominant, others subaltern or marginalized. To illustrate with Wallace's stylization, in 1990 the "Anglo-Saxon" discourse appeared to be deeply embedded in the media and education, whereas the "European" discourse circulated mainly among the elite. It follows that discourse analysis of Britishness at the level of society could go a long way in helping us outline the temporal, spatial, and ethical parameters within which British state action occurs (Hansen 2006, 40–5; see also Gaskarth 2011; 2013, chap. 4; Berenskoetter 2014, 264–6). Those working in the tradition of the "traditions and dilemmas" approach of Bevir and Rhodes (2003) would almost certainly agree (Daddow 2015, 73; see also Hall 2012; Bevir and Daddow 2015; Bevir, Daddow, and Hall 2013; Bevir, Daddow, and Schnapper 2015).

An extensive literature has indeed emerged since the publication of Wallace's article that can help us examine the role national identity plays in shaping foreign policy choices. The wager I make building on this literature is that *discursive fit* can help us grasp the political dynamic between national identity contestation on the one hand and foreign policy on the other. Also known as resonance, match, or congruence, the concept of discursive fit is associated with multiple disciplinary and social-theoretic traditions (inter alia, see Vucetic 2011b, 12–13; Vucetic 2016b, 210–12; Holland 2013, 53–5; 2020, 69–73; Bevir and Daddow 2015, 279; Daddow 2015b, 76; Colley 2019, 2). In social psychology-inspired theories of identity management, for example, ruling elites succeed in reframing national identities as a way of achieving a more positive social evaluation only if their cues fit with the prevailing attitudes, opinion, and feelings of the public (Ward 2019). Likewise, in securitization theory, the framing of issues or events as security or existential threats depends, in part, on the willingness and ability of the target audience to accept the claim that its reality has changed such that extraordinary or emergency measures may be implemented (Croft 2012). And virtually all neo-Gramscians approaches would say that hegemony, although plural, complex, and fluid, is ultimately bounded by some sort of goodness of fit between the material structure and the predominant mental superstructure (Hall 1996a).

British foreign policy scholars have thought about discursive fit or similar concepts before. For example, writing with Christopher Tugendhat in 1988, Wallace draws our attention to "domestic acceptability," which they define as a constraint on British foreign policy-makers (Tugendhat and Wallace 1988, 101). Writing ten years later, Beatrice Heuser (1998, 5) argues that the emphasis on "independence" and "alliance solidarity" in British nuclear deterrence strategy persisted because it resonated with prevailing "collective mentalities" – and with more generally held British beliefs, images, allusions, and commonly held points of reference.

Identity-based explanations of British foreign policy rely more explicitly on discursive fit than do other explanations. In Amelia Hadfield-Amkhan's (2010, 204) nominally neoclassical realist account, national identity appears as "a political and cultural mechanism that obtains in foreign policy at moments of crisis."[28] The reason the pound-versus-euro debate of 2003, to use one of her case studies, was never much of a debate, she contends, had to do with the utter misfit between the new monetary structure and the prevailing national identity in Britain at the time – namely, a self-referential, particularist, and conservative "ethos of Englishness" (185; on the essential Englishness of British foreign policy identity, see also Doty 1996b).

The same argument might be extended to "England's Brexit" (Barnett 2017, chap. 10) – that is, to the failure of the pro-EU stance of the UK's official and unofficial mind to prevail over what many scholars argue were deeply rooted, and primarily English, objections to "loss of sovereignty."[29] Accordingly, *one* good reason Remain lost the 2016 referendum and the general election of 2019 lies in the pervasiveness of the belief in the idea of British exceptionalism among voters concentrated in "England without London" and parts of English-speaking Wales.

Questions of Britishness, as Oliver Daddow and James Gaskarth remind us, have *always* kept UK leaders awake at night: "does the course of action fit in with Britain's view of itself and how it wishes to be seen by other actors in world politics? Would the British people support and identify with the policy? Which communities that Britain belongs to are

affected by the issue at hand?" (Daddow and Gaskarth 2011, 17; see also
Bevir and Daddow 2015, 274–5; Gaskarth 2013, 61). The authors' own interpretations of foreign policy-making under New Labour demonstrate
this empirically (Gaskarth 2011; Daddow 2011), as do, for example, Jack
Holland's (2013) analysis of Blair's rhetoric and the "War on Terror," and
Nick Whittaker's (2017) examination of the "island race" trope in the context of the UK's struggles with globalization and with Brussels.

Role-theoretic approaches to British foreign policy recognize the importance of this dynamic as well. They do so through a number of analytical links: role conceptions or (discursive) self-understandings
regarding the state's international role and purpose; role performances,
or enactments of roles through policy choices and outputs; and role
orientations, which are foreign policy strategies that take into account
one's material and social constraints. Observing British foreign policy
debates circa 2010, Gaskarth (2014, 48) distills six such orientations: "iso-
late, regional partner, influential (rule of law state), thought leader, op-
portunist interventionist and great power." These, he argues, are bounded
by social expectations such that "governments that deviate from script
can face punishment or the very least confusion from domestic audiences
or other international actors." So, if the UK can no longer fight major
wars alone, or even make division-sized contributions to deployments
with allies, then a great power role orientation will only create inconsis-
tency and confusion at the level of British identity discourses.[30] The mutual constitution of identity and roles seems to be important even for
David McCourt (2014a), who argues that the key to understanding post-
1945 British foreign policy is not British identity but, rather, context-
dependent expectations that emerge from the international process of
"role-taking," "role-making," and "alter-casting." His key finding is that
the US and France continually cast Britain in a "residual great power"
role. But apparently so do the British people themselves: McCourt *also*
finds British leaders "framing their behavior in certain ways to make it
fit" with prevailing ideas "at home" – in the House of Commons, with the
media, and with public opinion.[31]

Building on the above, we might say that *any* theoretical framework
that purports to trace how political authority in British foreign policy is
"legitimized," "narrated," "framed," or "performed" requires an account

of discursive fit. The problem is that *most* theorists focus only on the manoeuvres political elites use to dominate meaning-making and to control debate. This I find reductionist. Here is a much-quoted paragraph from Sir Oliver Franks's Reith Lecture 1, broadcast on BBC Radio on 7 November 1954:

> The action of a Great Power can decisively affect the fate of other Great Powers in the world. It is in this sense that we assume that our future will be of one piece with our past and that we shall continue as a Great Power. What is noteworthy is the way that we take this for granted. It is not a belief arrived at after reflection by a conscious decision. It is part of the habit and furniture of our minds: a principle so much one with our outlook and character that it determines the way we act without emerging itself into clear consciousness. (Franks 1954)

Franks's six-part Reith Lectures series offers a superb glimpse into the postwar official mind, partly because the lecturer carried them with all the gravitas one might expect of a diplomat who had helped to negotiate both the Marshall Plan and the North Atlantic Treaty.[32] It is also a startlingly accurate prediction of the future. Even after empire, he declared, the kingdom would stay the course.[33] But in the above passage we see that Franks lectured as a sociologist, too. Great power pursuits are a matter of habit, a belief so routinized and solidified that most people never even stop to think whether the label still makes sense. This is a conceptualization of discursive fit with a twist, one in which mass culture and "high" politics work together to generate Britain's mental furniture.

Following this model, elite agency is deeply constrained by what is intelligible and accepted in civil society at the level of "who is who," that is, in the everyday discourses of who "we" are and who "they" and "Others" are, or were, or aspire to be. Accordingly, a foreign policy (framing, narrative, performance) will make sense if it (continuously) resonates with the quotidian habits of the nation's elites and masses (Gaskarth 2013, 92; see also Hopf 2010). Attlee's decision to quit India in 1947, Macmillan's push for EEC membership in 1961, Wilson's "creative incompetence" during Turkey's invasion of Cyprus in 1974, or Thatcher's welcome of Zimbabwe's independence in 1980 – a few examples of unconventional, far-sighted British foreign policy action – were all contentious but not absurd. Conversely, a foreign policy performance characterized by a complete discursive misfit lacks intelligibility, while one that fits only a marginal discourse lacks acceptability. Either way, that policy performance lacks legitimacy and likely cannot go on for long – think of that moment during the Suez Crisis when the government in London found itself near-isolated internationally (unacceptable), or, for that matter, a counterfactual situation in which a post-1945 government decided to pay reparations to former colonies (unintelligible).

Reconstructing the habit and furniture of British minds is a worthy goal because it can help us make and evaluate non-circular claims about why some foreign policy frames and narratives – and so some foreign policy decisions and strategic choices – resonated and were supported, while others struck a false note and were rejected. Interpretivists would always say that "Suez" did not speak for itself, and neither did Britain, certainly not with a single voice. Instead, various political actors – primarily but not exclusively those at the apex of the Westminster-Whitehall system – fought hard to frame the crisis in some ways but not in others. But what a good interpretivist account of the crisis *also* needs, I argue, is an independent account of what then British society instinctively knew and felt about "us," "them," and "Others."

Discursive fit can be, and often is, conceptualized as a causal mechanism. That said, fit between foreign policy on the one hand and prevailing discourse or discourses on the other does not, and cannot, imply a perfectly linear one-to-one match between a particular construction of national identity and a particular foreign policy (Gaskarth 2014, 47). Instead, discursive fit means that dominant discourses construct truths and realities within which policy is made and unmade. This is precisely why many if not most constructivists draw a distinction between *why* and *how* (or *how-possible*) questions. To go back to Doty (1996a, 4) again, *why* questions put aside identity, while *how* questions problematize it. As in: Why did the government replace the UK nuclear deterrent with another US-made, US-controlled system? Versus: How did the act of throwing the country's strategic lot with Washington become normal and legitimate? The latter question is far more focused on productive power – that is, on the production of particular subjects, objects, and interpretive sensibilities upon which the (nuclear) special relationship rests (Croft 2001b).[34]

All this being said, basic factual questions are still important, especially for an account that sets out to cover colonial, Cold War, and post-Cold War contexts – namely, the period from 1950 to 2000. Although no professional historian –cultural, diplomatic, or otherwise – would recognize this book as history, I do borrow historical methods, scale, and sensibility (on historical IR, see Little 2008; Lawson 2012; Leira and de Carvalho 2016; on discursive construction of temporal identity, see Hansen 2006). Consider the following questions taken from the conventional historiography of decolonization, as articulated by Wendy Webster (2003, 3): "What was the impact on narratives of Britishness and Englishness of a diminution of British territories and a contraction of its frontiers? How were the legacies of empire portrayed? Were habits of mind associated with colonialism dismantled as rapidly or as extensively as British colonial rule, or did they outlast the end of empire?" We could add a few more: To what extent did Suez or the endless crises of the 1970s affect the identity repertoires through which British society brought itself to life? Did the government push into the Common Market follow significant transformations in dominant structures of feelings at either elite or mass levels? Was the Thatcherite "New Right" successful in redefining the national *senso comune*, as Hall famously predicted it would in January 1979, four months before Thatcher came to power? Did the new 1988 National Curriculum for England, Wales, and Northern Ireland in any way disrupt the dominant "Anglo-Saxon" discourse, as Wallace hoped it would? Did shifts in the gendered and racialized reproduction of the British state and society correlate with any discernible change in Britain's foreign policy ambitions?

Engagement with these and similar questions is necessary in my account for two reasons. The first is essentially Gramscian: if, as the Italian philosopher argued, powerful elite-run institutions, such as political parties and mass media, reproduce a national common sense that is shared by the elites *and* masses, it is likely that the identity of a country will remain stable for some time. But if agreement on central categories is thin and highly contested, such that said "vertical" consistency is

missing, national identity is likely to remain fluid, with discourses changing in accordance with historical action.[35] Either way, a broader and
deeper account of Britishness is a precondition for understanding, not
only in terms of continuity and change but also in terms of policy alternatives that never came within the reach of actual policy.

The second reason relates to what IR scholars variously call "recursi-
vity" and "looping effects" (Jepperson, Wendt, and Katzenstein 1996, 62;
Whittaker 2017, 10; Doty 1996b; Mattern 2005). The basic notion here is
that national identity simultaneously influences and is influenced by
state policy action, and that both processes have continuous and over-
lapping relations with the structure of the international system. Analyses
of foreign policy conducted from the perspective of "tradition and dilemmas" put these dynamics at the forefront, too: to what extent to traditions evolve upon the resolutions of dilemmas? (Bevir and Daddow 2015,
275, 283; Bevir, Daddow and Schnapper 2015, 8). Therefore, in addition
to examining how discourses of Britishness influenced the shape of British foreign policy performances in certain historical contexts, I also pay
due attention to how British foreign policy performances wrote British
identity. This brings into play counterfactual reasoning – that is, reflection on how the British decision makers would have responded to key
watersheds had identity topographies been different at the time or had
they evolved differently.

To sum up: I consider British foreign policy as a dynamic, three-way
interaction between decisions makers themselves, discourses of British
identity into which decision makers are socialized and within (or against)
which foreign policy is made, and broader processes – generational, cultural, and international – that confront decision makers with different
challenges within this nexus. Now I turn to the methodology I use to
evaluate this framework.

Finding Britishness

All too often in the social sciences, national identity is approached via
positivist methods. Scholars come up with a list of national identities
they expect to find in a community and then they proceed to look for

them via public opinion surveys, for example. The interpretivist goal, in contrast, is to allow the subjects to speak for themselves as opposed to having the analyst speak for them. We see this sensibility at work in a number of recent studies of British political culture and citizen understandings of politics. Nick Clarke, Will Jennings, Jonathan Moss, and Gerry Stoker (2018) mix textual data from Mass-Observation studies – that unique archive of British everyday life – with a quantitative analysis of responses to public opinion surveys to examine repertoires of cultural resources that defined British "anti-politics" in the postwar period. Matthew Jones (2018) looks at what Mass-Observation reports said about the nation's wars in the Falklands, the Gulf, Kosovo, Afghanistan, and Iraq. Thomas Colley (2019) relies on interviews to examine how ordinary British citizens narrate stories of Britain's role in war and Britain's identity more generally.

I reconstruct the content, contestation, and evolution of post-1945 Britishness using inductive discourse-analytic research that my collaborators and I conducted under the auspices of Making Identity Count (MIC), a project to assemble the first constructivist database of national identities for use in IR and in social sciences and humanities more generally.[36] The analysis is based on an archive of textual artefacts sampled in six ten-year intervals: 1950, 1960, 1970, 1980, 1990, and 2000. The texts are drawn from an assortment of everyday experiences and institutional centres in the UK, with one eye on different forms, modes, and media of elite versus mass communication. Leadership speeches; newspaper editorials, op-eds, and columns; and secondary school history textbooks were taken to be sources of elite discourse, in contrast to more mass-oriented letters to the editor to said newspapers, novels, and commercial feature films. Table I.1 is a summary of the documents used, with further details in Appendix A.[37]

My sampling strategy raises a number of questions. To begin with, the elite-mass distinction is, sociologically speaking, loose. This is by design. Rather than differentiating between policy and cultural elites, or between elites and sub-elites, or between different types of masses, I simply collected texts that can be credibly described as much talked about, highest circulating, must-read, bestselling, or most watched, the theoretical principle being that elite and mass publics are "co-authoring" the national

Table I.1 Finding Britishness, 1950–2000

Year	Speeches	Newspapers	Textbooks	Films	Novels
1950 (Lab)	Attlee. King's Speech, 1.3.	Daily Express	Carter & Mears. History of Britain	The Blue Lamp	Christie. A Murder Is Announced
	Attlee. Margate, 3.10.				Shute. A Town Like Alice
1960 (Cons)	Macmillan. Scarborough, 15.10.	Daily Mirror	Rayner. Short History of Britain	What the Butler Saw	Fleming. Dr No
		Daily Express	Barker & Ollard. General History of England	Doctor in Love	
1970 (both)	Macmillan. Queen's Speech, 1.11.	Daily Mirror	Strong. History of Britain and the World	Sink the Bismarck!	Christie. 4.50 from Paddington
	Wilson. HC Deb on Address 2.6	Daily Express	Titley. Machines, Money and Men	On Her Majesty's Secret Service	Christie. Endless Night
1980 (Cons)	Heath. HC Deb on Add. 2.6.	Daily Mirror	Larkin. English History	Battle of Britain	MacLean. Force 10 from Navarone
	Thatcher. Brighton. 10.10.	Daily Express	Hill. British Economic and Social History 1700–1975	Life of Brian	Forsyth. The Devil's Alternative
1990 (Cons)	Queen's Speech. 7.11.	Daily Mirror	Sked & Cook. Post-War Britain	McVicar	Smith. Wild Justice
	Queen's Speech. 7.11.	The Sun	Kavanagh & Morris. Consensus Politics	Shirley Valentine	Forsyth. The Negotiator
	Major. "First Speech," 4.12.	Daily Mirror	Connolly & Barry. Britain 1900–1939 & May. Economic and Social History	The Krays	Smith. A Time to Die
2000 (Lab)	Blair. Brighton. 26.9.	The Sun	Walsh. Modern World History.	Chicken Run	Rowling, Harry Potter and the Goblet of Fire
	Blair. "Britain speech," 28. 3.	Daily Mail	Culpin & Turner. Making Modern Britain	Gladiator	Rowling, Harry Potter and the Philosopher's Stone

Notes: Coding was done from June 2015 to December 2017. For more on source selections, including complete bibliography, see Appendix A. For complete reports, detailed coding guidelines and coding examples, and other supplementary files, go to the project website https://www.makingidentitycount.org The reports for 1980, 1990, and 2000 are co-authorships with, respectively, David Orr, Kristen M. Olver and Alyssa Maraj Grahame. Kazim Rizvi, Melanie Mitchell and Kalathmika Natarajan provided invaluable research assistance in identifying and collecting historical materials.

identities contained therein. The former's political domination over the latter – even as "mere" consumers of texts – is thus an empirical question.

Next, the term "British" was invested with modern meaning through imperial projects dreamed up in England – from the seventeenth-century colonization of Ireland to the 1707 Act of Union between England and Scotland and its subsequent westward enlargement into Ireland in 1800. Always centred on London, this union of unions was furthermore con-stitutionalized as a multinational, polyglot, and hegemonic empire whose patterns of historical development bear a resemblance to similar polities elsewhere.[38] The Britain I analyze in this book, however, refers to its post-1945 iteration – what Edgerton (2018b) calls "national UK."[39] This is in line with Gaskarth's textbook definition of Britishness: an overarching national identity shared by *many* members of the UK's sub-state nation-alities within the UK as a polity (Gaskarth 2013, 197–8n1; cf. Schnapper 2011, 3–4; more generally, Gilroy 2004; Ward 2004).

One advantage of this definition is that it is sufficiently sensitive to the variability of both "British citizenship" and "national UK" in the period under study.[40] Indeed, the focus on national identity categories must not preclude paying due attention to how non-national categories become articulated within a British "we." That being said, the reader will rightly inquire about the *Manchester Evening News* and *Liverpool Echo* or, in nod to a proper "four nations" approach, the Swansea-based *South Wales Evening Post* and Scottish history textbooks. Why produce another study that treats the English as *the* British nation rather than as *a* British nation (Gamble 2003, 3)? An equally strong case can be made for a less print-centric archive, not least because radio and, from 1970 onwards, television were at least as popular as movies.[41] So, where are documentaries, soap operas, sitcoms, the FA football cup finals, and cooking shows? And why not sample mass discourse from Mass-Observation, too?

My defence here rests on both principled and pragmatic reasons: prin-cipled, because my analysis deliberately privileges England and, more specifically, London as the dominant site for the discursive production of national UK; pragmatic, because an inductive recovery of a repertoire of ideas from which the postwar elites and masses drew to identify them-selves as British is time-consuming even for a single year, much less for six. Doubtless, adding the *Liverpool Echo*, the BBC's *To the Manor Born*

and *That Sinking Feeling*, and Bill Forsyth's Glaswegian comedy film
would have enriched and diversified the corpus of texts for 1980. But it
would also have required hundreds of more coding hours. (The multi-
modal nature of discursive meanings contained in film and television
suggests that a single scene might contain *dozens* of relevant references.)[42]
As for ordinary people-authored texts from Mass-Observation, no such
material exists for this particular year – the project was discontinued in
the mid-1960s and was revived only in 1981. So, while I would agree that
the historical documents I use are far from optimal, I would also say that
optimal sources do not exist for the issues explored in this book.

The reader will note that my analysis heavily intersects with some
social identities, specifically those of privileged white men of a certain
age and class. Among the leaders whose speeches are examined here, for
instance, all but one were white men and all but one were Oxford-
educated. The rest of the corpus is thankfully less Oxonian, yet there,
too, the overrepresentation of white men is nearly as overwhelming with
regard to both authors and characters.[43] But locating the discursive imagination and articulation of a nationalist UK in its white "malestream"
is not necessarily a methodological shortcoming since it gives me an opportunity to apply and evaluate select ideas drawn from feminist and
postcolonial scholarship. From the bomb to assorted invasions and re-
invasions, postwar British foreign policy produced and reproduced gendered hierarchies not only "abroad," as between the West and non-West,
but also "at home," as when some leaders feminize and emasculate their
opponents by calling them weak, risk-averse, or backward (McClintock
1995; Doty 1996a, chap. 5; Doty 1996b; Webster 2005; Basham 2018).

Figure I.1 is a step-by-step visualization of the analytical process. The
aforementioned sampling strategy is shown as step 1. In step 2, dubbed
finding identities, my collaborators and I began with an *effort* to put
aside any prefabricated ideas about what Britain meant or what it meant
to be British.[44] We then used three basic inductive coding rules to code
every reference to "we" and "us" that appeared in the actual texts: *valence*
– that is, positive, negative, neutral, or ambiguous; *aspirational/aversive*
– that is, whether or not the identity is one that the Self aspires to or is
trying to avoid; and *significant Other*, which refers to any broadly na-

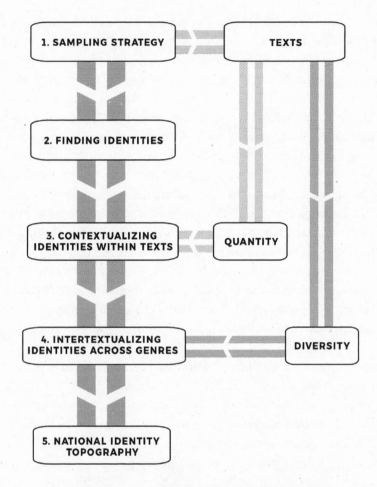

Figure I.1 Discourse analysis: From texts to topography

tional categories to which the Self compares itself in time and space (i.e., not just other countries but also historical events, such as the Second World War or the Scottish Enlightenment, or ideologies, such as liberalism or communism). The method forced us to differentiate mere themes ("leisure is good") from actual national identity categories ("the English like good leisure") as well as to examine local particulars and contingent meanings that might otherwise be lost when analysis accepts either platitudes ("the British are militaristic") or statements drawn from the media or public opinion research ("young Britons rank Spain as a top vacation destination").

By way of illustration, here is my coding of "No Trumpets," an editorial published in the *Daily Express* on 15 September 1960:

> Where are the drums? Where are the trumpets? They do not sound for today's preliminary session of the Commonwealth economic conference.

> The sad truth is that nothing of importance is likely to come out of this conference. It may be that Empire lands like New Zealand, already worried about its tariff preferences, will learn that the British Government means to reduce those preferences still more.

> The Government is more concerned with getting into the same trading system as Dr. Adenauer than with developing the Empire trading system.

> Who supposes that Dr Adenauer would give a fig for Europe if he had an empire?

In this text I observed four discrete identity categories: imperial, Germany, Europe, and trading. I coded *imperial* as positive, with a note about the empire-Commonwealth interchange in which New Zealand appears to be subsumed under the British Self. *Germany* and *Europe* were both significant Others. The former, epitomized in the figure of its chancellor, was negatively evaluated because of its ambition (regional domination) and inferiority (no empire). The latter was merely neutral. Finally, though Britain was a *trading* nation, its aspiration was not free trade so much as "the Empire trading system."

Subjecting the entire 1960 corpus to the same procedure, I distilled numerous other identity categories from what the texts said about who or what is excluded , and where the boundaries between "us" and "them" were in those days versus where they were before and where they might be in the future. Inspired by Gramsci's theory of common sense, I likewise looked at the meanings of "the good life" – what was a desirable way of life in 1960, a just and normal way of ordering British society, its politics, economics, culture, spirituality, and so on. While reading and coding, I also ran a tally of raw identity category counts and their prevailing valence, first within texts and genres, and then across all five genres. This yielded a long list of identity categories – 155 in this case – arranged by salience, from most frequent to least. The top categories – the top 25 per cent of all identity categories coded and counted for 1960 – were the ones I discussed in detail, with ample examples provided. The category "patriarchal" topped this list, followed by "class-based," "statist," "modern," "just," "technological," "anti-Soviet," and so on.

In figure I.1, these two steps stand as "contextualization" (step 3) and "intertextualization" (step 4). The purpose of this method is to balance the interpretivist commitment to an inductive recovery of British identities in their local, historically constituted contexts with a method that is more systematic, transparent, and replicable than is usually the case with more traditional interpretivist measures of importance and prevalence of intersubjective meanings.[45] Looking at the findings from across all six years at once, I could thus identify postwar Britain's most significant Others as well as a dozen cross-cutting and reoccurring identity categories (categories in brackets refer to their intersubjective near-synonyms) across political, cultural, economic, and social dimensions. These include statist, modern, class-based (unequal), democratic, patriarchal (manly), orderly (civilized), capitalist, partisan, influential, declining, just (fair), and benevolent. I could likewise observe identities that were specific to one or more years under study: post-imperial (from 1960), educated (to 1970), diverse (2000 only), and so on.[46]

The final step in the analytical process, step 5, involved a reconstruction of a British identity topography, or a map, for each year under study. This step was the most theoretical in the sense that I clustered coded identity categories into prevailing (hegemonic, dominant) and alternative (counter-hegemonic, subaltern) "discourses of Britishness" according to the observed main discursive patterns: elite-mass unity versus elite-mass division, most significant Others, and different identifications alongside political, economic, social, and cultural dimensions of what

Britain or British meant in a given year. For 1960, for example, I identified three: a dominant discourse, which I labelled Modern Britain, and its two challengers, Socialism and Traditionalism.

I did this for all six years under study, thus completing what we might call a comparative-static analysis (in which a compare-and-contrast is performed at different points in time but without accessing data corresponding to the in-between period). This allowed me to take a transversal view of the evolving British "we" and to see how different discourses might overlap *and* how past discourses influenced future ones (Hall 1996c, 202; Hansen 2006, 55–66). A quick summary of the main findings shows that British society perceived and conceived Britain as fundamentally special: modern and prosperous, free and democratic, fair and just, capitalist and industrial, beautiful and orderly, and peaceable and benevolent. These categories of identity were "vertically shared": they circulated not just among the ruling elites but also, to various degrees, among the masses, and not just in what I call hegemonic discourses – I give them labels such as "Recovery" and "Adaptable Britain" – but also in counter-hegemonic discourses such as "Socialism" and "Traditionalism." They were also "sticky": they existed in all six years under study. So, however heterogeneous the understandings of Britishness and however radical the generational and cultural transformations in society, the British "knew" they were, or were supposed to be, unique. This construction could also be spatial, temporal, and/or ethical, as in a claim that our empire was not only the largest and historically most consequential but also essentially and uniquely liberal. British exceptionalism, then, is the first essential component for understanding the drive towards global power in British foreign policy long after such an approach became all but unaffordable financially.

Britain – the noun I use to talk about a state that in fact prefers to be called "the UK" – was predominantly, though not exclusively, an English project. This was more explicit in 1950, when every other text seemed to conflate Britain (England, Wales, and Scotland) and even the United Kingdom (of Great Britain and Northern Ireland) with England, than after the 1970 Scottish devolution referendum, much less after actual devolution of power under New Labour. Yet England was always Self, except when it referred to an unhappy past version of itself, as in "Victorian England," while Wales, Scotland, and Ireland, both north and south, wavered between Self and Other, depending on the context. Similarly persistent was the deictic centring on the UK and, more specifically, on England in phrases such as "the Home Counties," "the island nation," "the mainland," "the British Isles," and, indeed, "the British."[47]

The failure of the English to conceptually separate themselves from other British nations went hand in hand with a tendency to view empire as something that England/Britain possessed, not something that England/Britain was. This configuration changed from 1960, with the rise of national as well as of postcolonial and post-imperial self-identifications – a "Socialist" embrace of the Movement for Colonial Freedom, for example. It changed even more in 2000, when "multiculturalism" was grafted onto cosmopolitanism to further emphasize the nation's diversity, inclusivity, and tolerance. What stayed the same was a practice of separating the state from its violent imperial and colonial past – and from coloniality as a present condition – and the nation from the presence of non-white citizens. And whereas mainstream discursive practices eventually came to address sexism overtly and often in considerable depth ("we are a queendom now"), this was never the case with racism, where the most common response was "we are not as bad as others."

Empire and its legacies configured the world map throughout and with variable effects on Britain's ontological security. The West was white, meaning majority populations of Western polities were always racialized as white. Australia, Canada, and New Zealand were proper "British," or "white Commonwealth," countries and so peaceful, orderly, well governed, or just simply lucky. The US, a.k.a. America, was Self and Other at once – not a Canada on steroids but certainly part of the shared "English-speaking world," to use Churchill's parlance. Related, while virtually everyone acknowledged American presidents as true leaders of the West, only a minority accepted that the special relationship was *the* flying buttress to Britain's own leadership and privileged international status.

The United States' liminal status never extended to other former colonies, irrespective of how much they shared with Britain its history, politics, culture, economics, law, media, and familial ties. The "New Commonwealth," later also described as "the Third World," was consistently on the outside, as were, with various degrees of separation and

aversion, apartheid South Africa, the Irish and French republics, the
two Germanys (West and East), and "Europe" (in latter years also known
as "Brussels"). Soviet Russia was as menacing as Nazi Germany, the defeat
of which was a constant source of pride and of moral supremacy. Neither
India nor China were coded as top identity categories.

Britain *also* viewed itself as declining. Though present in all years, this
identity category was most systematically repeated and reworked in 1970
and 1980, when the kingdom's industrial economy and its masculine
ideals – strength, pride, and independence – came under severe attack.
The question of what needed to be done about decline was subject to
contestation, both intra-elite as well as elite-mass. In some years, elite
celebrations of economic progress (as in Recovery) or socialist institutional life (as in Socialism) struggled to convince the masses, committed
as they were to certain traditions (as in Traditionalism). In other years,
the discourses advanced by Thatcher and her adherents ("Thatcherist")
regularly clashed with civil society's memories of *le temps perdu*. However, the more important finding is that most discourses in most years
were still bloated with affirmations of, and aspirations to, collective greatness – scientific, civilizational, moral, and so on. Continuously reproduced and circulated, "greatness" shaped how the British experienced
historical change in the first place.

Understanding multiple and layered elements of British identity in
this way is useful, I argue, because it helps us recreate the ever-changing
daily experience of both the governors and the governed – that is, both
the elites and the masses – and therefore the deeper intersubjective structure within which Britain's leaders operated in the post-1945 period.

Finding British Foreign Policy

The constructivist framework I develop and evaluate in this book sets
out to illuminate British relations with the rest of the world rather than
particular British foreign policy choices. Some empirical focus, however,
is necessary. I begin with foreign policy *debates* – public exchanges about
merits and demerits of particular British foreign policies or policy situations. If my framework is right, these debates should reflect and rein-

force elite-mass connections and disconnections at all times. Accordingly, the object of discourse analysis now shifts from civil society to "the British foreign policy elite," which is a convenient shorthand for texts produced by influential individuals embedded in Whitehall, Westminster, and the London media, a.k.a. Fleet Street (Sanders and Edwards 1994, 415–16; cf. Towle 2009).

To put temporal and spatial constraints on debates, I broke each of the six decades under study into four "events," for twenty-four in total, as listed in table I.2.

In principle, events include anything from external shocks and crises, government policy U-turns – think Suez or East of Suez – to new information, knowledge, and broader processes that mark the modern world, whether in the economy and politics, in ecology and technology, or in migration and ethics. "Eventfulness" is a useful perspective from which to view history in order to observe temporality and the logic transformation.[48] War is a classic case because winning in war make states ontologically secure – just look at the many ways in which Thatcher tried to position the success of the Falklands War as the decisive locus of Britishness. Conversely, endless, unwinnable wars on terror are likely to produce ontological anxiety (Suboti and Steele 2018).

In this study, I focus specifically on "foreign policy events," which I selected in accordance to three selection rules: temporal proximity, spatial diversity, and paradigmatic relevance (Appendix B, figure B.1). The first rule has to with the underlying causal logic: the idea that the temporal gap between an identity topography and the corresponding event should be shorter rather than longer. This is why, for example, I decided to look at de Gaulle's "first veto" of 1963, not his "velvet veto" of 1967.

The second rule follows from the aforementioned wager that topographies of Britishness can shed light on multiple developments in British foreign policy during a given period. Accordingly, for each decade under analysis I selected events corresponding to each of Churchill's famous "three circles" of British foreign policy: one for the British Commonwealth and Empire, one for the United States and other "English-speaking peoples," and one for "Europe." As many scholars have noted, "three circles" was never so much a heuristic device for describing the competing priorities of British world power as the reigning "framework"

Table I.2 Parliaments, governments, ministers, and events, 1950–2000

Parliament	Gov't	Prime Minister	Foreign Minister*	Events (incl. Defence Reviews)	
1950	Labour	Clement Attlee	Ernest Bevin	*1950s*	
			Herbert Morrison	Korea	
1951	Cons.	Winston Churchill	Sir Anthony Eden	Suez Crisis	
1955		Anthony Eden	Harold Macmillan	Schuman & Pleven	Sandys (1957)
			Selwyn Lloyd		
		1957 Harold Macmillan			
1959			Alec Douglas-Home	*1960s*	
				Winds of Change	
1964	Labour	1963 Sir Douglas-Home	Richard Austen Butler	Skybolt Affair	Healey (1966)
		Harold Wilson	Patrick Gordon Walker	De Gaulle veto	
1966			Michael Stewart		
			George Brown		
1970	Cons.	Edward Heath	Michael Stewart	*1970s*	
			Sir Alec Douglas-Home	East of Suez	
				Nixon Shocks	
1974	Labour**	Harold Wilson	James Callaghan	EC Entry	Mason (1975)
1979	Cons.	1976 James Callaghan	Anthony Crosland		
			David Owen		
1983		Margaret Thatcher	Baron Carrington	*1980s*	
			Francis Pym	Falklands Islands	Nott (1981)
				Trident purchase	
1987			Sir Geoffrey Howe	Thatcher's rebate	

1992	1990 John Major	John Major Douglas Hurd Malcolm Rifkind	*1990s* Gulf War Bosnia Maastricht	King (1990) Rifkind (1994)
1997	Labour	Tony Blair Robin Cook		
2001		Jack Straw	*2000s* Iraq War on Terror The euro	Hoon (2002) Hoon (2003)
2005		Margaret Beckett		

*In 1968 Secretary of State for Foreign Affairs became Secretary of State for Foreign and Commonwealth Affairs

** Labour (minority) from February to October 1974 and again from 1976.

that configured postwar Britain as sitting at "the very point of junction" of these three spaces and the go-to "conceptual prism" through which, for decades, actual foreign policy events were processed.[49] The expression "squaring the circles of British foreign policy" is still being used (Hill 2019, 8, 180).

Paradigmatic relevance refers to events that have already been used to evaluate or highlight constructivist and interpretivist claims concerning postwar British foreign policy.[50] I followed this rule on the assumption that my book would not be readers' first (or last) exposure to the historical period, debates, and events under discussion. This led to two benefits and one drawback. The first benefit is range. In looking at the event now simply known as Suez, for example, I draw on studies of the crisis attuned to the role of political rhetoric and discourse and, for additional context, on studies dealing with the press and the parties, including their "backbench tribes" (e.g., Onslow 1997; Mattern 2005; Towle 2009; McCourt 2014b; Thomas and Toye 2017). Similarly, I pay close attention to secondary interpretations of "paths not taken," "missteps," and "missed opportunities," meaning the conditions under which British leaders could have legitimately broken alternative paths, such as "more Europe" or alignment with Washington *à la française*.[51] This literature provides crucial insight into the policy options British leaders considered before they chose some and rejected others.

The second benefit is greater attention to "silences" – vital areas not addressed in policy discussions. As Heuser (1998, 5, emphasis in original) notes, actual foreign policy debates were rare in postwar Britain: "Typically, basic concepts are *not* spelled out, but taken for granted, just as consensus on them is taken for granted." Attention to the unspoken, implicit references can be found in most such analyses but especially in discourse analytic accounts. I naturally heed the contextual aspects of said silences, as when all decision makers agreed that foreign policy is special policy because of, for example, "immutable structural dictates" or "the need for secrecy."[52]

Reliance on secondary sources poses assorted risks: priming, bias, misinterpretation and omissions, among others. I minimized this drawback in two ways. First, I consulted secondary literature only *after* completing steps 1 through 5 (figure I.1) for all years under study. Second, to estimate the influence and centrality of the people quoted and cited to the debates under study, I worked with multiple histories and analyses, occasionally analyzing primary sources directly. Whenever major interpretative differences emerged I flagged the reader in an endnote.

Wading beyond foreign policy, I added a selection of defence reviews to my analysis as well. I did this for two reasons. First, as Denis Healey, one of most influential postwar defence ministers, remarked, defence policy often "came to determine foreign policy due to the fact that all commitments were considered to be vital" (quoted in Rees 2001, 30). In other words, there is evidence that high military expenditure had the effect of determining the nature of Britain's post-1945 global role rather than the latter determining the degree of the former. Second, defence reviews, as declaratory policy (Dorman 2001, 9), are in principle deeply "eventful." Produced by bureaucrats under the direction of the government (minister) of the day and then presented to the legislators and the public, these documents – also called statements on defence or defence white papers – are indeed elaborate documents that address the past, present, and future of defence policy, laying out both geostrategic rhetoric (cf. Porter 2010) and (the ever more difficult) budgetary considerations. As such, they tend to prompt public contestation about national priorities and policy trade-offs, thus giving constructivist researchers yet another vantage point from which to analyze the (putative) pathologies in Britain's relations with the rest of the world (Croft 2001a).

Table I.2 lists at least one defence review for each decade (for bibliography, see Appendix B). In addition to analyzing the textual content of each, I combed through relevant historical studies to determine what parts, if any, of said documents were publicly debated, and with what effects for my analysis of the identity-foreign policy nexus overall.

Together, these methodological choices provide a chronologically structured, geographically diverse, and relatively efficient discussion of postwar British foreign policy. In addition to crossing colonial, Cold War, and post-Cold War contexts, the chapters that follow thus cover Britain's relations with the individual states of the First, Second, and Third Worlds, both bilaterally and within multilateral international institutions. And although "security themes" predominate, the empirical testbed is still broad enough to cover a myriad of separate yet, from my perspective, conspicuously intertwined phenomena.

To sum up, my goal in this book is to demonstrate the validity of a properly constructivist reading of Britain's international (mal)adjustments after 1945. Although many British foreign policy analyses now routinely incorporate identity, discourse, and habits, they rarely attempt to recover these intersubjective structures inductively, much less over time and across the elite-mass divide. This is a lost opportunity from both theoretical and analytical viewpoints for only a wide-angled lens allow us to see patterns of continuity and change in said structures as well as to locate relevant parallels among them.

Plan of the Book

The next six chapters are arranged chronologically, covering the six decades between Attlee's "New Jerusalem" and Blair's "New Labour." Each is structured as a three-part discussion:

- Summary of the main findings and arguments.
- Discussion of top British identity categories with examples drawn from the corresponding MIC report. For presentational purposes, I plot top identity categories measured by frequency in word clouds, where larger and darker words represent categories that were coded as most frequent.
- Reconstruction of a topography of contemporary Britishness and a reconsideration of select foreign policy events in light of said topography.

In the conclusion, I summarize the findings and compare them to other accounts of British foreign policy. And while this discussion is primarily about competing interpretations of the past, I end on a speculative note, briefly considering what the future might hold in store.

1

Between the Actual Superpowers

In 1950, Britain was still in the midst of postwar reconstruction. Following a landslide victory in the general election of 1945, the Labour Party, under the leadership of Prime Minister Attlee, introduced a host of tax-and-spend reforms aimed at achieving greater fairness and equality as well as full employment. These included a free NHS, nationalization of transport and heavy industry, and the funding of welfare provision and education. Abroad, his government oversaw the withdrawal from South Asia and the rebranding of the British Empire into a modern, "multiracial" commonwealth. The same government also handled the early days of the Cold War, once again bringing the Union Jack – whether alone or embedded in various iterations of the Red Ensign – close to the American Stars and Stripes. Attlee proceeded to win the 1950 general election, albeit with a slim House of Commons majority of five. Only twenty months later, Churchill-led Conservatives were back in power.

My analysis of the textual sources discussed in the introduction points to three mainline discourses of Britishness in 1950. Dominant at both elite and mass levels was a discourse I label "Recovery." Emphasizing industrial modernity, innovation, order, freedom, democracy, benevolence, collective responsibility, leisure, and beauty, this discourse stressed pride in the country and its ability to lead the world. This made Recovery not simply exceptionalist but also exemplarist, given that it configured the UK as so great that others must emulate and cite our example in producing their own lived realities. This logic of domination and subordination was often overtly gendered and racialized, as in the references to the militarily feeble Europeans or the politically immature Asians.

Recovery was contested on two dimensions. One was in the realm of politics and economics, where a challenger discourse I call "Socialism" foregrounded working-class values and interests and attacked the status quo supported by Britain's capitalist elites. Socialism was primarily an elite-level discourse, but it claimed to speak for the voters of "the socialist Labour Party." The other contestation involved "Tradition." Finding institutional representation in the monarchy and parts of the Conservative Party, this discourse resisted political, social, and cultural changes, especially those espoused by Socialism.

These contestations did involve all identity categories, however. All three discourses normalized the conflation of England with Britain, commitment to empire – a.k.a. the Commonwealth – Second World War victor's pride, anti-communism, support for traditionally defined masculinity, and a view of the British people as fundamentally peaceful. Another nostrum was that American cash and the American atomic bomb were temporary compromises and that Britain would soon be in a position to exercise leadership of the "free world" on its own again.[1] Together, these findings help explain Britain's expansive foreign policy in the period leading up to the Suez Crisis and the Sandys review – the defence white paper Defence Minister Duncan Sandys issued in 1957. If both Recovery and its Socialist and Traditionalist alternatives configured Britain as a legitimate global problem-solver, then we can see why postwar Britain would think and act much like prewar Britain. In other words, it was not just the ruling elites – Labour, the Tories, Whitehall officials, and other power-holders sitting in London – but also the ordinary people who believed that their country should order and reorder "their" parts of the globe.

1950: "Where Men Have Been the Most Free"

Figure 1.1 is a word cloud of the top fifth of all identity categories measured by raw counts as I coded them in my discourse analysis of high-circulating British texts in 1950.[2] Looking at the very top category, *modern*, we see that it typically referred to some combination of capitalism, industrialization, trade, socioeconomic progress, and the diminishing role of religion in public life. In all of these areas, the British saw themselves as *world leaders*. A newspaper editorial published mid-summer made both points by discussing the nation's permanent seat on the United Nations Security Council. "We also sent our films to thirty-four different countries – from Iceland to Indonesia – telling the British story. The value of this alone has been enormous" (*Daily Mirror*, 15 June 1950, editorial).

Both the elites and the masses accepted capitalism as a fact of British life. Judging by the surveyed history textbooks, capitalist modernity was understood to have increased the quality of life overall – it raised the *wealth* and the living standards of all Britons. The term was not at all problematic, while enabling exciting new *leisure* activities like going to the cinema or, for the well-off, airplane vacations. Capitalism was also a major source of *pride*, given the kingdom's penchant for creative imagination and path-breaking *innovations* in modern industry, science, and technology. Victory in the Second World War proved this beyond a doubt, and so did, for example, Britain's leadership in the development and production of jet engines (*Daily Express*, 15 September 1950, op-ed). But capitalism also carried problems. Examples include increased materialism, social alienation, and detachment from work (Carter and Mears 1948) as well as pressures on marriage and the family (*Daily Express*, 15 December 1950, op-ed). Readers of the *Daily Mirror* had good reason to be worried about the economy. One threat was automation: As machines were increasingly replacing workers, the result was mass unemployment in a number of areas of the country (*Daily Mirror*, 15 February 1950, letter). Another threat was oil-powered modernization: "British greatness will be bound up with the prosperity of coal," said one writer (*Daily Mirror*, 15 May 1950, op-ed).

For some, a smart response to these problems was *statism* – the idea that state action could and would improve society.[3] Leadership speeches and textbooks evaluated this category positively, while newspaper pieces were mostly critical. Judging by Attlee's speech at the party conference in Margate that year, Labour was the agency of all major statist projects, especially in the economy (Attlee's Margate Speech). The pro-Labour newspaper, the *Daily Mirror*, was less gung-ho: it had misgivings about the introduction of unnecessary new taxes (15 August 1950, editorial) and

Figure 1.1 Top British identity categories in 1950 by frequency

the scandalous deficiencies in the fight against tuberculosis (15 December 1950, editorial). The pro-Tory *Daily Express* was similar. Though it questioned the Attlee government's policies in toto, it recognized that state interventionism was "now" supported by most "industrial workers" – a group that also happened to be the dominant voting bloc (*Daily Express*, 15 April 1950, editorial). Letters to the editor in both newspapers were less sanguine and less absolute about the idea that state action was rational, much less that it constituted the heart of Britain's success. Compulsory, state-subsidized holidays were a folly, argued one of them: "If this sort of thing is allowed to develop there will be no need for the masses to do anything but fill in forms and apply for anything necessary" (*Daily Mirror*, 15 September 1950).

Looking at the meanings of the same category in high school history textbooks, we see claims that industrial workers' well-being was proportional to "interference by the State" (Carter and Mears 1948, 755). In this view, laissez-faire economics was always bad news, and *trade unionism* was a "triumph" (Rayner 1948, 478). Furthermore, statism was *always* positively evaluated in the wartime context; indeed, having lived through two world wars in a single generation, the kingdom understood and appreciated the value of standing together. Britain won the war, wrote Carter and Mears (1948, 1,034), because its government successfully "mobilized the whole nation," including through unpopular policies such as rationing or the billeting of women and children. Statism and trade unionism sometimes bled into a moral opposition to individualism.

The two newspapers disagreed about free trade – a top forty identity category. While Lord Beaverbrook argued in "his" *Express* on 15 November that free trade made British consumers happy while increasing local productivity, the *Daily Mirror* called for protecting British farmers (15 February 1950, op-ed). The newspapers also recognized themselves as *partisan* – this, too, was seen as a sign of Britain's healthy democracy. As for the political-juridical composition of this democracy, "Britain" and "England" were almost always construed as one and the same, and the national "we" was at once extended to, and separated from, the rest of the Union: Wales, Scotland, and Northern Ireland. Northern Ireland was most consistently on the outside and the *Irish* Other was typically configured as threatening, as in these words of the police inspector in Agatha Christie's novel *A Murder Is Announced*: "He could have shot her from behind a hedge in the good old Irish fashion any day of the week, and probably got away with it."

That being said, the British – elites and masses alike – greatly worried about matters of *justice* and *fairness* in 1950. The lack of housing and high cost of living were almost universally seen as class issues and therefore as deeply unfair. In the film *The Blue Lamp*, the murder of the unarmed policeman is explicitly attributed to the rise of youth delinquency, which, in turn, is framed as a symptom of larger problems in society, including the collapse of fathering and (heterosexual, nuclear) family life and the lack of work and education opportunities. In Christie's *Murder*, the source of corruption is the age-old practice of money-worshipping: "I'm afraid I know only too well the really terrible things that people will do to lay their hands on a lot of money." Another theme related to this identity category was the pervasive belief that crime and corruption were corrigible through state and civil society action. For example, an article penned by a regular columnist in the *Daily Mirror* talks of the "black market millions" (15 June 1950). To solve the problem of under-the-table economic transactions, the government needed to demonstrate to the people that it could spend their tax dollars prudently.

In the same spirit, the British were always on the watch for government incompetence and various forms of corruption in society – political, moral, and social. (This is best thematized in *The Blue Lamp*, which focuses on wayward urban youth.) The British were likewise comfortable with self-scrutiny. Whether it was real citizens writing in newspapers about continuing food shortages or a character like Jean Paget in Nevil Shute's *A Town Like Alice* expressing misgivings about gender relations in London or Aboriginal social inclusion in her new Australian town, the British were supposed to always ask questions about themselves and their country, no matter how uncomfortable these might be. From a letter published in the *Daily Express* (15 July 1950): "We certainly have a fine capacity for self-criticism. It may be the secret of our continued survival as a force in the world."

No text in the entire corpus denied that Britain was socioeconomically unequal and *class-based*, meaning divided by material wealth and education. In the fictional texts, the perspective was always that of the working class. This is significant, as both elite- and mass-oriented texts at the time agreed that working-class people were slowly gaining real political power. For individuals, however, a key to power was money. The richer you are, the more rules you can bend, observed one letter writer in the *Daily Mirror* on 15 March 1950.

Britain further defined itself as *masculinist*, meaning as a country in which the male was, and was supposed to be, culturally and economically dominant. In both elite- and mass-oriented texts, women are either non-agents, like in the movies, or the self-evidently weaker sex. In newspaper discourse, government always needs "good men," the breadwinner is always male, and the caretaker of children is always female. Yet gender inequality was beginning to be addressed. An op-ed in the *Daily Mirror* (15 March 1950) titled "Men Must Learn It Pays for Wives to Be Educated" explains that women's education in developing countries could be greatly facilitated through radio and film. A letter in the same newspaper, published in response to a different topic, disagreed: "I'm all for making sacrifices to give a boy a good education. But I really can't see that it pays with a girl" (15 July 1950). Similar ambiguities emerge elsewhere. The textbooks duly celebrate the triumph of universal suffrage, but they do not follow up on the facts of *patriarchy*. The two novels, *Murder* and *Alice*, are to some extent stories of female empowerment, yet they, too, stop short of questioning the dominance of men in modern society.

Gender hierarchy was implicated in a national obsession with physical *beauty*. Much like with women's physical appearance (*Daily Mirror*, 15 November 1950, column; *Daily Express*, 15 August 1950, column), the British were keen to closely examine, and occasionally lament, their built and natural environments. To Earl, one of the main characters in the film *What the Butler Saw*, Britain has a major problem with the latter – its awful climate. Other fictional characters focus on the former. Chipping Cleghorn, the English village in Christie's *Murder*, "self-consciously" staged itself as picturesque to attract visitors and new residents. Unkempt property was uncivilized. To Joe Harmon, the Australian protagonist of *Alice*, post-Second World War England looked unattractive, "bombed and muggered up," in contrast to Alice Springs, the ideal "bonza town" of the Australian outback that he imagines as having cinemas; ice cream parlours; luxury shops; fresh milk, fruit, and vegetables; a swimming pool; and many young women. (Willstown, his actual Australian hometown, has none of the above, plus no radio and no telephone.) Law and order had a certain beauty too. In *The Blue Lamp*, criminals are threatening but only temporarily, thanks to the ordinary people who dutifully help the police.

Britain was unequivocally *Western*. Further to its "invincible" industrial capitalism (*Daily Express*, 15 May 1950, letter to the editor), the West was distinguishable on at least four additional dimensions: *democracy*, *freedom*, *Christianity*, and *civilization*. Prime Minister Attlee, in his Margate Speech, agreed but emphasized that Britain's democratic socialism could be a beacon to the world as well:

The course of the next few years may well decide the future of civilisation for decades or for centuries … We are called upon to give
a lead to the peoples of the world because of the strength of our
movement in this country and because our policy of democratic
socialism is the only dynamic alternative to totalitarian communism. Only through that policy can we get peace and social justice.

The people of the kingdom were similarly *responsible* and selfless. This
was especially strong in the elite discourse on history and world politics.
For example, in international peace and security, "Britain was under no
treaty obligation to Czechoslovakia, but her moral responsibility to the
Czechs was clear" (Carter and Mears 1948, 1,010). And in world health,
Dr James Simpson's research into the benefits of administering chloro-
form during operations was widely shared, thus lifting "an immense
burden of human suffering" (896). A sense of service was closely tied up
with an *imperial* commitment to the Commonwealth, which was the
new name for the British Empire – an awesome entity that stretched
west and south across the Atlantic to Canada, the Caribbean, and sub-
Saharan Africa, and then east across the Indian Ocean to Arabia, Malaya,
and Australasia. There, the business of combating human suffering went
hand in hand with the business of obtaining raw materials at below
world prices.

The best part of the empire was the old settler empire, where loyalty
and pride in Britishness have always been plentiful, especially during the
world wars. "Britain and the Dominions … are the areas where democracy has proved reasonably successful and where men have been the most
free"; as such, they are "the best hope for the future progress of mankind"
(Carter and Mears 1948, 1,031). In addition to controlling the seas, another
textbook explains, "Britain had taken over nearly all the lands where
Europeans could make permanent homes" (Rayner 1948, 479). Of course,
the white-majority Australia and Canada were imagined as much closer
to home than, say, the two Rhodesias.

The British were, or aspired to be, *educated*. Education helped the
economy and made the country stronger, while being moral and civili-
zing, which was an end in itself: "education is to make life interesting …
boredom is a disease of the self" suggested an op-ed in the *Daily Mirror*

(15 March 1950). The textbooks lauded past governments who invested in science and engineering education, while also celebrating various "men of letters" in British history. In the latter narratives, high-calibre writing and speaking skills were synonymous with power and authority even for individuals outside politics.[4]

The link between imperial and Western identities was not obvious. The newspapers argued that Britain had distinct responsibilities as a member of "the Western world" (*Daily Mirror*, 15 March 1950) and, together with the US and France, as a member of the "Western 'Big Three'" (*Daily Mirror*, 15 May 1950), on the one hand, and as the centre of the Commonwealth (*Daily Express*, 15 November 1950), on the other. The former focused on anti-communism in Europe, the latter on paternalist development in "the Third World."[5] Civilization, religion, and race were usually so intertwined that it was hard to code them as separate categories. When explicitly hailed, the kingdom's religiosity was either broadly Christian or more specifically centred on the Church of *England*. Monarchism was not a top identity category either, but it does appear in the archive, as when the prime minister patted himself on his back for bringing the Indian *Republic* into the Commonwealth (Attlee, Margate Speech).

Britain's civilizational world leadership was evident in the way that both the British elites and the British masses regarded themselves as superior vis-à-vis other nations. The Australian Aboriginals, Malays, and Chinese in *A Town Like Alice*, much like "Mittel Europeans" in *A Murder Is Announced*, were feminized, while the Japanese were more likely to be hyper-masculinized as militarist and barbarian. The textbooks, both published after the war, divided the world into the West and the "half-civilized," "uncivilized," and "backward" rest (Carter and Mears 1948, 998; Rayner 1948, 448, 473). The Japanese prison camp in *Alice* is hailed as unnatural, impermanent, and subject to a degree of British agency. Both Jean and Mrs Horsefall refuse to be cowed by the Japanese military, while Joe dares to steal the Japanese captain's beloved black Leghorn chickens, an act for which he is literally crucified (but survives).

In these constructions, Britain variously emerges as white, Anglo-Saxon, Christian, Protestant, Western, developed, and modern. Importantly, in this context the British saw themselves as *benevolent* towards the inferior Other. In *A Murder Is Announced*, the fictional village Chipping Cleghorn is the permanent home to moody Mittel Europeans (Mitzi and Rudi) as well as "the local atheist" (Butt). Benevolence extended to the vanquished and divided *Germany*, Britain's second-most significant and mostly negatively evaluated Other. The plight of the "unfortunate civil population of Germany" inspired sympathy among the elites and masses alike (*Daily Mirror*, 15 February 1950; *Daily Express*, 15 August 1950). Mrs Swettenham, one of the characters in Christie's *Murder*, declares: "I never really cared for dachshunds myself – I don't mean because they're German, because we've got over all that."

"Getting over all that" was a function of the incredible masculine resilience of the British people. In Shute's novel, Joe not only survives the sadistic torture inflicted on him by Captain Sugamo but defiantly asks his torturer for a bottle of beer at the end. In *The Blue Lamp*, the protagonist loses his only son in the war but treats a newbie colleague like his son. Christie recognizes this in her novel, too: the adults are bemused that the young Julia has difficulty believing that once upon a time people could buy "heaps of coke and coal" rather than being at the mercy of the Fuel Office for strictly rationed bits and pieces of the same. That said, no text pausing over the war failed to remind the reader that patriotism meant loyalty, duty, responsibility, and sacrifice.

Though the British elites and masses always positioned themselves in the very centre of the universe, they also accepted – most of them, anyway – that Britain was no longer *the* world leader. In history textbooks, the fact that "Britain would eventually be caught up and passed" (Carter and Mears 1948, 896) in medicine, as in so many other areas, had to do with forces beyond Britain's control, the main force being the events of the Second World War. Having sacrificed itself in those years, and especially in 1940, Britain was in material *decline*, the crowning proof for which was its *dependence* on the *US*. According to the simple frequency count, the US, a.k.a. America, was by far Britain's most significant Other in this year. The Rayner (1948, 516) textbook gushes over America's "immense power," as did the newspapers over America's wealth. America's ability to set cultural, economic, and technological trends was so overwhelming that *any* British victory counted as newsworthy. This includes the United States Air Force's transition to Royal Air Force-style uniforms

(*Daily Mirror*, 15 August 1950, column) and the fact that British tennis stars bested their American counterparts at a darts game. "I fear these will be our only victories against the Americans," wrote one columnist (*Daily Express*, 15 June 1950).

A source of security, aid, and credit to the free world, the US was Britain's most valuable ally – a commonplace view illustrated in a *Daily Mirror* editorial from 15 December expressing "sincere gratitude" for the "generous friendship" offered by Washington (see also *Daily Express*, 15 June 1950, op-ed). However, gratitude sometimes went hand in hand with resentment, as when a *Daily Express* (15 February 1950) columnist protested Britain's "increasing dependence on American strength and American leadership" in the context of Bevin's Spain policy. Concocted as a way of striking a balance between the government's commitments to the British socialists (who wanted to renew the boycott against the fascist country) and the US (who wanted Britain to renew relations with Franco, the country's dictator), argued the columnist, the policy achieved nothing, making London look weak on the international stage. Others were more understanding: in an ideal world, Britain would not be reliant on the aid of others, but we do not live in an ideal world, argued one letter in the same newspaper (*Daily Express*, 15 November 1950).

The Soviets and their *communism* threatened Britain in fundamental ways. This threat was civilizational – the *Daily Express* ran an op-ed on 15 March 1950 concerning shocking revelations about Soviet Russia's no-weekends labour policy, for example. No text evaluated communism positively. The prime minister unequivocally noted in his Margate Speech that communists did not belong to Labour. He also argued that *socialism* had nothing to do with the militaristic, hypermasculine Marxist-Leninist behemoth that was the main error of modern times. More from the prime minister's Margate Speech:

> Now, there is no other alternative. Capitalism, you know, has lost faith in itself. When this Party was formed 50 years ago there was still the buoyant optimism of liberal capitalism. Except by socialists, its moral and its economic bases had hardly been questioned ... We have our socialist faith, built up on our belief in the brotherhood of man ... We have our faith in freedom. We have our belief in the

dignity and worth of the individual in society. We have our faith in
toleration. We have our faith in social justice.

In other words, a good Labour socialist fought against the status quo
policies of both the Conservative and Liberal parties *and* against "totalitarian communism," as Attlee put it.[6] Echoing Gramsci, he also added
that Labour socialism had a spiritual quality, something that capitalism
utterly lacked yet hid from view through institutional means: "Herein
these publicists show their quite unconscious bias, because they always
regard conservatism as normal and socialism as abnormal. It is our task
to change that so that people will consider it normal to have a Labour
Government and an aberration to have anything else."

Although Britain defined itself as *pacifistic*, diplomatic, and trade-
oriented, nothing in the texts surveyed here implies that the nation ever
shied away from a good manly fight if and when necessary (*Daily Mirror*,
15 September 1950, op-ed). British *military* prowess was a reality in Korea,
a historical axiom, and a matter of cross-partisan consensus. Not all Labour voters supported military spending, but, as the prime minister explained at Margate: "It is unpleasant to all of us to have to devote so much
of our resources to defence, but we have a clear responsibility to this
people and to the world to see that freedom shall not go down for lack
of defences." The Soviet threat was the reason that continued investment
in nuclear weapons trumped concerns about their tremendously destructive potential (e.g., *Daily Express*, 15 December 1950, op-ed) or hopes
for the UN (*Daily Express*, 15 June 1950, op-ed). In addition to being
taught that the nation had appeasers but not Quislings, high school history students learned that their "responsibility to the world" did not cease
in the nuclear era (Carter and Mears 1948, 1,001).

My analysis of a set of political speeches, newspapers, history textbooks, movies, and novels that British elites and masses produced and
consumed in 1950 has given me insights into the content and contestation
of Britishness at the time. In the next section, I begin by identifying the
competing discourses of British identity, which I then use to shed new
light on British foreign and defence policy in the 1950s.

Old Empires Die Hard

Judging by the distribution of valences and their mass-elite breakdowns, British identity in 1950 was subject to both consensus and contestation. The consensus was that Britain was emerging from the shadow of the Second World War in ways that made its people fully appreciate the importance of sustainable peace, state power, imperial power, democracy, freedom and justice, civic and patriotic pride, benevolence, and personal and international responsibility. Maleness is the taken-for-granted norm; strong military capabilities and partisanship were necessities, not ideals; no one apologized for being materialistic. I call this discourse "Recovery."

According to Recovery, the ideal Briton was a middle-aged Englishman with a well-paying job, a wife, and multiple children (in that order). Living in his own house with modern furniture and furnishings – in addition to ample food, drink (especially tea), and movies – was his idea of a dignified life. He would sleep better if his government were better able to fight crime and corruption. In this regard, he would also like to see a nuclear-armed Britain as this would help keep the Soviet menace at bay. Loyally supported by its far-flung dominions and colonies but also allied with the all-powerful America, his Britain steered the world in the direction of a more humane and peaceful politics, always erring on the side of generosity.

The two baseline divisions in the British identity topography at the time were Socialism/Recovery in politics and economics, and Traditionalism/Recovery in the sociocultural realm. With respect to the former, it was obvious that the British elite struggled to articulate the country's raison d'être in unison. Although "everyone" in the ruling class agreed on the importance of prodigious exports and of fiscal and technological sovereignty, a strong minority, led by the prime minister, believed that the future belonged to democratic socialism, not the sort of capitalism supported by the Conservatives and Liberals at home and the Americans abroad. While the working class – the backbone of the British masses – unequivocally supported collectivist principles that gave rise to trade unions and state action, there appeared to be no consensus on how the state should facilitate economic growth. A significant segment of said masses felt that it was consistently being made an instrument for the benefit of the rich elite. Consequently, they welcomed policies that taxed the rich and allowed for more leisure time and more education opportunities – in short, policies that made Britain less unequal.

Most of these divisions came naturally to parties on the left and the right. Supporters of the socialist Labour Party saw Britain as a country where prosperity for all was always aspirational – consigned to the future rather than hailed as a feature of the present or of the past (this does not apply to Britain's identity relationship with the "poor countries"). Contrast this with the Conservatives and Liberals, whose supporters disagreed that capitalism was lacking either vitality or moral integrity. That being said, my discourse analysis suggests that the left-right jousting over the political economy was mostly an elite phenomenon, with Recovery dominating at the mass level of understanding.

British identity was furthermore split between two different social and cultural self-critiques. According to Recovery and Socialism, one key problem with Britain was that it was unequal, half-educated, and deferential to traditional authorities, especially the old establishment figures. The two discourses accepted the social and cultural change wrought by modernity, even if they often struggled with its celerity and scale. What was not widely accepted, however, was revolutionary change, including the Socialist idea that Marxist politics and economics could put an end to self-absorbed, immoral, and irresponsible behaviour. Only a small number of voices contended that women could very effectively run their own affairs (to say nothing of defending the idea and practice of divorce). Challenging both of these views, the Traditionalist discourse argued that the reformist impulses of the current establishment undermined order, resilience, responsibility, freedom, independence, loyalty, and other proven forms of social and cultural expression considered characteristically British. Some Traditionalists added that human inequality was the natural, God-given order of things and that the British ought to feel pride in being treated more fairly and more justly by each other and by their state than any other people on the planet. From this perspective, contemporary Britain should always think twice before closing the door on its Victorian Self.

The foreign policy implications of the identity topography centred on Recovery are as follows: (1) defend freedom and democracy, (2) help out the poor and semi-civilized, and (3) reduce dependence on US fiscal and military aid. Socialist and Traditionalist Britons agreed with these missions, but they emphasized different means for making the nation more powerful. Of the three, the Traditionalist discourse was the least conventional in the sense that it posited that many modern developments represented a transgression against a natural order of things. Indeed, it was nostalgic for the bygone era when Britannia went to church, ruled the waves alone, and invented things that brought home huge profits.

Let us begin with Churchill's first circle of British foreign policy, starting with the ongoing transition to Empire 2.0, a.k.a. the (British) Commonwealth. Only Traditionalism had a problem with aspects of this policy: Why downgrade the world's largest and most successful empire? The prevailing answer was that an empire-to-Commonwealth transition was actually an upgrade: a modernization entirely consistent with Britain's democratic, freedom-loving, just, fair, peaceable, civilized, and benevolent Self. Rather than a truly post-imperial future, the best the British elites could do was dream up "a new ideology of 'partnership,' in which empire was the instrument of social, economic and political uplift, the imperial counterpart to the welfare state at home" (Darwin 2009, 546).

The discourses of Recovery and Socialism supported "decolonization" on the assumption that the newly independent countries would remain in the Commonwealth. The fact that India, Pakistan, and Ceylon had all flocked back into the fold – only Burma said no – confirmed this expectation (as did, later, the Gold Coast's announcement that it planned to do the same once it became independent as Ghana). Also consistent with these versions of British identity was the practice of peacefully controlling the flow of Middle Eastern oil, which at once helped balance books and strengthen military vehicle engines, as well as Commonwealth trade, which was more extensive during the 1950s than at the height of imperial power (Edgerton 2018b). Then there was Whitehall's preference for continuous investment in the so-called sterling bloc, in which Malaya played an important role, with an eye to restoring all but parity with the dollar as a trading currency. Though more than a few political and business leaders argued for more free trade and less imperial preference, especially in the post-1955 period, the governments in London stuck to the status quo (Schenk 2010). This, of course, was consistent with Traditionalism as well, and in particular with the argument that British power could be strengthened through closer ties with the Commonwealth and, especially, the "old Commonwealth," a.k.a. the "kith and kin" of the "white Dominions."

Premised on the idea of British moral primacy, all three discourses wanted Britain to act responsibly in the world, especially in "its" part, the Commonwealth. In rhetoric, this meant setting the colonies free and bringing their white rulers back to Europe – precisely what communists had argued would be impossible. In reality, however, responsibility always meant paternalism: helping the former colonies develop, democratize, and appreciate the benefits of maintaining close ties to the white metropole. This reality was also deeply racialized. India was said to deserve independence earlier than Ghana because the Asians were inherently more independent-minded than the Africans. Consider also the decision to support the creation of a complex new federation of Nyasaland (today's Malawi) and the two Rhodesias (later the independent states of Zambia and Zimbabwe) in 1953. This case was different because it was about the future of British settlers, hence the preservation of the old hierarchy: supported by metropolitan power, a white European minority would continue to rule over millions of inferior black Africans. The same rationale justified support for South Africa, where white supremacism was more explicit and more brutal. Although Labour routinely accused the Tories of being imperialist and hostile to the "new" Commonwealth, the Attlee government quietly moved to expand colonial policing and intelligence in reaction to unrest in Malaya and riots in the Gold Coast.[7]

With both the political class and the masses being at ease with illiberalism overseas, British policy-makers never hesitated to resort to coercion when they deemed it necessary for the preservation of the natural order of things. The imperial impulse coupled with anti-communist identity helped justify a number of military actions, from the swift intervention to suspend the British Guiana Constitution in 1953 to the counterinsurgency campaign in Malaya from 1948 to 1957, the longest-lasting counterinsurgencies in the imperial periphery at the time. As Darwin (2009, 546) puts it, "the conflation of 'containment' (to safeguard Britain at home) and 'imperial defence' (to secure its overseas spheres) was one of the ways in which any residual opposition to imperial burdens could be readily neutralised." The conflation of containment and imperial defence framing illuminates the events in Kenya. There, practically throughout the 1950s, the British-supported forces fought an anti-colonial movement on the part of the Kikuyu people known as Mau Mau, and they did so by resorting to extrajudicial killings, mass detention camps, forced population displacement, and torture. (However, focused on white victims, actual or imagined, the metropolitan public would not actually learn about most of British brutalities until 1959.)[8]

Churchill's second circle of British foreign policy was "the English-speaking world," which he defined as consisting of Britain, the US, and "British Dominions."[9] The deep bonds to this world – cultural, political, social, economic, and military – were self-evident in all three discourses, though Socialism also insisted that Britain now had bonds with "other socialist countries." This consensus helped legitimize not only support for US efforts to build NATO and fight in Korea but also dependence on American cash and the American atomic bomb. First, the Attlee government famously overruled the military's advice – but not Churchill's demand for a parliamentary vote – and joined the US-led, UN-approved "coalition of the willing" hours after the UN condemned North Korean aggression (Self 2010, 108). Second, that same year, US Air Force B-29 bombers stationed in Britain received nuclear weapons. The first decision was of course discursively legitimate, whatever the protestations of the military, not only in relation to British society but also in role-theoretic terms – namely, in defining Britain as "a world leader" and "an upholder of international law" (McCourt 2011). As for the second decision, recall that British society constructed the US as lying between a complementary Other and an extension of the Self. Little wonder the Attlee government allowed the stationing of the bombers even without securing any veto powers over their use, at least initially.[10]

Two years later, the Service Chiefs decided that deterrence was the only effective defence against a nuclear attack.[11] It is here that we see the beginning of the multiple "paradoxes" of British nuclear policy that Andrew Pierre wrote about almost fifty years ago.[12] First, the UK invested heavily in nuclear arms but asked other states to abide by non-proliferation – a policy that continues to this day.[13] This could be seen as a clash of identities, between a masculinist one that inspired status-seeking via military means and a pacifist one. But, as we have seen in the previous section, none of the discourses of Britishness in 1950 configured this contradiction as contradiction: Britain was always both.

Second, the UK insisted on possessing an "independent nuclear deterrent" while in reality being technologically and strategically subordinate to the US – a reality that the UK-US Mutual Defence Agreement of 3 July 1958 only formalized (Baylis and Stoddart 2015, 91–2). Some "maverick" officials aside, London did not see dependence on the US as total or final.[14] Indeed, the expressed goal of both Labour and Tory governments was to first rebuild and then recoup Britain's natural position as a top-tier great power – that is, as the third superpower. Bevin's much-quoted remarks to his cabinet colleagues about the British atomic bomb from 25 October 1946 captures this consensus: "We've got to have this thing over here, whatever it costs ... We've got to have the bloody Union Jack flying on top of it" (Harrison 2009, 5).

"Old Commonwealth" leaders mostly shared this sentiment, which is why the countries they governed remained pro-Britain in diplomacy, economics, and defence well into the 1950s. A good example is the assistance Australia provided in the making of the British nuclear deterrent, sometimes called "the Empire bomb," at Monte Bello and later at Maralinga and Woomera (McKenzie 2006; also see Vucetic 2011, chap. 3). The Suez Crisis is an even better example. As IR theorist Janice Bially Mattern (2005, 139, 131) argues, this was essentially "a zero-sum competition for credibility" between two empires claiming leadership of the freedom-loving West. Yet this was not a competition that Britain could ever win, and the best London could do was to accept the policy of junior partnership. Apart from anti-Soviet diplomacy, intelligence, and military cooperation, the two sides indeed worked hard in those years to sustain the UN, free trade, and other institutions that American IR theorists would later come to call the "liberal international order."[15] More on this later.

Pierre's third paradox concerns Britain's policy towards Churchill's third circle, "Europe." By hugging the US so close, Britain further distanced itself from the European integration projects, from the Schuman Plan in 1950 right through the ill-fated plans to create a European nuclear force later on. Doubtless, Europe was a significant Other in 1950: nothing in either Recovery or its two challengers indicated interest in the talk of a new economic union on the Continent. Consequently, British officials had no reason to support the Schuman (May 1950) and Pleven (October 1950) Plans, much less Jean Monnet's "federalist" project, which appeared to begin to materialize with the establishment of the European Coal and Steel Community in 1951.[16] Minister of State Christopher Mayhew captured this consensus in 1950 thusly: "It is not ideology, but logic and common sense, plus the brute facts of Britain's world-wide entanglements that prevented Britain from forming a bloc with other West European states" (quoted in Blackwell 1993, 72). Britain's "character," Bevin said, made it different from "them."[17] So viewed, the *only* way for Britain to participate in the European integration project would have been as a leader of a Third Force (see introduction). The British position remained unchanged even five years later at the Messina Conference, where the UK was represented by a low-level Whitehall official, and in the subsequent negotiations at Brussels, where London received an offer to become a founding member of the European Coal and Steel Community and therefore a member of the EEC as well.

This path was not taken, which, in hindsight, could be classified as a high-profile misjudgment, for Messina proved to be a critical juncture in European history. Yet, calling this an "abdication of British leadership" goes too far (Dell 1995; cf. Barker 1983, 155–62). If British society in 1950 constructed the German Other as a twice-vanquished enemy, then the British political class could not see the Federal Republic of Germany as anything but a protectorate. (This was of course not wrong: the Western allies *did* create West Germany in 1949, the same year as NATO and the Council of Europe.) It was similarly beyond the realm of fantasy for any British person to imagine that economic opportunities in a French-led continental club could one day come to match those in the "British overseas market." A sentence that one then high-ranking official (allegedly) directed to Lord Plowden at the Treasury captures this particular *senso comune*: "We were being asked to join the Germans, who had started two world wars, the French, who had in 1940 collapsed in the face of German aggression, the Italians, who had changed sides, and the Low Countries, of whom not much was known but who seemed to have put up little resistance to Germany."[18] Daddow's analysis of what he calls the "outsider tradition" is very helpful here: "By the end of 1955, [the outsider tradition] had clearly become the *leitmotif* of British European policy, an achieved and ascribed which resonated inside and outside Whitehall" (Daddow 2015, 76).

The Six – Belgium, France, Italy, Luxembourg, the Netherlands, and West Germany – would of course proceed towards the Treaties of Rome, signed in 1957, thus creating the EEC and the European Atomic Energy Commission. At that point, the UK leadership began to view continental Europeans with less contempt and the European project as something other than "nonsense and a mere French attempt to evade realities," as another high-ranking bureaucrat (allegedly) put it (Sir William Strang, overheard in private conversation [Dell 1995, 52]). But even after years and years of strategic thinking and rethinking that decade, the most the Macmillan government could do was to say that the national interest lay not in EEC trade but in a rival arrangement: first, the short-lived Free Trade Area, and then, from 1960, the European Free Trade Association (EFTA), a.k.a. the Seven – Austria, Denmark, Norway, Portugal, Sweden, and Switzerland, plus Britain as the bloc's unquestioned leader. Its reasoning was straightforward: what EFTA allowed, and the EEC did not and could not, was preferential trade with the Commonwealth, thus letting British foreign policy come full Churchillian circle. (By the same token, as I explain in the next chapter, Britain's first application to join the Common Market was not straightforward.)

Rather than Messina, it is of course the Suez Crisis that usually counts as *the* turning point and the greatest British foreign policy fiasco since the Hitler era, starting with Munich in 1938. The 1956 crisis is a thrice-told tale: it refers to the decision by Prime Minister Anthony Eden's government to reverse Egypt's nationalization of the Suez Canal Company by military means, in collusion with France as well as, secretly, with Israel, and in defiance of nearly all British allies. The first part, the intervention, was not particularly controversial from the perspective of British identity at the time, but the second and third parts were. Eden's decision indeed proved to be disastrous. Under US financial pressure (Dobson 1995, 170), Britain and France were compelled to abandon the invasion after just a few days and then to withdraw their forces by December 1956 (Israel evacuated Sinai three months later).

The government got away with its Suez plan for a while.[19] The main claim, which Eden made publicly on 2 August 1956, was that Egyptian president Nasser's action was illegitimate and that Britain had the right as well as the duty to protect Western interests, not just British ones. This made sense to most Conservatives, particularly the right-wingers who still could not believe that the British military was earlier ordered to give up its large Suez Canal Zone base. As Eden did not make a case for the use of force right away, he received considerable support in the House of Commons. Hugh Gaitskell and Herbert Morrison, speaking authoritatively as leader of the opposition and former foreign secretary, respectively, agreed with this framing, with the former going so far to compare Nasser with Mussolini and Hitler. Even the seemingly anti-militarist and anti-imperialist Bevan supported the government at first, likening Nasser to a thief from *One Thousand and One Nights*: "If the sending of one's police and soldiers into the darkness of the night to seize someone else's property is nationalisation, then Ali Baba used the wrong terminology."[20]

Much like the surveyed general public, Fleet Street rallied behind the government as well, with some newspapers identifying Nasser as a Soviet agent and outlining invasion scenarios. Historical accounts of the crisis suggest that the consensus weakened by mid-September and then rapidly fell apart in late October as, under increasingly confusing circumstances, the shooting began. However, it is also true that the government's propaganda lines on the intervention's rationale generally resonated with the press and public opinion until the very end. This is consistent with my reading of what it meant to be British. All three identity discourses called for trust in government and full support of British troops – in Suez these were indeed British, not imperial – while constructing Britain's power and global reach not as an end in itself but, rather, as a means for making the world a better place, which in this case meant supporting international law and safeguarding the industrial well-being of Western Europe and parts of Asia.

As the crisis escalated and Eden's relationship with the Americans deteriorated, the opposition – Labour and Liberal members of Parliament (MPs), including Richard Crossman, Desmond Donnelly, Clement Davies, William Warbey, and James Griffiths – became more critical as well as more united. The idea of resisting American pressure at all costs had little discursive support outside Traditionalism, nor did, arguably, crude realpolitik, because even those who viewed world politics as a dog-eat-dog jungle in which the strong devour the weak obsessed about moral superiority. On 12 September 1956, Gaitskell made a case for diplomacy and arbitration, which was a reversal of his own initially belligerent position, albeit in ways consistent with the discourse of Recovery. This framed Eden and his hawkish backers in the Conservative "Suez Group" as hopelessly retrograde imperialists. Harold Macmillan, Eden's successor at 10 Downing Street, jumped on the bandwagon as well, suggesting that UN involvement constituted a success. (This, too, was ironic considering that he had been the most hawkish cabinet member during the crisis; indeed, at one point, Macmillan even threatened to resign as chancellor if the invasion did not happen.)

Looking back at the analysis in the previous section, such a U-turn was not illegitimate. On the contrary: framing "the special relationship" as a function of "shared history" – a trope that brings to mind the English language, liberal values, wartime experiences, the Christian ethic, and more – was eminently resonant with what the British held to be true circa 1950.[21] Yet, it is also true that the Americans were able and willing to solidify and, when appropriate, repair this partnership – a development that would be emphasized in any role-theoretic analysis of British foreign policy (more on this in a moment). Already in January 1957, President Dwight Eisenhower had invited Macmillan to a "Big Two" summit in Bermuda. The meeting produced a number of defence- and intelligence-sharing agreements, which led to a spectacular deepening of the special relationship the next summer. In June, the repeal of the MacMahon Act formally reignited UK-US nuclear cooperation; in July, a joint Anglo-American military ("peacekeeping") force intervened in Jordan and Lebanon; and in August, the first of the sixty US Thor nuclear missiles arrived in the UK (Self 2010, 85). That this was a relationship of unequals was obvious to many in Whitehall, but there was nothing fundamentally illegitimate about it.[22] Even the Traditionalism discourse, in which anti-Americanism was usually explicit, accepted that close cooperation with Washington offered opportunities for the pursuit of imperial policies by other means.

Moving next to defence policy, we see further consistencies with a discursive coalition of Recovery and Traditionalism. Jumping in response
to Korea, where the UK sent no fewer than fourteen thousands troops in
total, defence spending sharply went up, such that, in 1951, Britain was
spending more per capita in the domain than even the US, and "total
numbers in the British army and navy were far larger than the empire's
apogee in 1920 – almost twice as many, if the RAF is included."[23] The text
of the Sandys white paper in fact fits my interpretation of Britishness.
The document promised radical reforms on the assumption that the then
level of defence spending – around 10 per cent of GDP – was severely
hurting the economy (Dorman 2001, 12–13; Self 2010, 163–4; Gaskarth
2013, 135). First, there is an acknowledgment of the amorphous nature of
"the Communist threat" and the need to solidify Britain's "financial and
economic strength," including "export trade," as a way to counter this
threat. Next, there is a call for the rebalancing of defence spending away
from human workers and towards technology. Rather than full conscription, the document explained in detail, what Britain needed was new
technology, especially nuclear. But, consistent with both the dominant
discourses and its two challengers, the empire was not forgotten either.
The East of Suez role was preserved, against the defence minister's wishes
(Dorman 2001, 13).The defence of "British colonies and protected territories against local attack" – that is to say, the defence of colonial order
itself – was an imperative as well. This, as Robert Self notes, meant that
"Britain was still trying to remain a world-class nuclear and military
power – a mini-superpower – but with more limited resources than at
any time since the early 1930s" (Self 2010, 164). Finally, and also consistent
with identity discourses, we see a jab at the European allies in the context
of their poor burden-sharing within NATO.[24]

Though defence spending remained formidable until the mid-1960s
– the numbers placed the UK among NATO's top three spenders – the
Sandys reforms did abolish conscription and create a new force that had
only very limited war-fighting capabilities (Harrison 2009, 90, 93–4).
Bureaucrats were generally well aware of such limitations. Having processed new information on population estimates and other long-term
trends in 1959, Arnold France, a top official at the Treasury, invoked
Churchill's three circles in coming to this conclusion: "I doubt whether

we shall be sufficiently skilful as a juggler to keep the three circles all in the air much longer" (Peden 2012, 1095). Politicians, in contrast, followed a different common sense. Scholars of postwar British foreign policy often talk about a bipartisan consensus in this period, based on a small set of basic principles, pillars, or tenets: (1) support of the Western alliance and US foreign policy goals, including above all the worldwide containment of communism; (2) pursuit of a (semi-)independent nuclear deterrent; (3) protection of British assets overseas by way of imperial military outposts; (4) stabilization of the pound; and (5) profound ambivalence towards the French-led European integration process (Self 2010, 35–9; Heinlein 2002, 12–15). All of these are consistent with the above identity topography – Recovery above all but also, with some exceptions, Traditionalism and Socialism. Crucially, said exceptions were controversial preoccupation only *within* parties (Self 2010, 34). This warrants a closer look.

Had Traditionalism been dominant in 1950, and had someone like Anthony Eden been in charge of Downing Street, the scope of legitimate foreign policy might have been very different in the sense that many more people in Whitehall and Westminster would have insisted on the imperial status quo and openly resented the idea of playing second fiddle to the Americans. Notwithstanding "the loss of India," London would have thus tried to strengthen the remaining empire-Commonwealth connections, while opting for a more transactional relationship with Washington. Consider a situation that has many parallels with Suez: after a new Iranian regime nationalized the enormous British oil refinery at Abadan in 1951, British decision makers at first thought about a military intervention but eventually opted for a more covert operation that, together with American intelligence services, effectuated the infamous coup two years later (Louis and Robinson 1994, 493–5; Walton 2013, chaps. 4 and 7; Cormack 2018, chap. 5). The lack of publicity notwithstanding, it is likely that Traditionalism would have framed this action as a temporary marriage of convenience – a traditional British foreign policy response and a model for future dealings with the Americans. At Suez, a properly Traditionalist foreign policy would have privileged the Entente Cordiale as a counterweight to American pressure. This, in reality, was what the

French expected, which is why the political fallout of the crisis also included a proliferation of Anglophobic images, both old and new, across the Channel: "perfidious Albion," "English abandonment in the Battle of France," and, as I discuss in the next chapter, "America's Trojan horse." Suez effectively turned France towards West Germany and European integration *sans* Britain.[25]

As for Labour, the institutional home for the Socialist discourse and therefore for resistance towards imperial policy, its internal division was more pronounced, especially in the period of opposition, 1951 to 1964, when party discipline was looser. The party's left wing in those years had around fifty backbenchers, including Richard Crossman, Barbara Castle, Michael Foot, and Ian Mikardo – a loose faction first known as "Keep Left" and then "Bevanite" after Aneurin Bevan, Attlee's powerful minister of health and later minister of labour. What it wanted was to end the empire sooner rather than later while also redirecting public monies away from defence and towards social programs, starting with the NHS. This position had some overlap with Foreign Secretary Bevin's idea of a Third Force (discussed in the introduction) in the sense that it duly configured British socialism as a *via media* between capitalism and communism. In the end, Bevanites lost to the "Keep Calm," a.k.a. "Gaitskellite," left, a group named after Hugh Gaitskell. As chancellor of the exchequer, Gaitskell famously responded to the Korean War with a "pragmatic" budget that diluted the free treatment promise of the NHS by levying some user charges – the so-called "teeth-and-spectacles" controversy that led Bevan and two of his more junior colleagues to resign from the government. The feud between the Bevanite and Gaitskellite wings of the party rocked Labour until 1957, with one of the main battlegrounds being foreign policy. In contrast to the generally pro-US Gaitskellites, the Bevanites were partial to more neutralist and less militaristic options – Bevan often railed against US-style capitalism, German rearmament, and the British hydrogen bomb.[26]

The dominance of Recovery precluded both of these counterfactual alternatives. A Traditionalist-Conservative desire for a global foreign policy made little sense in the 1950s because Britain literally needed time to recover from the war before it could jostle for influence with others. (This proposition would have been vindicated by the middle of the decade, considering the measurable improvements in the kingdom's balance of payments situation, industrial production, and many other economic trends.) Furthermore, a US-led bloc, however flawed, provided strength and safety both in numbers and in terms of the nuclear deterrent. This argument foreclosed the Bevanite Labour option too: Britain was now part of the Western alliance, not a state so exceptional as to bravely pursue a go-it-alone foreign policy, much less sufficiently socialist to throw in its lot with, say, the Third World. Put differently, the Gramscian common sense in Britain then was *much* closer to Bevinite consensus than to either Tory imperialism or Bevanite neutralism.

The literature on British "roles" generally agrees with my analysis as well. Exemplifying historians' approach is Brian Harrison's broad *New Oxford History* sweep of postwar Britain, which builds on both secondary sources and diaries and memoirs penned by the elite. In his view, six roles or self-images competed for attention from 1951 onwards: imperial power, beacon of democracy, global governance expert, ideological pragmatist, cultural leader, and moral leader (Harrison 2009, 543–4; see also Harrison 2010, 547–8). None of these roles contradicts my map of British identity discourses in 1950. Global governance expert and moral leader, for example, had everything to do with a view that Britain and the British people were responsible, benevolent, and world-leading. These were not always delusions. Though Churchill's plan for a summit with Soviet leadership in 1953 failed, UK diplomats did exceptionally well at, for example, the Geneva Conference on Indochina that took place the next year.

A partial exception to Harrison's argument about the ideological prag-matist role is the Socialist discourse. Like Recovery and Traditionalism, Socialism saw many benefits in pursuing alliances based on shared lan-guage, culture, and history. Like Traditionalism, it also occasionally supported the idea that Britain must go it alone, while also engaging in anti-American grandstanding (Socialist anti-Americanism was arguably more principled than the Traditionalist version, which came from a com-bination of petty resentment and moral superiority.) As Harrison (2009, 544) himself notes, many in London argued that Britain *could* stand for "the potential 'middle way' between Communism and capitalism." One of the best articulations of this position was Bevan's resignation speech of 23 April 1951:

> This great nation has a message for the world which is distinct from that of America or that of the Soviet Union. Ever since 1945 we have been engaged in this country in the most remarkable piece of social reconstruction the world has ever seen. By the end of 1950 we had, as I said in my letter to the Prime Minister, assumed the moral leadership of the world. It is no use hon. Members opposite sneering, because when they come to the end of the road it will not be a sneer which will be upon their faces. There is only one hope for mankind, and that hope still remains in this little island. It is from here that we tell the world where to go and how to go there, but we must not follow behind the anarchy of American competitive capitalism which is unable to restrain itself at all, as is seen in the stockpiling that is now going on, and which denies to the economy of Great Britain even the means of carrying on our civil production.[27]

A Socialist vision of the aims and ethos of the empire/Commonwealth was consistent with this position too, given that Socialism emphasized responsibility towards newly independent and soon-to-be independent nations. Even the new international institutions such as the UN stood to benefit from British democratic socialism.

Another interpretation of British roles can be found in McCourt's constructivist analysis of post-1945 British foreign policy. Building on symbolic interactionism in sociology, he argues that foreign policy action emerges from role dynamics – that is, from social expectations generated in and through interactions between and among states and non-state actors. He finds that the Suez Crisis is a marker of transition from a "great power role" to a "residual world power" in British foreign policy (McCourt 2014a, 68–71).[28] He also argues that the intervention – the actions between 27 July and 6 November 1956 – was made possible by "the co-construction of mutually supportive sets of expectations by France and Britain in the form of residual great power roles" (70). The governments in London and Paris likewise attempted to "altercast" the United States into a particular kind of Western alliance leader – the kind that would support gunboat diplomacy even in the twentieth century.

McCourt's analysis is a valuable contribution to constructivist IR. What is less convincing is his insistence that roles and identities are rival explanations. It is undeniable that state-level interactions with France, the United States, Nasser's Egypt, and the Soviet Union all contributed to the particular understanding of Britain's (residual) great powerhood in 1956 and therefore to the emergence of a political space that enabled the intervention. Yet the same construction emerged from British society as well. I say this not only from the vantage point of 1950, but also, as we shall see next, from the subsequent years. Simply put, the main lesson British society learned from Suez was not that Britain should *never* intervene in the old empire, only that it should not do it so recklessly.[29] So, while it is true that Suez greatly illuminated Britain's relative decline – Sir Oliver Franks described it as "a flash of lightning on a dark night" (Hennessy 1996, 97–8, cited in Harrison 2009, 106 and Peden 2012, 1075) – it is equally true that, many years later, British society carried on much as before 1956, taking British greatness entirely for granted.

2

African Winds, Atlantic Anchoring

"Great Britain, attempting to work alone and to be a broker between the United States and Russia, has seemed to conduct a policy as weak as its military power." These words are from US secretary of state Dean Acheson's speech from December 1962, in which he famously chided Britain for losing an empire but never finding a role. Among many scholars who closely read this speech was Kenneth Waltz, the future star of structural realist thought in American IR. As he put it in his 1967 book, British foreign policy after the Second World War was simply "bewildering": "to derive influence from a nuclear force while depending for component parts upon another country; to pose as a first-class power by maintaining a third-rate military establishment; to play a global role with the world's seventh-ranking army" (Waltz 1967, 177). Waltz then explained this outcome with a combination of institutional and social variables, such as prevailing national attitudes, traditions, ideologies, and habits, which he argued prevented policy-makers from adapting to the reality of the bipolar international order and Britain's subordinate place in it (174, 178–80).

The theoretical framework I outline in the introduction allows us to revisit Waltz's explanation with an interpretive analysis of the national attitudes, traditions, ideologies, and habits that he claimed were deeply "ingrained" in British society (Waltz 1967, 252). My analysis of the discourses of Britishness in 1960, four years after the Suez debacle, leads me to conclude that Waltz was right. Little or nothing in either elite or mass texts suggest that British society was ready to have its state play the more modest role of a medium-sized power. On the contrary, the fact that Britain had now become the third-ranking world power meant that the discourses of British identity replaced claims of military and economic superiority with claims of the moral and political high ground.

My findings are as follows. The dominant discourse, which I label "Modern Britain," acknowledged modernity's material basis; the importance of wealth creation through technological innovation, industrial production, and exports; the power of heteropatriarchy; and the need for order, freedom, justice, and fairness. Viewed through this lens, the British were doing better than ever before. Against Modern Britain stood a mass-based discourse that criticized Britain for its inherent elitism and excessive respect for inherited wealth. I label it "Socialism" to signal continuity with my topography of Britishness in 1950, the caveat being that the earlier iteration was an elite discourse.

Modern Britain saw a close alliance with America as necessary in the context of the Cold War and argued that the kingdom still could, and should, claim co-authorship and shared responsibility for anti-Soviet efforts globally. The same discourse likewise argued that empire had to be replaced by a "multi-racial," 700-million-people-strong "family of nations" – a sensible option given that the year under study was also the year of "Winds of Change" and mass decolonization. As in 1950, the European integration project was mostly out of sight at the level of civil society, distanced by a general view of Western Europe as divided between the former Axis powers and the nations that the British rescued from the Axis powers. Socialism was slightly more ambivalent on foreign policy, but only because it focused its attention sharply inward, towards the protection and expansion of the British welfare state. Waltz was, therefore, right: neither version of Britishness offered an alternative to the old Churchillian idea that Britain should continue to act as the linchpin between and among Europe, America, and the Commonwealth. And this helps explain the puzzling character of the kingdom's hyperactive foreign policy at the time, or, in the words of the American theorist himself, "a pursuit of a world influence for which the material basis is lacking" (Waltz 1967, 306).

1960: "Britain No Longer Leads the World"

Figure 2.1 captures the most commonly reoccurring identity categories in the corpus for this year.[1] In contrast to 1950, the top identity category is now *patriarchal*.[2] In Agatha Christie's *4.50 from Paddington*, British society is presented as treating women as unreliable, deferential, instinctive, naïve, and irrational. Lucy Eyelesbarrow, whom Miss Marple hires as an investigator, upsets the local order of things simply because she is "poking about." In his retirement speech to a group of physicians in *Doctor in Love*, Sir Spratt advises his junior colleagues they had "better get married as quickly as possible." This is because marriage "makes you respectable. Saves you from amorous patients. Prevents gossip. Gets phone answered, something to do on your time off. Most men don't like doctors mucking about their wife unless the doctor has a wife at home." In the same movie, Dr Nicola Barrington is "always" mistaken for a male doctor named Nicholas. In her conversation with Dr Sparrow, she observes that "women doctors are still rather novelties" and that "most men want to examine me." Other high-paying professions were similarly unwelcoming to women: "I don't think it is suitable for women to be found on the stock exchange floor," wrote a *Daily Express* columnist on 15 September 1950.

Dr Barrington and Second Officer Davis, Commander Shephard's able assistant in the blockbuster Second World War movie *Sink the Bismarck!*, are exceptional for being seen as indispensable to the workplace. They are unexceptional, however, for being depicted as younger and therefore more substantial. Physical appearance was understood as essential for women, bordering on obsessive. In *Doctor in Love*, Dr Sparrow has to turn away six candidates for a newly opened secretarial position, all six of them young attractive blondes. "Girls in our office still come to work wearing flimsy high-heeled shoes," says Sparrow, with "still" referring to the winter. Newspaper discourse was similar: Cliff Richard, a popular pop singer at the time, is reported as having a "Date Book," in which he evaluated the "sorts of girls" with whom he interacted (*Daily Express*, 15 March 1950).

The second most frequent identity category was *class*. Its meanings varied between elite and mass sources but usually referred to the idea that Britain was profoundly unequal or that the British people were divided by class consciousness. Markers of class were wealth and civilized manners – practices like polite rapport and regular reading that were said to be common among the "upper class" and rare or non-existent among the "working class."[3] Also varied in meaning were *justice* and *fairness*, their common denominator being an aspiration for equal respect for the law and equal opportunity for all citizens. Judges, civil servants, and soldiers who acted on behalf of the British public were regarded as impartial professionals; politicians less so, given that their public and private faces were understood as different. Fairness also meant better housing for the ordinary people.

History textbooks confirmed that Britain was *statist*, meaning that it was a nation accustomed to the idea and practice of state action. According to Barker, Aubyn, and Ollard (1960, 17), the Victorian age was miserable because workers and women were not "recognized as an essential element in the social and economic machinery of the state." The moment this changed, the kingdom grew happier and healthier. The government of the time basically concurred. Macmillan, the man who restored the Tory morale after Suez and had recently led them to a third successive general election, argued at the party's annual conference in Scarborough that a degree of state interference was acceptable, one key exception being "nationalisation or rigid State control of industry."

Being *modern* variously meant being industrial, productive, urban, and progressive. The two history textbooks examined for 1960 were similar to their counterparts for 1950 in the sense that they viewed the past as moving into the present in a straight line, with British political, social, and cultural life constantly improving for most British people most of the time. The newspapers agreed: there was more consumer choice than before.

As always proudly *democratic*, Britain saw itself as being divided into two *ideological* (or *partisan*) camps: conservative, represented by the ruling Conservative Party, and socialist, represented by the opposition Labour Party. In the Scarborough Speech, Macmillan explained what the people of Britain wanted and did not want in the 1960s. The first list, which harmonized with "Conservative policy," included "opportunities to get on in their jobs and to use intelligence and imagination and initiatives"; higher wages; lower income tax; homes; "more new hospitals,

Figure 2.1 Top British identity categories in 1960 by frequency

houses, roads and schools"; and a wide social safety net ("We have the biggest social programme in our history and we are spending on it a bigger proportion of our national wealth than ever before"). The second list, which was code for Labour's socialist policies, included local council housing and "nationalisation or rigid State control of industry." The British, it was thought, were deeply sceptical about more radical bases for social and political change.

Again, as in 1950, the texts under analysis regularly subsumed "Britain" and "British" under "England" and "English." England/Britain's nucleus was unquestionably London, particularly from the point of view of the kingdom's defenders – namely, James Bond in the Ian Fleming novel *Dr*

No and the protagonists of *Sink the Bismarck!*, a blockbuster about the naval battle involving the eponymous battleship, the symbol of German military might in the Second World War. *Doctor in Love*, a film comedy, suggests that all young doctors want to live in the capital rather than in the countryside. Other British nations are once again Self and Other. In the Queen's Speech for 1960, Scotland is Britain, yet Scottish "Highlands and the Islands" are said to lack "modern standards of living." In *Doctor in Love*, Dr Banks pretends to be "Dr McGregor" through an overwrought impersonation of a Scottish accent in front of Sir Spratt, who, in turn, is fond of mocking Scots. (Although more populous and geographically larger than Northern Ireland, Wales rarely appeared as Other.)

In yet another continuity with 1950, the nation also configured itself as *civilized* and *wealthy*, both relative to the rest of the world as well as to its past self. Britain was also fundamentally *orderly*, meaning respectful of the law, clean, and moral. This is made evident by the behaviour of the over-the-top characters in *Doctor in Love*. Sir Spratt, for example, declares that he has been running red lights "since Port Said in 1920," while the young "to-hell-with-the-ethics,-think-of-the-fun" Dr Banks keeps pornography at work and shows interest in tax avoidance. The British likewise saw themselves as *peace-loving*, both historically and in terms of the contemporary pursuit of peaceful co-existence with the Soviet enemy (more below).

Technological modernity is what made Britain a *world leader*: "Britain's booming canning industry, which pioneered the preservation of food is celebrating its 150th birthday" (*Daily Express*, 16 May 1960, letter). "The great spread of agricultural machinery has lightened the task of the farmer," suggested the prime minister in his Scarborough Speech, adding that "it is worth recalling that our agriculture is the most highly mechanised in the whole world." Indeed, the Conservative government of the day presented itself as a well-oiled machine taking the country forward to a better future.

Continuity and *tradition* advanced Britain's world leadership too. Worried about the "soaring" crime and violence in the country, the *Daily Express* called for more corporal punishment, against "modern penal methods" (15 November 1960). Britain's Christian identity was important to the prime minister. "Divinely ordered, the family it is at once the most natural and the most intimate of our institutions," he said in his Scarborough Speech. And if Britain were to not help the underdeveloped African countries: "then we have no right to call ourselves either democrats or Christians."

As in 1950, *capitalism* caused stress to the British, and it was understood that different classes experienced this stress differently. Working-class frustrations with capitalism centred on high house prices and rents, low wages, price inflation, and long hours. A letter written by a country inn landlord to the editor of the *Daily Express* expresses outrage over a government proposal to extend shop opening hours and working time in his sector of the economy: "84 hours a week, excluding holiday extensions. What other class of worker is called upon to do this, without some compensation?" (15 November 1960). The elites understood that it was good government policies that harmonized economic growth with personal prosperity.[4]

Modern capitalism was routinely linked to *industry* and Britain's penchant for *trading*. "We all depend," said the prime minister, "on the expansion of world trade" (Scarborough Speech). And modern capitalism was neither for the meek nor for the weak-hearted: "The world does not owe us a living. We have to earn it. That means that we have to compete, and to compete with some very efficient countries" (Scarborough Speech). Historically, Britain had done well for itself under this system (Barker, Aubyn, and Ollard 1960; Strong 1958). The contemporary trade deficit and poor competitiveness were therefore exceptions, not the rule.

Equally important were the limits of state action vis-à-vis individual *freedom*. The challenges of police work, argued a columnist in the *Daily Express* on 15 March 1960, must be respected, but so must the rights of citizen within the existing laws. Dr No hides in a mountain stronghold on Crab Island, which he had previously purchased from an American society for the protection of rare birds. He dismisses Bond's threats by invoking habeas corpus and private property rights:

So the police come, the soldiers come. Where are a man and a girl? What man and what girl? I know nothing. Please go away. You are disturbing my guanera. Where is your evidence? Your search warrant? The English law is strict, gentlemen. Go home and leave me in peace with my beloved cormorants.

Going back to the earlier finding about patriarchal identities, freedom in 1960 Britain was understood within a male-centred and heterosexual universe in which Others are feminized and therefore inferior. Among the fictional characters in the archive, Bond and at least two physicians in *Doctor in Love* are portrayed as sexually magnetic. Bond never once misses an opportunity to ogle women, and he is especially drawn to the "queer, beautiful" and "childish" Honeychile Rider. She responds to his advances immediately (the secret agent's lifestyle is better than aristocratic in the sense that he is not only well travelled, educated, and confident but also cash-rich, physically superior, and technologically savvy). Bond's masculinity is underscored through contrasts with the sexually impotent, grotesque Dr No. The philandering Tony Banks in *Doctor in Love* is a Bond parody of sorts, but his sexual success is at the Bond level.

The British masses understood themselves as more sexual than before. While multiple texts acknowledge that moral and social mores against nonmarital sex can be, and are, easily transgressed, the consequences of such transgressions are always configured as greater for women than for men. In the movie *Doctor in Love*, where everyone is both sexual and sexualized, men are far freer to pursue women than vice versa. It was also perceived that boozing went hand in hand with sexual encounters. Bond downs three hard drinks before bedding Honeychile, and the two young physicians bed two female strip club dancers with a bottle of Canadian Club disguised as medicine. Indeed, all men, rich or poor, were meant to like to drink – cognac for Sir Spratt, Scotch for the doctors (and for Bond), beer for the masses. Wildewinde, Dr Cardew's off-the-wall assistant in *Doctor in Love*, is tolerated despite his habit for "getting plastered from time to time," and in *4.50 from Paddington*, Mr Crackenthorpe offers Inspector Craddock, who is on duty, a drink (the inspector declines).

If accents and alcohol divided the country, the nuclear-armed Cold War united it. "There is no question where Britain stands here. Britain stands with *the West*," declared Macmillan in his Scarborough Speech.

He was correct in the sense that not a single text in the archive questioned British membership in the capitalist and democratic Western alliance against the *Soviet* bloc. Elites and masses alike agreed that the Soviets were perennially dangerous, partly because of their pernicious Marxist ideology and their awesome military-industrial complex, and partly because of their trickery. Soviet leader Nikita Khrushchev was always looking for ways to split the West (*Daily Mirror*, 15 May 1960, letter). All British *communists* were Moscow-controlled too.

Standing with the West meant close cooperation with the *Americans*. In *Dr No*, for example, it comes as no surprise to anyone that the British Secret Service and the FBI would work closely together or that Turks Island, one of Britain's Caribbean territories, would be so essential for the US military's missile testing.[5] In addition to being a source of security, America was also the avatar of modernity, a nation with seemingly endless freedom, wealth, and opportunity. In *Doctor in Love*, Dr Cardew's estranged wife prefers California to London, and Dr Banks is impressed with American marketing methods and also with a rich female American professor.

But the new centre of the universe was also resented. The rise of American power, a textbook explains, had everything to do with the advent of the "third stage of the Industrial Revolution," which emerged thanks to "atomic energy, electricity, and [the] internal combustion engine ... aluminum, steel, concrete and plastic." The same factors explain why "Britain no longer leads the world" (Barker, Aubyn, and Ollard 1960, 65–6). Unable to monopolize these new technologies, the country *declined*. The great sacrifice of the British in the Second World War accelerated Britain's technological subordination to America, especially in the nuclear domain.

Macmillan's own view was that Britain, while second only to the superpowers, was again rising in the world. "With President Eisenhower and Mr. Khrushchev addressing the [UN General] Assembly, it seemed right that the British Prime Minister should go and try to speak for Britain" (Macmillan's Scarborough Speech). The rest of the elite merely desired a world-leading Britain alongside the US. This emerges clearly in *Daily Express* editorials on the future of a British nuclear deterrent (15 April

1960) and the American veto on Britain's cooperation with Europe on space research (15 June 1960), as well as in textbook treatments of new factors "conditioning" British foreign policy (Barker, Aubyn, and Ollard 1960, 283). This was not merely an aspirational identity. The concluding message of both *General History of England* and *History of Britain and The World* is the same: although we are in material and imperial decline, it would still be a political and moral mistake to underestimate our contributions to global security, trade, and freedom. *Dr No* makes the same point, given that it is a story of a heroic British secret agent who uses British state resources to protect the free world. In contrast to 1950, the British *Empire* was now a much more ambiguous Other, with some texts taking historical pride in it, others dismissing it as a "drain on resources," and still others equating modernity and civilized behaviour with anti-colonialism. The empire was also "over there," in a sense that the British saw their "home base" as racially homogenous.

The depictions of *Germany* mostly stayed the same. In the film *Sink the Bismarck!*, the Third Reich is depicted as much stronger than Britain – as a terrifying military-industrial juggernaut bent on world domination. This is clarified at the outset by the voices of the London-based American correspondent ("There is something special about the people of this island, this nation ... Britain is fighting alone steadfast, unflinching") and First Sea Lord ("If we had a hundred more ships we still wouldn't have enough"). The movie opens with documentary footage of Hitler cheering on the battleship's official launch in 1939, alongside hundreds of Nazi flag-waving Germans, and the *Bismarck*'s commander is portrayed (counter-historically) as a fanatical Nazi.[6] What ends up winning the battle against the warship is prudence and *determination*, not material power. The hero is the head of Naval Operations, Captain Shepard, the officer who had earlier lost a ship in a battle against the same German commander who led the *Bismarck*. This time he moves with competence, commitment, and the legendary British stiff upper lip. Shepard thus convinces a superordinate that "calculated risks" are different from gambles, and he proceeds to set up a bed in his Admiralty office, demanding the same dedication from his subordinates ("Either you have discipline or you haven't"). And although his only son, a Royal Navy sailor, happens to get in the way of the mighty *Bismarck*'s onslaught, the officer calmly chooses duty over family ties: "Emotions are a peacetime luxury." This is in line with the machine-like Agent Bond, who thinks of his Beretta as an "extension of his right hand."

Germany's latent ability to out-modern Britain is likewise evident in history textbooks. The beloved National Insurance Act of 1946, the bedrock of Britain's welfare state, was essentially an adaptation of German social legislation introduced in the actual *Bismarck* era, German musicians historically influenced English ones, and the West German plastic industry impressively reassumed its world-leading position within eight years. On some modern trends, however, Germany was behind: "German girls in England are changing their apron strings for G-strings," said an op-ed (*Daily Express*, 15 February 1960).

Views of the non-European world in 1960 similarly stayed the same in relation to 1950, especially in mass discourse. The movie *Doctor in Love* explicitly insists that modern medicine is not the work of "African witch doctors," while a newspaper column describes a certain Lord Craigmyle's interest in a new business venture in Africa as a collective good of sorts: good for the seasoned businessman himself, good for Britain, and good for the Africans (*Daily Express*, 15 February 1960). For the prime minister, Britain had a "special duty" towards the *Third World,* meaning the Afro-Asian, a.k.a. non-white, Commonwealth world that it had once ruled from London (Scarborough Speech). This duty was also articulated as uniquely British *benevolence*: absent our help, the Third World would fall prey to injustice and excessive brutality, as in Nasser's Egypt, apartheid South Africa, or the Belgian Congo, which in that year descended into a vicious war. As a *Daily Express* op-ed put it on 15 August 1960 in regard to Cyprus: "The Greeks and Turks on the island would long ago have torn each other to pieces if British soldiers had not kept them apart." (No mention was made of Britain's vicious partition of India.)

The British elites understood that the colonized populations resisted colonial rule. It was not controversial that some local students would boo and jeer the British prime minister in Nigeria (*Daily Express*, 15 January 1960, op-ed), nor was it controversial to say that "the enemies of the African people" are "the white men who are prematurely casting away their responsibilities" (*Daily Express*, 15 July 1960, op-ed). Yet not every text, at either the elite or mass levels, agreed that the years of the British Empire were numbered or that all (new) Commonwealth countries should be "helped to independence." The case in point is Jamaica, as imagined by the fictional agents of the British state in Fleming's *Dr No*. In the novel, the ultra-modern, cosmopolitan Bond happily goes along with the everyday racism of the colonial secretary, such as his references to common and uncommon "mixture of bloods" (the Chigroes, the "half Chinese, half German" Dr No), "the usual hysteria of the Chinese," the bravery of Cayman Islanders, or the trickery of the Russians. The movie *Doctor in Love* is not radically different, as when Sir Spratt diagnoses Dr Sparrow: "Is your father a Chinaman? Then it's simple. You have jaundice."

Such explicit racial slurs were not present in the newspapers. "No one who believes in Jesus Christ may be excluded from any church on the grounds of colour or race," declared a *Daily Express* op-ed on 15 December 1960. This was especially obvious in comparison to apartheid South Africa (15 April and 15 July 1960) and the US's "Deep South" (15 November 1960), as observed by various authors in the *Daily Express*. Yet, the fictional Pleydell-Smith would no doubt agree with the pieces that argued that the African people lacked political maturity (15 February 1960, op-ed) or that South Africa should be neither embargoed nor expelled from the Commonwealth because of "700,000 loyal white people who voted for the monarchy and share our traditions and ideals" (15 October 1960, letter). What we observe here is variation in the *means* of racialized differentiation from behavioural and institutional traits to skin colour. The "kith-and-kin" Commonwealth was not the same as the Commonwealth writ large.

In sum, Britishness in 1960 had many continuities with Britishness in 1950, but it also had a few discontinuities. In the next section I first take stock of these, and then I proceed to consider British foreign policy of the ensuing decade, focusing on decolonization, the Skybolt Affair, and the failed push into the Common Market.

Ce n'est plus grand-chose?

The topography of Britishness in 1960 can be conceptualized in terms of a single consensual core, which I label "Modern Britain," and three sets of more contested identities labelled simply "economic," "political," and "sociocultural." In general, Britain and the British imagined themselves to be modern, post-imperial, declining (in power), orderly, Western, civilized, democratic, and world-leading (in status). Most of these identity categories were evaluated positively across the five genres, the notable exception being "declining," which was always an aversive identity. Internationally, Britain belonged to the capitalist and democratic West, which implied alliances with the United States and West Germany against communist powers led by Soviet Russia. The Third World, including both the current and former colonies in Asia and Africa and other countries outside the Atlantic region, was regarded in the mass discourse as the antithesis of Modern Britain. The British elites generally shared this view, but they also related to the Third World with altruism and hope, as in the prime minister's statement, in his Scarborough Speech, that "we have given our new emergent territories a good training and a good chance."

Beyond Modern Britain, I identified several key divisions. Judging by the elite-level texts, the ruling establishment saw the country as progressing thanks to its commitment to democratic norms and institutions, capitalism, material wealth, technological innovations, the Western alliance, and international peace and development. The masses occasionally disagreed. On the economy, the masses were more likely to worry about capitalism, even if they agreed with the elites on the value of industry, trade, technology, and wealth creation. An example of a desire for a less capitalist Britain comes from Mr Crackenthorpe, a character in *4.50 from Paddington*:

> I live here because my father built the house and I like it. After I'm dead they can sell it up if they want to – and I expect they will want to. No sense of family. This house is well built – it's solid, and we've got our own land round us. Keeps us private. It would bring in a lot if sold for building land but not while I'm alive.

His fight against wear-and-tear capitalism was also a protest against urban sprawl, which, in the 1950 report, I coded as an element of Traditionalist discourse: "'Nowhere to walk outside this place,' growled Mr. Crackenthorpe. 'Nothing but pavements and miserable little band boxes of houses. Like to get hold of my land and build more of them. But they won't until I'm dead.'"

In the area of politics, the British masses were less negatively inclined towards the fact that Britain was divided politically and ideologically. Indeed, the masses did not see the collectivist ideology supposedly cultivated by the Labour Party as excessive. The masses were also more willing to evaluate class in a neutral fashion – possibly because they did not think class divisions were malleable. They fretted less over the fact that Britain was militarily and therefore politically dependent on America during the Cold War. On social and cultural issues, the masses indicated a desire to see Britain as a manly, heteropatriarchal society, albeit not necessarily traditional. They also cast a sceptical eye on elite benevolence and government prudence. The chaos of decolonization had little to do with the path to a better life in Britain, and no text in the archive, elite or mass, examined Britain's imperial record in a critical fashion or spoke against the vassalization of the country vis-à-vis the US.

To what extent did the botched Suez invasion change how the British defined themselves and their country? Historians William Rogers Louis and Ronald Robinson contend that Suez led to a regime change of sorts – that is, to a replacement of Eden's "imperialists" with "the pragmatists" à la Macmillan (Louis and Robinson 1994, 480–1). Yet, we also see that the old foreign policy impulses survived this transformation. So, while Suez and subsequent developments reconstituted the West, the East, and the Third World all at once, some things did not change. The quick recovery of Britain's imperium in the Middle East is a case in point (Verrier 1983, 180–2; Louis 2004: Thomas and Toye 2017, 226). The same goes for the decolonization waves of the 1950s and the early 1960s. While by any reasonable measure this process thoroughly redefined internal/external boundaries of Britishness and so understandings of a British citizen located within these boundaries, British society mostly stuck to the old scripts. As Harrison (2009, 543) notes, Acheson's remarks were upsetting in 1962 precisely because the empire was not imagined as lost just yet.

My discourse analysis confirms that, in 1960, most British people, elites *and* masses alike, conceived of their country's position in the world in much the same ways as they did in 1950: as a great power and America's second in command. We see this in the two identity topographies. Recovery evolved into Modern Britain, but the two discourses were broadly similar. Socialism, which I argue in chapter 1 was mostly an elite discourse, was now marginalized, while Traditionalism almost completely disappeared from the identity topography.

The one change was that being "America's second in command" now looked permanent. True, we were still rising and recovering, but the room for manoeuvre was now severely limited, partly because of the seemingly unsolvable problems with the economy (the kingdom continued to struggle with a massive balance of payments deficit), but more importantly because of the changing nature of the nuclear face-off between the United States and Russia. Barker, Aubyn, and Ollard (1960, 283) explain in their textbook that, although Britain and France had managed to develop, produce, and test the bomb, "no one imagine[d] that they or any other of their imitators [would] be able to catch up the giants."

If we accept that there has been as much continuity as change in British identity in this period, then we should expect to see a foreign policy leading not to an abrupt Hollandization of Britain, as Macmillan feared in 1956, but, rather, to a steering of a familiar postwar path. This meant that London would continue to claim co-leadership of the West but in reality, at least in most situations, act as a cheerleader for US foreign policy. Accordingly, in the rest of this chapter I evaluate this prediction against a selection of events from 1960 to 1966, a period spanning three governments – the Conservative governments of Harold Macmillan and Alec Douglas-Home and the first Labour government of Harold Wilson.[7]

My first focal point is Macmillan's "Winds of Change" Speech of 3 February 1960. Delivered in Cape Town, the political heart of apartheid South Africa, during his six-week African tour, the prime minister's speech addressed a community of Old World whites – "the British, white South Africans, and whites in East and especially Central Africa alike" – arguing that it must yield to the wind of "African national consciousness (Buettner 2016, 58). This ushered in the next stage in Britain's imperial retreat: a decision to give up formal colonial rule on the continent. Prompted by a combination of metropolitan, colonial, and international factors – these include the financial weakness and defence cuts at home, the visible collapse of the French and Belgian Empires in Africa, and the horrors of the Kenya Emergency mentioned in the previous chapter – this was nevertheless a controversial policy shift, not least because many nationalist movements in Africa had clear communist inclinations. Macmillan nevertheless insisted that the retreat was in fact an opportunity, given that the Empire had to evolve and modernize in "the flood of its greatness, undefeated in war." This, he added, "has been an evolution, not a revolution – a process, I firmly believe, not of decline but of growth" (59).

Macmillan's rhetoric fit the mainstream discourse. Once racist South Africa was de facto expelled the following year, this newest Commonwealth *almost* looked not simply like a family of like-minded nations (Macmillan also called it a "brotherhood") but, rather, like an embodiment of Modern Britain on an intercontinental scale. It had the Queen (who had indeed claimed the title "Head of the Commonwealth"), Westminster-style political constitutions, a customs union, rich resources, cheap capital via the city of London money markets, the British pound as its master currency, and, as of 1965, a permanent secretariat in St James's. Even Cyprus, which had no "proper" British settlers and "only" British military bases, joined the club in 1961.

In this framing, "Winds of Change" resonated with the Socialist discourse as well. The same goes for many Labourites. Some, like party leaders, were merely hypocrites: although the party's 1964 election manifesto called for an end of colonialism, in practice Labour supported a foreign policy status quo (Darwin 1991, 27; Grob-Fitzgibbon 2016, 290–2; Shilliam 2018, 146). Others were merely strategic: if colonial policy is inseparable from anti-Soviet policy, then the "family of nations" was precisely a means of defanging anti-colonial campaigns led by India and other Third World nations (for context, see Hyam 2006, chap. 4; Heinlein 2002, chap. 5; Harrison 2009, 6, 101–4; Darwin 2009, 633–4; Toye 2013). And still others, much like most Britons, were wilfully ignorant of the Commonwealth's history – that is, the fact that the British Empire was built upon economic and ecological devastation and maintained through divisions, inequalities, and imperial violence.

"Instead of the loss of empire spelling Britain's decline," Elizabeth Buettner (2016, 46) remarks, "the growth and metamorphosis of the Commonwealth would attest to Britain's resilience, adaptability, and ability to dictate the course and pace of change, as well as indicate dedication to racial inclusivity and equality." Of course, civil society was well aware that "inclusivity" and "multi-racial" character always applied only to Britain's "exterior."[8] This is precisely why both parties supported the new Commonwealth Immigration Act, 1962, which, by putting controls on African and Asian immigration, severed family ties both figuratively and literally (Doty 1996b; Paul 1997, chaps. 5–6; Buettner 2016, chaps. 1 and 7; Shilliam 2018, chap. 5.). (Note also that attempts to curb immigration and citizenship rights of people from the old imperial territories has continued since, right down to the time of this writing.)

In a racist interpretation of global affairs, overseas "police action" or "emergencies" – whether in Yemen, Kenya, Uganda, Tanganyika (today's Tanzania), Malaya, Brunei, or dozens of other places – was in the natural order of things, as was the maintenance of "multi-purpose" bases in Aden, the Persian Gulf, Malaysia, Singapore, and Hong Kong long after the imperial retreat. The same sensibilities guided British policy when a white settler-ruled Southern Rhodesia unilaterally declared independence in 1965 and when the US asked Britain to "clear" Diego Garcia in 1967.

This brings us to the Skybolt Affair, which is the name of a crisis in UK-US relations caused by the American decision to cancel a missile program that the British military intended to use as its main nuclear delivery system (for discussions, see Pierre 1972; Lee 1996; Murray 2000; Baylis and Stoddart 2015, esp. chap. 5). The tiff was deep and entirely public, with Acheson making things worse with his jibe about a post-empire Britain going aimless in the world. That same month, December 1962, Macmillan met with President John F. Kennedy in Nassau, where they struck a deal very much in the spirit of the special (nuclear) relationship between the two countries: the transfer to Britain of a superior US-made nuclear missile system, Polaris. Much as with the Trident system later in the century – one of the topics of chapter 4 – the deal was available only to the UK.[9]

Considering Acheson's comment, and also that in 1961 Macmillan was unceremoniously excluded from Kennedy's summit with the Soviet leader Nikita Khrushchev in Vienna, the Nassau deal was a coup for exceptionalists because, with Polaris missiles, Britain (technically) retained an "independent" nuclear arsenal and, with it, a "disproportionally large influence" in NATO nuclear strategy.[10] As he received his honorary US citizenship in April 1963, Churchill had his son Randolph read out a note of thanks that included this response to Acheson:

> It is a remarkable comment on our affairs that the former Prime Minister of a great sovereign state should thus be received as an honorary citizen of another. I say "great sovereign state" with design and emphasis, for I reject the view that Britain and the Commonwealth should now be relegated to a tame and minor role in the world.[11]

In other words, Nassau was a coup *if* London decision makers used it wisely to maintain Britain's rightful position in the hierarchy of states.

For McCourt, the Skybolt Affair was primarily a clash of "role expectations." As before, Britain was acting as a "residual great power," attempting to maintain its "independent" nuclear deterrent in order to "keep up with the Joneses," as Macmillan actually put it to the Americans at Nassau (McCourt 2014a, 91). There was nothing odd about this statement: every British official from Bevin onwards has publicly argued that Britain needed its own nuclear weapons for this reason, too, and not just to deter and prevent foreign aggression. However, as we saw in the previous chapter, already in the 1950s Britain put itself in a unique position among nuclear powers by relying on another state – the US – for developing, producing, and servicing key parts of these weapons and their delivery systems (Heuser 1998; Croft 2001b; Beaumont 2014; Baylis and Stoddart 2015, chap. 5, appendices 2 and 5). The move to cancel an indigenous strategic missile program, Blue Streak, which duly received criticism in the news media in 1960, including in the *Daily Express* (15

April, editorial), and instead buying the US's Skybolt missile, was consistent with this trend.

The challenge for British leadership, once again, was to find a rhetoric that could accommodate a paradoxical relationship with the US. As McCourt notes, the Macmillan government achieved this by concocting new phrases. One of them was "UK-US interdependence," which underscored various British contributions to the defence of the West. A good example of interdependence at work was an agreement in 1960 to permit the use of Holy Loch in Scotland as a base for the US Navy's submarine-launched ballistic missile deterrent force. The other key phrase was "supreme national interest." The Macmillan-Kennedy joint statement issued at Nassau stated that Polaris missiles would be used to deter and prevent Soviet aggression against NATO countries, except where Britain's "supreme national interests are at stake." But while the two sides never agreed on what would constitute this exception, the phrase was eminently usable politically, especially to British policy-makers who claimed that Britain maintained independence over the use of nuclear weapons (McCourt 2014a, chap. 3). In private, however, they realized exactly where the UK stood: "We find American support for our overseas policies virtually indispensable," wrote Foreign Secretary R.A. Butler in 1964 upon interacting with Kennedy's successor in the White House, Lyndon B. Johnson. "They find our support for theirs useful and sometimes valuable" (Darwin 2009, 638).

So, why did the UK not seek a non-US alternative to Skybolt? A new system to be co-developed and co-produced with France was eminently conceivable, not least because the Cold War détente opened up avenues for more independent foreign policy orientations.[12] The answer once again lies in the discourses of Britishness. If America was an extension of the British Self and the French were viewed with a degree of condescension, then doubling down on the special relationship was easier than pursuing the alternative.

The Skybolt Affair had adverse consequences for Britain's relationship with Europe in the sense that Nassau confirmed French president Charles de Gaulle's belief that Britain was America's "Trojan horse," which, in turn, compelled him to veto Britain's applications for EEC membership in January 1963 and again in December 1967 (McCourt 2014a, 103–7). This is another well-trodden chapter in British foreign policy textbooks, usually explained in terms of changing trade patterns. As Saunders and Houghton show, in those years the Commonwealth progressively lost a larger and larger share of British trade to the EEC, a.k.a., the Six.[13] Yet, as we saw earlier, changing immigration patterns mattered at least as much. Once the settlement of non-white Commonwealth workers began to turn permanent, the government moved to close the empire door for good. Either way, Britain "turned to Europe because it had nowhere to go."[14]

Well aware of the new realities, and also supported by the US, the Macmillan government moved in July 1961 to apply for EEC membership, with then Lord Privy Seal and future prime minister Ted Heath in charge of negotiations. The tactical goal was to broker special arrangements for Britain's imperial bloc. As for the strategic goal, Macmillan had already articulated it in 1956: since even as an imperial power Britain cannot compete with the American and Soviet "big units," maybe London should consider working together with the Europeans.[15]

The problem for Macmillan and Heath was that British identity compelled them to negotiate from a position of superiority and exceptionality. As the one Western European power who had vanquished the Nazis, and who was firmly in the nuclear club, British society expected Britain to have certain privileges in the EEC, including keeping the Commonwealth customs union. Furthermore, among the Tories, France was seen as weaker than before – a view shaped by the French military's defeats in Vietnam and Algeria and the subsequent regime change in Paris.[16] As for Labour, its National Executive Committee was still adamant that the Commonwealth was a "much larger and still more important group" than the EEC (Grob-Fitzgibbon 2016, 291), while its leaders, first Gaitskell and then Wilson, hardly differed from the Tories in terms of high expectations regarding Britain's role in the EEC and conditions on a set of demands that all but guaranteed a European veto.

The notion that "we" could maintain world leadership and create wealth through trade was also shared among media, business, and academic leaders. And, as before, exceptionalism regularly bled into exemplarism. "More than most Powers, we can still presume to precedence in teaching nations how to live," wrote the journalist and historian

James Morris in 1962 in the context of an *Encounter* magazine debate on whether to join the Common Market (quoted in O'Toole 2019, 8).

None of this went well on the Continent. At the (in)famous press conference of 14 January 1963, de Gaulle intimated that the British were delusional to think they would receive special treatment, while making no less than five references to the Nassau agreement. The general also expressed his view that the Macmillan application was a step in the right direction, one that "one day perhaps will lead [Britain] to dock with the continent."[17] As for his "l'Angleterre, ce n'est plus grand-chose," or "England is not much anymore," a statement so contemptuous that all English-language history reproduces it in the original French, he did not actually say it at the press conference but months later (Peyrefitte 1994, chap. 18; Milward 2013, chap 14). As we see in the next chapter, Britain's request for special privileges in the EEC was a challenge that took twelve years of discontinuous negotiations and continuous policy learning to solve.

Like Heath, Wilson, who was the prime minister from 1964 to 1970 and again from 1974 to 1976, deserves a great deal of credit for Britain's turn to Europe. The rest of Wilson's foreign policy, however, was remarkably status quo-oriented (Vickers 2011, 5). Though he famously rejected President Johnson's demands for British troops to join the US-led war in Vietnam, Wilson actually supported most other US foreign policy goals, including the one that banned cross-bloc attempts to broker peace, and he stuck with the US-provided "independent" nuclear deterrent, despite promising to get rid of it in Labour's 1964 election manifesto and despite strong opposition from the left wing of the party and various peace groups, including a formidable Campaign for Nuclear Disarmament.[18] This is consistent with my analysis of Britishness in 1960: a commitment to the special relationship was a good fit with the discourse of Modern Britain, whatever the protestation from those on the party's left.

The special relationship also helps explain the puzzle of Wilson's defence or, rather, imperial policy. Commissioned by the prime minister in his first year in office and dubbed the Healey review after Defence Secretary Denis Healey, the white paper and its accompanying statement on defence estimates were released on 22 February 1966, a week before a general election in which Labour would go on to win a comfortable majority.[19]

· The Healey review called for a major budget cut and a partial overseas retrenchment. As Andrew Dorman (2001, 17) notes, "declaratory policy was allowed to remain largely unchanged although in reality the majority of commentators recognised that this marked the beginning of the withdrawal from East of Suez and the down-playing of the world role." Looking at my analysis for the year 1960, this reality did not fit British identity all. From the perspective of both Modern Britain and Socialism, imperial withdrawal was not a moral injury but, rather, proof that "we" are exceptional and exemplary, given that no other power could lead a multi-racial family of nations. Secondary literature suggests the presence of more niche elite discourses, but there, too, we see mostly dissonance with Wilson's policy. For Tory right-wingers, for one, being a *modern* world power still meant being a modern *world* power. Labour's left-wing, in contrast, wanted neither world nor power.[20]

But here is where the special relationship comes in again. In 1965, Wilson struck a secret deal with the Johnson administration, which offered American cash to support the pound in exchange for Britain's continuing East of Suez presence, meaning its military presence in Asia, with over fifty thousand soldiers in the Far East and almost thirty thousand in the Middle East.[21] Though the prime minister would later proceed to renege on this deal, the logic of the deal reflected and reinforced a foreign policy of the status quo.[22] The broken deal, as we see in the next chapter, exacerbated UK-US tensions over Vietnam, among other issues.

Another interpretation of the Healey document comes from Waltz (1968, 156), who read it as setting a defence policy of "keeping the roles, reducing the means, and changing the rationalizations." The Wilson government indeed stayed the course, however level-headed its assessment of Britain's commitment-capability gap: "In the long term, a partial reduction of global military obligations would be inevitable." But rather than concluding that Waltz was right to harshly criticize British foreign policy, let us give the last word to IR scholars Harold and Margaret Sprout, who, in 1963 wrote:

> It is one thing for American observers to delineate the unresolved dilemmas of British statecraft. It is perhaps more difficult for us to appreciate the degree to which feasible solutions are unacceptable

and acceptable solutions are unfeasible under the political and economic conditions prevailing in Britain and in the larger world arena today. (Sprout and Sprout 1963, 688)

The Sprouts were right. It was one thing for Acheson and other American observers like him to look at the last Macmillan years – not to mention Home's interregnum in 1963–64 or Wilson's government that followed it – and see Britain's declining position in world affairs. It was another thing for British society to have some kind of perfect bird's-eye view of itself.

3

Between Europe and Nixon

How did the great imperial retrenchment of the 1960s affect Britain's view of itself? What of the dire financial circumstances of the first Harold Wilson premiership, including the painful devaluation of sterling in late 1967? In the preceding chapter I detail the ways in which British society maintained an exceptionalist narrative after Suez. Britain wanted to have it both ways – to support decolonization and also to retain a Commonwealth imperium. But 1970 was a much more ontologically insecure year, given the confluence of ongoing industrial strife, the "Troubles" in Northern Ireland, and the vigorous culture war in some parts of British society over the meanings of gender and sexuality. A general election happened in 1970 as well, resulting in an unexpected change of government from Wilson's Labour to Heath's Conservative.

The weight of evidence points to more continuity than change. "Modern Britain," the dominant discourse of Britishness in 1970, is similar to its 1960 predecessor in terms of its overall positive evaluation of national outlook and of the glories of being a world-leading country. This Britain defined itself in terms of democracy, modernity, law and order, social freedom, technology, leisure time, and, especially, justice and fairness. It was also less English and patriarchal than before, even if the aesthetic standpoint from which to interpret all of these axes of identification was still that of an adult heterosexual English male. In thinking about the nation's economy, this average citizen had two discursive prostheses at his disposal: the "Socialist" discourse, represented by Labour, emphasized strong state intervention and stronger unions; the "Traditionalist" discourse, embodied by some Tories, asked for more individual responsibility and more competition. Foreign policy was not subject to contestation. Modern Britain was threatened by communists and the Irish or, rather, by the violence instigated by Catholics in Northern Ireland. It believed in supporting American and European allies, opposing the Soviet Union, and helping the Third World.

These continuities set us up for a puzzle for in the 1970s Britain "finally" turned away from the Empire and towards Europe in a credible fashion. East of Suez, followed by the budget-cutting 1975 Mason defence review, indeed constituted a major foreign policy shift. This goes double for the entry into the Common Market – a decision that required a referendum. Even the temporary distancing from the US in the Heath years in response to the so-called Nixon shock of 1971 constitutes a significant break that appears to be at odds with the dominant discourse of Britishness. How, indeed, do government leaders legitimate foreign policy change when society – that is, "the habit and furniture of our minds" – might be predisposed towards the status quo? I argue here that three factors were decisive, two agentic and one structural. First, the Heath and Wilson governments framed East of Suez as consistent with the modernization of the kingdom and "its" Commonwealth; second, they framed the dilemma of Europe versus the Commonwealth as a false one – Britain could participate in both; third, they were helped by the fact that Britishness had indeed evolved in ways that allowed them to recast, or at least rebrand, the prevailing definition of greatness. Two and a half cheers for elite agency, then.

1970: "Natural Inheritors of the Traditions That Made Britain Great"

Figure 3.1 captures the most commonly reoccurring identity categories in the corpus for this year.[1] *Fair/just* is the top identity category, partly because it is an amalgam of two heretofore separately coded identity categories. Consider first the words of Wilson, in his address to Parliament as a former prime minister following the victory of the Heath-led Conservatives in the election of 18 June 1970, about what his Labour government had achieved:

The fairer social climate ... fair, not only because social justice is an end in itself and one of the first duties of government, but also fair, as the right hon. Gentleman will rapidly discover, because there can be no solution to Britain economic difficulties unless all of those who are asked to contribute to that solution, by their efforts, by their restraint – their sacrifices, even – can feel that what they are asked is fair and part of a justly ordered society.

In other words, Britain, under Labour, had aspired, and under the Conservatives should aspire, towards being ever fairer. To underscore the message, Wilson proceeded to criticize Heath's cabinet for being too male and too rich, the Conservatives for being too "reactionary" and "regressive," and fellow parliamentarians for failing to make "the cricket grounds of Britain safe for racially selected teams to play on."

The archive confirms the presence of a collective awareness of the nation's ongoing economic, social, and political divides: between the wealthier Home Counties and the poorer North; between the disorderly and violent *Northern Ireland*, sometimes simply called Ulster, and the *orderly* rest of the country; between the old and the *young*; between men and women; between *tradition* and progress. Some of these divides correlated with *partisanship* and ideology, at least according to the discourse of the ruling elite. On the left was Wilson's Labour, which preoccupied itself with working-class struggles, with *trade unions*, and with human rights – both in Northern Ireland and with respect to Commonwealth immigration ("open" and "anti-immigrant" are both categories in 1970, though neither appears in figure 3.1). On the right was the Conservative Party, whose interests were said to align with business interests. Heath, the new prime minister, prioritized "restoring freedom of choice to the individual" as well as curbing "permanent immigration" (Heath Address). He also wanted to see less partisanship and more unity: "We had a surfeit of politics and very little responsible Government. It will be exactly the reverse in the second half of 1970 under this Administration." He added that "the greatest challenge which faces us still today" is "to create within freedom in Britain one nation."

As in previous years under study, in 1970 Britain identified as a *modern, capitalist,* and *democratic* nation with an *activist state.* According to the

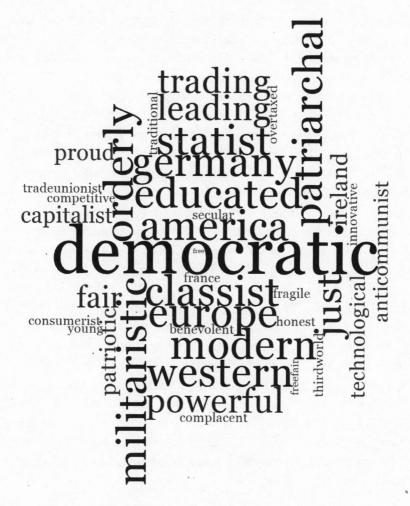

Figure 3.1 Top British identity categories in 1970 by frequency

history textbooks, the UK became great through empowering its people and through trade and profit-making, which then came together to propel the Industrial Revolution, expand commerce, and create prosperity.[2] *Class* was again among the top categories. On the elite end of everyday discourse, the modal point of view was that of a politically conscious middle-class subject, whether individual or institutional, asking why some groups in Britain were marginalized or proposing ideas on how to make the weaker less dependent on decisions made by the stronger.

Larkin's (1964, 144) textbook explicitly connects the rise of industrial capitalism to the changes in British society and politics: "The contrast between extreme wealth and extreme poverty became more glaring, and the battle between capital and labour more clear-cut."

In the elite discourse, class divides were progressively narrowing. They were also contingent on events. In the texts about the Second World War, class matters but nowhere as much as does *patriotism*. Consider the blockbuster *Battle of Britain*: in contrast to the other squadron leader, Skipper, Cranfield, an aristocratic Royal Air Force officer played by Michael Caine, appears out of touch and uncaring but willing to die for king and country. In Alistair MacLean's novel *Force 10 from Navarone*, a Second World War bestseller, the whisky-sipping Jensen, the chief intelligence officer behind the commando raid and a "prototype for the classic British naval captain," is an able warrior, as is Miller, one of the commandos, who just happens to be a brandy-loving West Londoner who "uses a napkin at meals." Going back to class, upper-class men are loved when they are stoical, fearsome, and resilient – like regular British men.

Elsewhere, class was more fixed. *Endless Night*, Agatha Christie's whodunit novel, centres on the doomed marriage of Ellie Guteman, a bored, fragile American heiress who "thought nothing of taking a plane over to England for twenty-four hours and then flying back again," and Mike Rodgers, a handsome local chauffeur keen to "move up" and "make good." Poorly educated, Mike is confused about the difference between Cézanne and tzigane ("which I gather is a gipsy orchestra") and therefore insecure in front of Ellie:

> Ellie: "I wish you wouldn't be so obsessed with class distinctions."
> Mike: "Me! What's your American phrase – I come from the wrong side of the tracks … I don't know the right way to talk about things and I don't know anything really about pictures or art or music. I'm only just learning who to tip and how much to give."

The elites and the masses agreed that capitalist modernity came at a cost. In principle, "anyone" could succeed but "everyone" had to work – perform tasks or produce goods that other people wanted. But, in reality, the free market was often unforgiving regardless of one's hard work.[3]

In the elite discourse, Labour supporters were utopian idealists – as well as "democratic socialists" – who sought to reduce class inequality by transforming most aspects of capitalism, including private property. Conservative supporters, in contrast, were less sanguine about *statist* ideas and practices and especially about intervening in the economy. This is evident in the op-eds. In the Labour-leaning *Daily Mirror*, the Labour government receives high marks for its plan to spend money on "single women, pensioners, and lower-paid workers" (15 April 1970). In contrast, op-eds and letters published in the pro-Tory, pro-Empire *Daily Express* – in the film *On Her Majesty's Secret Service*, this is Bond's pre-ferred daily – describe Britain as *over-taxed* and statism as a cause of economic and social ills, including, to name a few examples, underpaid farmers and nurses (15 January 1970), poor communication with the British diaspora (due to a high tax on mail to and from Rhodesia, 15 April 1970), and rising food prices (15 May 1970). In *Endless Night*, tax-ation is a source of major unease.

Trade unionism was closely associated with socialism, but Conservative and Liberal parties supported it because the alternative was a path to electoral oblivion. Indeed, anti-unionism was seen as retrograde; today's employers could not manipulate the employees as before. For Prime Minister Heath, trade unionism went too far, into a "chaotic state" as he put it in his address:

> The present rash of strikes, to such a large extent unofficial, is the symptom of impoverished industrial relations, of unsatisfactory machinery and of increasing disregard for obligations which have been undertaken. I believe that as a nation we are not doing justice to ourselves or to our history.

The elites and the masses consistently worried about the *fragility* of the British economy. This was expressed in the speeches given by the two prime ministers. The outgoing Wilson praised the strength of sterling and the strong balance of payments but not much else. For the incoming Heath, Britain was "a *trading nation*" dependent on international peace and stability, its economy suffering mightily from inflation ("the worst we have known for 20 years"), underinvestment in manufacturing, low

productivity, low reserves, strikes, and "substantial overseas debts." This
was the more dominant perspective at both elite and mass levels of everyday discourse.

Like in 1950 and 1960, in 1970 Britain understood itself as *patriarchal*.
British women were expected to be married in their twenties, supportive
of their children, and affectionate towards their husbands (*Daily Mirror*,
15 December 1970). That this arrangement curtailed their freedom was
dismissed. One male letter writer in the *Daily Mirror* put it thus: "Grumble
away, lady, and make the old man babysit for you now and again while
you have a natter with your girlfriends" (15 August 1970). From a French
perspective, Britain was a "man's country": "In France a woman dom-
inates everything. It is a country of women ... that's why my husband
likes to visit England. Because their women are of little importance"
(*Daily Express*, 15 May 1970).

The mass-oriented fictional sources echoed these sentiments. In *Endless Night*, Mike is not keen on working with women ("however efficient
and even handsome they are"), and Ellie thinks that marriage determines
nationality: "I'm American – or I was, but now I'm married to an Englishman so I'm an Englishwoman." Both movies centre on white, middle-
aged, and upper-middle-class men in charge of aspects of national
security who complain about women, but counter-perspectives exist. In
Battle of Britain, a female section officer, a sexual Englishwoman, refuses
to transfer to another base with her squadron leader husband, an abusive
Canadian: "I'm just not the type to wave a wet hanky in sooty stations."
(More on sexuality and gender below.)

Modern, capitalist Britain was understood to revolve around money.
Rudolf Santonix, a successful architect who designs Ellie and Mike's
house in *Endless Night*, wants Mike to be comfortable with his new life:
"Born poor doesn't mean you've got to stay poor. Money's queer. It goes
where it's wanted." Mike, for his part, professes discomfort as he splashes
money on "more and more super luxury ... bigger bathrooms and larger
houses and more electric light fittings and bigger meals and faster cars."

To illustrate the rise of *consumerism* at this time, consider the last two
items on Mike's list: meals and cars. In 1970, eating out was rising in
popularity – half entertainment, half "relief from kitchen chores" (*Daily*

Express, 15 April 1970). As for cars, their consumption, or at least the consumption of car culture, was soaring. *Secret Service* opens up with Bond
cruising a coastal highway in his Aston Martin, when a female driver in
a red Mercury overtakes him. Following a dramatic encounter with the
driver, Bond introduces himself but fails to learn her name. To his luck,
he later spots the same red Mercury at a casino parking lot, thus locating
the driver.

Though a fantasy scene in a fantasy movie, it arguably captures one
idea of the good life, at least among British men. As extensions of the individual self, cars were in high demand, and so, as good capitalists, British
carmakers were expected to welcome foreign competition as this was
thought to lead to the availability of better and cheaper cars. The newest
model of Renault, a French car, "will stimulate healthy competition
which, in turn, can only benefit the motorists in the long run," editorialized the *Daily Express* on 15 May 1970. And to fuel all those cars and the
rest of its economy, Britain needed to keep its energy industry robust.
According to an op-ed in the left-leaning *Daily Mirror*, British Petro-
leum's new oil find in Alaska should be celebrated as a huge business opportunity, not criticized for its potential impact on the life of caribou
herds (15 December 1970). In short, in 1970, British capitalism lost no
solidity in relation to 1960.

Britain likewise continued to define itself as *innovative*, primarily in
science and *technology* but also more generally – in war, for example. An
op-ed published in the *Daily Express* on 15 August 1970 paints a portrait
of a young boy who built a computer in his bedroom, suggesting that
"these youngsters are the natural inheritors of the traditions that made
Britain great." Innovation was a function of good *education*, which is a
top ten identity category for this year –arguably a reflection of the sharp
rise of higher education in the 1960s. As an op-ed in the same newspaper
explains on 15 December, elementary and secondary schools should not
be a "comfortable conveyer belt" for feeding universities but, rather,
places where students develop interest in knowledge and learn skills. The
two newspaper pieces are indeed in agreement: with a new generation
of skilled and creative people, Britain's future may well be bright and glorious, much like its past. Alternatively, miss your opportunity to complete

school and you are likely to be stuck with hopeless low-wage jobs: "Petrol pump. Mechanic in a garage. Temporary clerk washer-up in a sleazy night-club restaurant" (Mike in *Endless Night*).

In 1970, the British saw themselves as being too *complacent* as well as rather *competitive* and resilient (the last category is not in the top fifth). Complacency emerged in trade, football, and politics. In this "straw-berries-and-cream election" – which conjures up the image of a lazy English summer (and the annual international tennis tournament at Wimbledon) – voters are naturally unlikely to show up at the voting booth, editorialized the *Daily Express* on 15 June, which is why the Conservatives needed to double their voter mobilization effort. On 15 September in an op-ed, the *Daily Mirror* made a similar point about union leaders, who appeared to be more interested in themselves ("Why do you dream only of money?") than in helping the Labour Party ("the Labour movement") come up with winning new ideas.

Competitiveness, in contrast, was imagined to be Britain's natural state. As the Larkin (1964) textbook explains, England became powerful by competing with other nations over many centuries. Resilience emerged in war. In *Battle of Britain*, the leadership, starting with Winston Churchill and his generals, are portrayed as resolute, aircrews as effective, and the London masses as defiant, refusing to be bowed by German bombs. In one scene a man in charge of the air raid siren is visibly unemotional when he learns about the approaching swarm of Heinkels. The novel *Force 10 from Navarone* follows the same model: the job of the British commandos, who are the soldiers of exceptional "initiative, self-reliance, independence in thought and action," is to "turn near-conviction into absolute certainty."

The British also understood themselves as essentially *benevolent* (a composite category including *compassionate* and *caring*) – towards each other, towards the former colonies, towards animals. For example, fox hunting, an upper-class pastime that some insisted was a traditional method of controlling the fox population, was rejected as woefully retro-grade: "There is a very humane method of trapping foxes without the need for horses and hounds" (*Daily Mirror*, op-ed, 15 January 1970). By the same token, all British aspired to be *honest* and expected honesty from their leaders. On 15 April 1970, an editorial in the *Daily Mirror*, the newspaper favouring the Labour Party, applauded the Labour chancellor for proposing an "honest budget" and refusing to "match the Tories in a perilous auction of lavish tax cuts." At election time two months later, a letter to the editors of the *Daily Express* commended Heath, as the Conservative candidate for prime minister, for his transparency and honesty and proposed that he "deserves voters trust" (15 June 1970). (The *Express* editorial on that day in fact agreed with this assessment, calling Labour politicians "mind-benders" and "brainwashers.") Similarly disappointing were dishonest practices in the marketplace. Companies were said to be lifting prices of tea for no other reason than to trick shoppers into believing that they were buying a better-quality item (*Daily Express*, op-ed, 15 August 1970). *Endless Night* mentions the "corruption of the rich," albeit only in passing.

British democracy was not contradicted by the existence of "the Royals." While the Queen stood for leadership, she was also understood as "entertainment." In one office scene in *Secret Service*, Bond downs his drink while nodding in the direction of the Queen's portrait on the wall. *Traditional* was a nebulous identity category. Those tired of the nation's class structure had no time for a gallery of titled aristocrats, gentry, and posh schools, from Eton and Harrow to "Oxbridge." However, those feeling disoriented by the pace of modern life aspired for a more traditional Britain, as did those who refused to give themselves over to the new industrial machinery, new medicines, new foods and food production practices, and new forms of entertainment. For still others, tradition meant safety and sensibility. Speed limits on British roads did not seem to apply to "car maniacs" (*Daily Mirror*, letter, 15 May 1970). The new computer age meant that fewer people were communicating with each other and more were communicating with machines, that electric bills were higher than before, and that Britain's new bank notes were "incomprehensible" (*Daily Express*, op-ed, 15 August 1970). On occasion, tradition also referred to the progress made in previous decades: the expansion of health service and education or the provision of council housing.

Several texts imply that Britain was Christian, but many more articulate it as *secular*. Virtually all fictional characters are the latter. Mike from

Endless Night is an example. For him, "God" is merely a metaphor for power. He recognizes that his mother provided him with a decent up-bringing but does not feel morally debased for participating in organized crime ("race-course gangs, and dope gangs, the rough and tumble dangers of life"). He dismisses superstition too. He builds a dream house on Gipsy's Acre, despite hearing from everyone that there was a curse on the place. In *Battle of Britain*, two government officials acknowledge that radar is the vastly outnumbered Royal Air Force's secret weapon. "We should be trusting radar and praying to God. Or is it the other way around?" Importantly, secularism characterized England but not necess-arily the rest of the country, where there appeared to be more interest in the supernatural and the miraculous. In *Force 10 from Navarone*, Captain Mallory is said to be of Scottish descent – "and everyone knew how the Scots indulged in those heathenish practices of second sight and peering into the future."

In 1970, Britain was a *free* society. National tolerance for sexual liberty, for one, was higher than ever before. In the Bond movie, for example, the eponymous protagonist is seen flipping through *Playboy*, a soft porn magazine. The British were conflicted over this development: some texts approved it, but most did not. Sexual liberty appeared to reflect and also reinforce a rising culture of permissiveness in British society. An author in the *Daily Mirror* described a new play that contained rape, murder, and orgies with "appalling fascination," while expressing confusion about the constitution of contemporary arts (op-ed, 15 April 1970). Controver-sial cultural agendas were understood to be pushed by the elites. As for the masses, their pleasures were simpler. An important feature of British identity was an affinity for alcohol and for social drinking. In some towns, "the drunks Olympics" were commonplace, keeping the police busy (*Daily Mirror*, op-ed, 15 August 1970).

Going back to the point about patriarchy, Britain's growing sexual lib-erty was gendered. Naturally men could engage in sexual innuendos and sexual promiscuity in ways that women could not. An op-ed in the *Daily Mirror* titled "Questions of a Revealing Nature" dared British women to assess their wardrobe to determine if they were a "hussy," a prude, or somewhere in between (15 December 1970). In comparison to their Aus-tralian counterparts, however, British women were by definition prudes

– consider one female columnist's fascination with "skimpy bikinis" Down Under (*Daily Mirror*, 15 April 1970).

The Bond movie goes an extra mile in hypermasculinity and swaggering male chauvinism. In the very first scene, Contessa Tracy di Vicenzo is literally saved by Bond – he stops her from committing suicide by drowning herself on a beach. In a following scene, Tracy's father Draco, a Corsican Mafioso with ties to MI6, attempts to give her to Bond for a "dowry of one million pounds in gold." Draco's explanation is that his traumatized daughter does not need a psychiatrist: "What she needs is a man, to dominate her, to make love to her, to make her love him. A man like me." In another scene, Bond hits Tracy, which makes her even more interested in him. By the end of the movie, Tracy gains more agency, albeit never vis-à-vis Bond. "Obey your husband in all things," says Draco at his daughter's wedding. "But of course I will, as I always obeyed you," she says.

In the Bond movie, sexism also goes hand in hand with racism. Bond, posing as a kilt-wearing heraldry scholar, arrives at Blofeld's health institute in the Swiss Alps and is invited to dinner, where he eats with the institute's dozen female patients from around the world. The curious aspect of the dinner is that each guest is given food from her part of the world: an Indian woman is eating naan; an East Asian woman is eating a bowl of rice; white European women are eating, variously, chicken, steak, pork, potato, and corn; and then an African woman is eating seemingly nothing but a peeled banana. The one most interested in Bond is Ruby, an Englishwoman, who creatively invites him to her room. In *Battle of Britain*, Czechs and Polish fighter pilots are mistrusted: a "menace to themselves and to us." Likewise, in the novels, racialized hierarchies and racist interpretations of society were commonplace. Three different characters in *Endless Night* describe "gypsies" as a "thieving lot." Andrea Stavros, the fun-loving, physical Greek member of the commando squad in *Force 10 from Navarone*, is also filthy.

Britain was also powerful, meaning *influential*, if not world-leading. A nation aspiring to be fair and just naturally pursued an ethical foreign policy or, as expressed by Wilson in his House of Commons Address, "a heritage of foreign and Commonwealth policies rooted in morality, idealism and concern for the dignity and equality of men everywhere –

a heritage which we fostered, a heritage of which we shall ever be proud." Wilson was disappointed with the Conservative government's decision to approve an arms deal with South Africa:

> I hope that the Government have worked out for themselves what it will mean for our standing in the United Nations. Have they thought this thing through? ... Have they thought of what it means in terms of the isolation of Britain in a small rump of colonialists and one or two ex-colonial Powers, with all that this means in terms of loss of influence in world affairs?

Taken together, the leadership speeches show a sense of ambiguity about Britain's *post-imperial* moment. In his address, Wilson spoke against "treating Commonwealth citizens, from the old and the new Commonwealth alike, as aliens" for reasons of "standing" and diplomacy. His Conservative rival Heath disagreed, believing Britain's foreign policy should be primarily about Britain. Sometimes that included supporting the former colonies – "our Commonwealth allies in Malaysia and Singapore, in Australia and New Zealand" – but not always. (In fact, Heath appeared keen on clinging on to the Empire a little longer: "The right hon. Gentleman did us a good turn by calling the election a year before he had to do so, and 18 months before the last date for our withdrawal from the Gulf and the Far East.")

Throughout the archive, *military* power emerges as a key source of British influence in the world. In the Larkin (1964) textbook, the kingdom is a great military power throughout. The Royal Navy is unsurpassed, and colonial misadventures – the 1883 Sudan intervention, for example – are thankfully rare. The military and war are part and parcel of British life in all fictional work surveyed. In *Endless Night*, the town's most powerful figure is a judicial officer named Major Philpot, and we learn that Ellie's brother died in the Korean War.

The novel *Force 10 from Navarone* and the movie *Battle of Britain* normalize war even further by linking Britain's greatness to the war-fighting prowess of its men in the Second World War. In the novel, the British commandos see the Mediterranean as a British lake, and Yugoslavia ends up being within the British sphere of influence: "We are the *only* people who are at present supplying them with rifles, machine-guns, ammunition and medical supplies." In the movie, the smallness of "the island" is emphasized to magnify the victory. In one of the early scenes, the British ambassador in Switzerland refuses to talk surrender with a German emissary: "We are not easily frightened. Also we know how hard it is for an army to cross the channel."[4]

Like in the previous years under study, Britain was obsessed with the *US*, with American modernity once again configured as simultaneously attractive and repulsive. According to the Titley (1969) textbook, once the US caught up with Britain in the nineteenth century, the US never looked back: their cars and their steel were cheaper, their financial capital more influential. *Endless Night* sends the same message. Compared to American breakfast – "coffee and a glass of orange juice and nothing much else" – English breakfast was fit only for a "Victorian squire," notes Mike. Americans were also reproduced not only as confident, hardworking, and innovative but also as individualistic, profligate, and racist. Closely allied to the US, the British celebrated American achievements and shared in the pain over the failure of the Apollo 13 mission. Human space travel may be pure hubris by default, but it is especially so if "we" forget that it is "courage, not computers, which advances human knowledge" (*Daily Express*, op-ed, 15 April 1970).

In 1970, *Europe* appears to be as significant as the US, or more significant if we add the raw identity counts for *France* and *Germany*. The Larkin (1964) textbook portrays *England* (as opposed to Britain) as a shrewd player of the European balance-of-power game. The Titley (1969, 70) textbook focuses on decline as Britain's industrial supremacy was lost by the end of the nineteenth century, and not just to Germany and the US: "Even France was outpacing us in motor vehicle production." Contemporary France was a close partner – that is, "now" that the reasonable Georges Pompidou had succeeded the intransigent de Gaulle (173), and "now" that the two countries spent almost a billion pounds to develop the Concorde supersonic passenger jet (255). Implicitly, this was a recognition of Britain's relative decline as a great power: while in absolute terms, the British were better off than in previous years, the Western Europeans were apparently doing better still. The one thing that could *never* decline relative to Europe was the higher

moral ground: in addition to standing alone in 1940, Britain's decolonization experience in 1960 was infinitely more civilized than was that
of the French in Algeria and Vietnam.

Contemporary France was now also a must-see place for the British
middle class rather than just the rich. An op-ed published in the *Daily
Mirror* is fascinated with the British fascination with this "naughty"
country where denied whims run wild – "a bidet is primarily for washing
the crotch" (15 December 1970). It is the same in the works of fiction: like
the Bond movie, *Endless Night* constructs Europe as a place of leisure
and high culture, whereby France is the top destination, followed by Italy.
The novel's protagonists thus spend their honeymoon on the French
Riviera and spend "fabulous sums for pictures and furniture" in Paris.
(The British masses at the time, note, still faced countless restrictions on
travel even to northern France.)

However, Germany was still viewed through the two world wars. Both
textbooks and Second World War-themed works of fiction show respect
for German military power: its warplanes, U-boats, Schmeisser machine
pistols, and tactical skills. Then there are sheer numbers: *Battle of Britain*
opens with the British evacuating all serviceable aircraft from the capitu-
lating France, stating that the UK has "650 planes compared to 2,500 for
the Germans." Both *Force 10 from Navarone* and *Battle of Britain* portray
German soldiers as sleek and arrogant (although in the movie they lose
their composure towards the end). Insecurity can be found elsewhere,
too. In *Endless Night* there is a German character named Greta, an au
pair and Elli's friend, who together with Mike plots Elli's demise. And
during the World Cup football tournament in Mexico, a gritty West German team recovered from two goals down against England to score in
extra time. This was a slap in the face: England's first-ever competitive
loss to West Germany and a payback for the last World Cup in which the
English gloriously beat the Germans in the final match played in London
(*Daily Mirror* and *Daily Express*, op-eds, 15 June 1970).

West Germany was consistently constructed as *Western*, like Britain.
In *Force 10 from Navarone*, the Iron Cross-wearing German officer Neu-
feld bemoans that he has to fight his Second World War in Yugoslavia:
"I wish to heaven that we were fighting a normal war against normal
people, like the British or Americans." Some pages later, Captain Keith

Mallory appears to sympathize with his German opponent: "It was a war which the Wehrmacht could never win, which the soldiers of no Western European country could ever have won, for the people of the high mountains are virtually indestructible." This might have described *Soviet Russia*, actually, because while the Soviet economy was regarded as no match for the West, its military seemed to be resilient and overpowering.

If the Soviet Union was Britain's living antithesis, then the *Third World*, with its conflict and poverty, came a close second. As before, in 1970 the British tended to think that Third World countries were unfree thanks to the centralization of economic decision making in the hands of small and often ruthless elites. The Middle East was described as tragic, a place riven by geopolitical struggles and political extremism (*Daily Express*, op-ed, 15 June 1970). The new prime minister's own preference was for Britain to stay out of these imbroglios. "Sometimes – I think particularly of Africa – decisions have been taken as a result of emotional pressures which, however sincere, have not always been fully reasoned, and neither have they been reasonable," Heath said in his address. Accordingly, he added, Britain should think twice before condemning apartheid South Africa for its "racialist practices" and jeopardize its "vital defence interests." (The London dockers, who, in 1968, hit the streets to show support for Enoch Powell and his "Rivers of Blood" speech, would have probably agreed.)

Comparison with the analyses presented in chapters 1 and 2 indicates the presence of multiple, layered, and mostly continuous elements of Britishness through time. In what follows, I consider how decision makers drew on these different representations of Self and Other, and to what ends they put them in the context of three events: the withdrawal from Asia, the Nixon shock, and the Common Market accession.

"World Status without Tears"

The above analysis suggests that the British in 1970 imagined Britain to be democratic and free-trading, and a synonym for a modern, secular, orderly, benevolent, and civilized country. As a manly, Western country, Britain was also more influential than the rest of the world as well as

allied with America and Europe against the Soviet Union, whose authoritarian government silenced dissenters, thus ruining hopes of the Rus-
sian people developing a strong economy and consuming modern goods.
Unlike them, the British were mostly or essentially free, honest, fair, and
just. The British were furthermore benevolent and tolerant, hence feelings of goodwill towards both Catholics and Protestants in Northern Ireland, and understanding even towards ostentatious immigrants from
Asia and Africa. And while the old imperial state was gone, the global
network of money and culture centred on London was still solid.

Mix all of these ideas together, and you get no shortage of discursive
continuity with the Britain examined in the previous chapter. Beyond
Modern Britain, which was again dominant, we can identify two more
Britains, which mirror the more ideological wings of the two main
parties: Traditional Britain and Socialist Britain. In general, both of them
agreed on the need to cultivate the institutions and forces that made
Britain great – its patriotic people, responsible government, strong military, solid manufacturing and service industries, competent professional
associations and media, and, of course, the world's finest schools and
universities. But they disagreed about what was to be done about the
nation's fragile economy. The Socialist discourse held that the British
state should continually intervene to make British life fair and just – and
to ensure that the working class was working. In January 1972, that is,
before the (first) oil shock and "the collapse" of Bretton Woods, 1 million
workers were unemployed. As I explain in a moment, a series of un-
precedented strikes that rocked the kingdom that decade can be seen in
the same context.

The Traditionalist discourse, in contrast, lionized competitiveness and
criticized over-taxation. In this view, a Britain ruled by proper Tories –
proper referred mainly to "One Nation" Conservativism, but with a dash
of free market liberalism present in the party's 1970 manifesto – would
rid itself of failing industries and aggressive trade union activities. The
Heath government (1970–74) was basically proper in this sense, given
that it set out to reform the tax system and industrial relations laws. (The
strategy quickly hit a series of road blocks, above all the miner strikes in
1972 and 1974.) Like before, the Traditionalist discourse was furthermore

characterized by nostalgia for a past Britain; a country, for example, where the youth was enamoured with the monarchy rather than feminism. The figure that arguably best represented this discursive stance was Enoch Powell, the maverick Tory politician then best known for said "Rivers of Blood" speech. By the same token, the pro-Europe Tory prime minister Health was a sell-out.

Having declared five states of emergency, the Heath government lasted until 1974, when Wilson won two elections, one in March that yielded a "hung" (minority) Parliament and one in October that led to a razor-thin Labour majority. In light of what appear to be major continuities in the British *doxa* between 1960 and 1970, we first need to go backward in time and consider once more the foreign policy moves of the first Wilson government, from 1964 to 1970. First, as detailed in the last chapter, in 1966 and 1967, this government started flirting with the idea of EEC membership, which de Gaulle quashed with his second, "velvet," veto. Then, in November 1967, it moved to devalue the pound. Technically, the policy was logical because it allowed the government to avoid yet another costly loan. From the perspective of British identity, however, this must have caused ontological insecurity because it ended Britain's vaunted position as the holder of the world's other reserve currency. (In 1972, the sterling bloc would end as well.) But the same month brought the hastened withdrawal from Aden, which foreshadowed "East of Suez" – a retreat from a vast part of the world that had seen continuous British presence for over three hundred years. This spelled Britain's future as "a major power of the second rank," as the foreign secretary, Michael Steward, publicly admitted at the time.[5] Announced in two steps, first in July 1967, then in January 1968, East of Suez had in fact been in the works since at least June 1965, which was when the cabinet entertained the idea of closing the base in Singapore.[6]

Multiple histories of postwar British foreign policy reference this period with an ironic phrase from Crossman, a well-to-do Labour heavyweight whom we met in chapter 1 and who now became one of Wilson's cabinet critics: "The status barrier is as difficult to break as the sound barrier. It splits your ears and it's terribly painful when it happens."[7] On one level, Crossman was right, for these moves are precisely the sort of painful, ear-splitting strategic adjustments that Waltz (1967) argued were "impossible" due to "ingrained" national attitudes, traditions, ideologies, and habits.

As barrier-breaking shifts go, Wilson's push into Europe and away from empire and the Commonwealth can be seen as the climax of a welter of circumstances and forces coming together, which, if one had paid attention, one would have realized had been foretold many decades ago. However, said shifts can only partly be explained by changes in Britain's identity topographies over time. As we see in chapter 2, the leading politicians from both Conservative and Labour parties could have legitimately argued, even in 1960, that the Empire had to change. Indeed, we say that *successive* iterations of Modern Britain accepted that colonies *should* receive their independence – African colonies in the 1960s, small islands in the Pacific and the Caribbean, and Arab polities in the 1970s – so long as they remain either in our family of nations or eager to follow our example in politics or at least in capitalism. This framing of the imperial retreat in fact rendered Britain ontologically secure since it resonated with the nation's image of itself as benevolent, liberal, and superior to its continental peers. Macmillan-styled tropes of greatness amidst decolonization were still alive. "We were not defeated, we withdrew out of our own volition," wrote Reginald Maudling, a Tory heavyweight and Heath's one-time rival, in his 1978 memoir.[8]

In the 1970s, Wilson (in his two mandates) and Heath were similarly able to reframe old foreign policy dilemmas and advance their reformist, "progressive" agendas. We thus see them using both rhetorical and institutional savvy to secure agreement for their policies piecemeal, first in the cabinet, then in the party, then more broadly, always taking advantage of day-to-day political dynamics – everything from the diminishing political and public interest in the Empire to the chaos of strikes and external shocks to the economy. We likewise saw both Tory and Labour politicians referring to the nostrums on modernization and progress in order to legitimate the military withdrawal from the territories East of Suez (Heath only made a point to slow down the withdrawal schedule).

Another key rhetorical move, common to the leadership from either party, was to argue that Britain's Commonwealth and European roles were essentially complementary rather than competing. This was not necessarily true, but it resonated in discursive terms. The same can be said about the early 1970s-vintage claim that the Six had moved away from its supranationalist and federalist impulses towards an arrangement that was more acceptable to Britain. However, given that nothing in my analysis suggests that the British masses in 1970 saw the European option as *the* future or even as a temporary solution to the never-ending budget and balance of payments deficits, Wilson's and Heath's push for the Common Market remains puzzling.

Here, too, we must pay close attention to timing and sequencing. Much like East of Suez, "entry into Europe" developed over several years, and it begins with Heath's decision to open accession negotiations anew as soon as de Gaulle was out of politics.[9] This time, the House of Commons and the business community were each sharply divided, and public opinion polls showed only a minority support for the policy. The Labour opposition was against, arguing that the UK deserved a much better deal than the one Brussels had offered to the Conservative prime minister. Supported by the press and with a white paper, which at 1 million copies solid, swiftly became the all-time best-selling official document of the British state, Heath marched on through almost fifty days of parliamentary debate (for a definitive history, see Saunders [2018]). His campaign succeeded. In January 1973, the UK become a formal member of the EC, together with Ireland and Denmark. (In 1967, the European Economic Community was reconstituted as the European Community [EC].)

Within months, Labour asked for a referendum on whether the UK should stay or withdraw, which it indeed got, in June 1975. This time, however, Labour was in power – Harold Wilson's 1974–76 government. Together with his foreign minister (and future prime minister) James Callaghan, Wilson first "renegotiated" Heath's terms – the quotation marks are necessary since Brussels hardly changed its positions, especially on Britain's contribution to the Community budget – and then endorsed "yes to Europe." Crucially, Wilson refused to take a leading part in the Yes campaign, and he also let members of his cabinet and his party campaign the other way. Tony Benn, Michael Foot, Barbara Castle, and many others did just that, under the Gaitskellite banner. The Tories, now in the opposition, had both their new leader, Margaret Thatcher, and their old one, Ted Heath, trying hard to secure a positive outcome for the referendum. In the event, after rollercoaster volatility in the polls, the pro-European cause was victorious: a large majority, 67 per cent, voted in favour of staying in, on a respectable turnout of 64 per cent.

Three discrete pieces of secondary analysis can help us evaluate the extent to which the pro-membership frames resonated with Britishness. Ludlow's focus is on the six-day run-up to the vote of 28 October 1971 – "the climax of over ten years of governmental and parliamentary debate, [which] had a cathartic value that not even the 1975 referendum could match" (Ludlow 2015, 19). What he finds is that the anti-Marketeer position was defended through the language of three "great British traditions": the Cobdenite liberal tradition of "cheap food," the related internationalist tradition, and Britain's tradition of parliamentary democracy. These positions, held by both Tory and Labour Eurosceptics, fit with aspects of each of the three discourses of identity that I discuss above, but especially with Traditionalism. Those in favour of EEC membership made two types of rhetorical moves. The first was to reject the anti-Marketeer interpretations of said traditions and to reject the EEC as a Franco-German plot as opposed to a common project that complemented Britain's own interests. The second was to reject the notion of tradition itself and to foreground the prospect of "an exciting future." Both of these can be said to fit best with Modern Britain, the dominant discourse. This might help explain why sixty-nine Labour MPs defied their party's then anti-EEC position, thus allowing Heath to move forward with his policy.

Compared to Ludlow, Gibbins (2014) offers an explicitly discourse analytic treatment. Looking at the 1975 referendum debate, he identifies the production of around two dozen identities coalescing into multiple British Selves.[10] His list of identities has more than a few overlaps with my analysis above – pragmatic, fading power, in crisis, militarized, defensive, militarily influential, interdependent, dominant, trade-driven, global, internationalist, free/peaceful, nonisolationist, unitary, democratic, socialist, and welfare-oriented, among others. He also finds that the "non-radical and friendly Othering" of Europe was made possible by "the temporal Othering" of Britain's warring past as well as by "the radical

Othering" of Soviet Russia (43–4, 54–5). The US Other was constructed as friendly and the US alliance as too constraining, while France was "consistently singled out as overbearing and imperial" (62). These observations have broad similarities with my interpretation, which suggests that most identities located by Gibbins were vertically shared, the outstanding exception being the Othering of Europe.

Another helpful discourse analytic treatment of the referendum debate is available in John Todd's (2016, chap. 3) study of the British discourse on European integration. His corpus is based on elite-level texts: the text of the main parliamentary ("white paper") debate itself, key referendum campaign literature, plus dozens of editorials in three newspapers – the *Times* the *Daily Mirror*, and the *Daily Express*. Todd locates four central, inter-linked themes – "Economy, Jobs, and Trade"; "Agriculture, Food, and Fisheries"; and "Sovereignty and Democracy" were the major themes, while "Consequences for Peace and Security" was a minor theme – and he finds that the pro-Market position had a slight upper hand. Interestingly, he also finds that the pro-Marketeers mostly opted for the language of fear: "fears of economic meltdown, fears of unstable food supplies, and fears about the UK's place in the world" (53). This suggests a mixed agreement with my findings. On the one hand, Modern Britain configured Britain and the British as fearless, not fearful; on the other hand, however, it is unsurprising that Britain's leadership found it difficult to make a positive case for joining "Europe." That all being said, had the Anti campaign been better run, the referendum would have probably resulted in a "no to Europe" (Saunders 2018, 131).

In defence policy, Britain's turn to Europe during the 1970s was less ambiguous. The Wilson government's Mason review, named after the state secretary for defence, Robert Mason, outlined a decidedly Euro-Atlantic geography: NATO gets the highest number of mentions at 33, the Soviet Union gets 23, West Germany 16, the US 15, and North Ireland 12. The Soviet enemy was to be deterred by nuclear weapons above all, but also by a land army in Germany and anti-submarine capabilities in the Atlantic. Out-of-area commitments, to use a twenty-first century moniker, were no longer in the national interest (Dorman 2001, 18). The Middle East, which was a top three category in both the Sandys and Healey reviews, barely registered as a top thirty in this review, and then only thanks to references to Oman. Here, too, we see a reflection of change in Britishness over time. Part 2 of the Mason review, published in 1975, was similar to the previous two white papers in that it fore-grounded budgetary considerations. This ten-year plan proposed further cuts, both in overall defence spending and in the size of the armed forces.[11] Air and seaborne transport capabilities were to be phased out, as was most of the British presence in the Mediterranean. In objective terms, the document reads as a farewell not only to East of Suez but also to the British world system and to Britain's world role as such (Dorman 2001, 18). According to Modern Britain, however, this would have been interpreted as rebalancing that role away from the purely military do-main rather than as accepting a more regional role. Protection of de-pendencies from Belize to Brunei continued, as did, under Thatcher, support for US-led military operations in the Middle East (Rees 2001, 41): "World status without tears," as the title of one of Wallace's (1970) essays put it at the time (see also Wallace 1991, 72–3).

Could the then government in London have pursued a third foreign policy option, one that was neither quasi-imperial nor European? Rather than offering many pages of counterfactual analysis, let us consider the 1970 topography again. From this perspective, it appears that the non-membership camp derived its cultural resources not from Modern Brit-ain but from the subaltern discourses, Traditionalism and Socialism. Between the two, Traditionalism was more extreme in the sense that it viewed continental Europeans with ill-disguised disdain: these people were variously enemies, rivals, or poor neighbours needing to be saved by British power and culture. Traditionalism was also weaker than So-cialism because it lacked institutional support outside a group of Tory politicians, led by Enoch Powell, who worried about the loss of national sovereignty to foreigners bewitched by supranationalism.

The Socialist discourse, in comparison, was well represented by La-bour, especially Labour left, by trade unions representing domestic and global firms, and by the left-leaning nationalist parties in Scotland and Wales.[12] So, would a Labour government under Benn (or Foot or Castle) have kept Britain out of the EC in those years? This is certainly possible, yet it is unlikely that *any* set of policies would have pulled Britain out of recurrent, externally generated economic crises. The fact that some called Britain "the sick man of Europe" captures the extent of the problem (it is also an apt reminder that a supply of *Schadenfreude* was steady in some European circles, to say nothing of those in the former African and Asian colonies). With record-breaking unemployment, blackouts, and the three-day week in those years, the Benn government would have governed under the same conditions as did the Heath government – an almost permanent state of emergency.

Counterfactuals bring us to the thesis that Britain's "Europeanization" was elite-driven. Pro-European demands made by some British politicians and business groups during the first half of the 1960s could not go very far because both the prevailing discourse of British identity and its main challengers insisted on tying Britain to the other two circles of British foreign policy, particularly the "kith and kin" of the Old Commonwealth. However, these demands were not vigorously resisted either: Europe's Otherness was not particularly salient in 1970 compared to later years. More important, pro-Common Market leaders were persistent. On the Tory side of politics, an outstanding case in point is Ted Heath, who, by any reasonable measure, was a life-long supporter of a more European Britain. Among Labour politicians, we see people such as Harold Wilson, Roy Jenkins (who, as home secretary, in 1965 had already teamed up with Foreign Secretary Michael Stewart), and Labour Deputy Leader George Brown trying to change the hard line on the EEC.[13] Both of these campaigns were successful in the sense that they helped make the European Other appear "non-radical and friendly," as Gibbins would put it, by the time of the referendum ten years later.

Considerations of elite agency are important in constructivist theorizing of foreign policy regardless of whether one privileges discursive fit, as I do here, or, as many poststructuralist theorists do, a view that foreign policy outcomes are but temporary and incomplete "arrestations" involving multiple processes and relations that neither precede nor inform action. Elite agency is likewise important to those, like Wallace, who would insist that national identity formation is always elite-driven. Going back to his distinction between "Europeans" and "Anglo-Saxons," it is tempting to interpret the entire turn to Europe in the 1960s and 1970s as a nationwide resocialization scheme designed by the former to inculcate a more European nation against the dominant Anglo-Saxon one, particularly given "the ignorance and incuriosity of the public about how the EEC worked, what it did and why it mattered" (Saunders 2018, 22). Whatever the theoretical angle chosen, no constructivist would deny that the causal arrow must also be reversed, such that foreign policy is not only an object of national identity contestation but also its means.

This point is useful for understanding the British reaction to the Nixon shock. Historians explain poor UK-US relations under Heath with reference to many factors, including the prime minister's desire to make Britain's commitment to the Common Market as credible as possible, thus minimizing the chance of a third veto (Self 2010, 87). An explanation from an identity perspective would emphasize American actions, starting with President Richard Nixon's unexpected – indeed, shocking – decision in 1971 to suspend dollar convertibility into gold. Given the impact this had on the Bretton Woods system and international financial exchange and the world economy, it is unsurprising that Britain's leaders paused to reconsider the benefit of acting as America's junior partner in world politics.[14] Being busy with their many great debates on EEC membership, however, they failed to articulate the one on the special relationship. Then, once the governments in both London and Washington changed in 1974, UK-US relations markedly improved, much as they did after Suez. Thus, rather than seeking emancipation from American tutelage as Heath might have done, both Wilson and his successor Callaghan cleaved to the US as closely as Macmillan had done.

Counterfactually, a second Heath government might have laid a bold plan for greater independence vis-à-vis the US. What is unclear is whether such a plan would have been sustainable. First, as with the case of the European Other, the British ruling class could draw on different cultural resources to construct Britain's unenviable position in relation to the superpower ally. Anchoring one end of the continuum was a threatening America, as in the Traditionalist and Socialist discourses, while on the other end was a friendly America, an image common to Modern Britain. The latter, however, was dominant. Second, US actions mattered. Had Nixon's successors in Washington pursued policies at odds with British identity, this would have created (even) more resentment among the British people, thus reconfiguring the dominant image of the US in all discourses of Britishness. The shift in Britain's position away from a reluctant stance towards the EEC to more constructive and generous policies would have then followed in this scenario.

Be that as it may, the 1970s saw two more shocks that put a question mark beside Britain's claims to greatness. As the oil industry in the Middle East grew during the twentieth century, the UK government claimed authority over it, first by granting concessions to favoured companies, then by directing the investment of oil revenues towards Britain. However, in 1973, Arab oil producers caused a global energy crisis by imposing an embargo and therefore an increase in the price of gas in response to Western support for Israel in the Yom Kippur (a.k.a. Ramadan) War against Egypt. However, the Heath government was not pro-Israel. Foreign Secretary (and former prime minister) Alec Douglas-Home, who had previously criticized the Jewish state, sought to demonstrate neutrality by suspending arms exports to the belligerents – the European position on the war. (The Saudis in return treated Britain as a special case during the embargo.)[15]

In any case, the upheaval hit the British economy very hard. High oil prices increased production costs, decreased corporate profits and stock market values, and deepened industrial strife. Within three years, the 1971 balance of payments tumbled from a £1 billion surplus to a £3.3 billion deficit, just as inflation climbed to almost 25 per cent. A large segment of British society experienced profound economic uncertainty. But this was only the first act in what proved to be a downright disastrous decade in which the entire postwar system of fixed exchange rates, capital controls, and wage policies collapsed. In 1976, the UK was officially an International Monetary Fund (IMF) "beggar nation," and so (almost) in the "another Argentina" territory. In 1978, the Iranian Revolution led to the fall of the British-installed shah in Iran, which, in turn, led to the second oil shock. At home a flurry of strikes engulfed an even deeper crisis, the "Winter of Discontent," which gave birth to Thatcher and Thatcherism. I discuss this and more, including the war with the actual Argentina, in the next chapter.

4

Down, Not Out

In the preceding chapter I analyze British foreign policy in the 1970s, a decade plagued with ontological anxiety. In this chapter, I further contextualize this by looking at British life in 1980. The main finding is a chronic sense of national crisis. In the previous year, Margaret Thatcher had inherited from Harold Wilson an economy in the doldrums, failing essential services, political fallout from chaos-inducing strikes known as "the Winter of Discontent," public spending cuts mandated by the IMF, and a balance of payments deficit.

According to the Thatcher government, the problem was with the principle of social intervention, which is why it called for radically new ways of rationalizing state-market relations – the essence of a reformist discourse that we could provisionally call "New Britain." On this view, the economic crisis had forever punctured enthusiasm for reducing class inequality and corroded individual energies and private enterprise. But most Britons did not see statism as a catalogue of errors, much less agree with attacks on organized labour. Instead, they called for a continuous commitment to broadly defined Keynesian economics, which the nation had developed after the Second World War and which had far more to offer than was usually allowed during hard economic times. This was an iteration of "Modern Britain," which we could provisionally call "Muddling Through."

These two discourses exemplified the partisan and ideological divisions over the methods and goals of public policy. However, these divisions did not apply everywhere. According to the texts surveyed, although many agreed that the country was slipping out of control and into financial ruin, most British people, elites and masses alike, retained a generally positive view of themselves vis-à-vis other nations. In this view, Britain might have been going down in the world economically and militarily, but at least its language, music, and culture more generally were constantly gaining new adherents. Furthermore, the idea that life under the aegis of American power, nuclear deterrence, and NATO was infinitely safer than going it alone in the world spoke to an already committed audience. Along the same lines, the consistently slow growth of the UK's economy compared with that of the EC, and other indications of the loss of national power and status, did not necessarily compel British society to accept the need for a change in the status quo.

The result was a paradox or at least a major internal contradiction: despite evidence of precipitous relative decline *within* both Muddling Through and New Britain, British society *still* tended to define itself as world-leading in many domains – developed, socially progressive, culturally attractive, technologically competitive, and, above all, free. In other words, the changing nature of the material realities of Britain was still being regulated by the familiar sense of exceptionalism. In the second part of this chapter I examine the extent to which this and other observed identity configurations enabled and legitimized four British foreign and defence policy performances of the early 1980s: the Nott defence review, the Trident purchase, the reinvasion of the Falklands, and a confrontation with the EC known as the Thatcher rebate.

1980: "Everything Has Gone Wrong in Cold Comfort Britain"

Figure 4.1 is a representation of top identity categories, by raw count, in 1980.[1] Compared to 1970, we see a significant change in how the British viewed themselves and their kingdom: weaknesses now outnumbered strengths. Core problems were economic and were reflected in some combination of poor growth rates, unemployment, sterling crises, rising prices (inflation in 1980 reached 18 per cent), troubles with wages and exports, and the fact that government – in particular the Tory government led by Thatcher – was now squeezing virtually every public service budget in the country. Whatever the angle, the elites and the masses agreed that the nation was crisis-ridden: *economically depressed* and *declining* above all, but also fearful of assorted terrorist attacks. "Everything has gone wrong in Cold Comfort Britain," declared the *Daily Mirror* on 15 February 1980 in its editorial on "the stench of unemployment." Ten months later, the crisis only seemed worse, with political leaders appearing either unable or unwilling to address it (*Daily Mirror*, 15 December 1980, editorial).

Importantly, national decline was understood as moral and social. Six letters in the sample lament the decline in "good" British manners on the part of, respectively, the police, government ministers, union leaders, television presenters, pubs, and retail workers. Also, this round of national decline was understood as qualitatively different. In their textbook, Sked and Cook (1979, 165) explain in reference to the 1960s that "Britain was still attempting to be a world power, without world resources." But it was only recently that the London stock market had experienced a "larger decline than had happened after the Great Crash of 1929," while inflation was "uncomfortably higher than in Europe or America" (333, 357).

For Thatcher and a segment of the ruling elite who supported her, the main culprit behind the persistent national malaise was *statism*, coded here as the top category. This year's Queen's Speech identified "the need to restrict the claims of the public sector on the nation's resources … to reduce the scope of nationalised and state industry, and to increase competition." Concretely, the government set out to work towards denationalizing the national oil company and introducing "opportunities for private investment" in transport and telecommunications.

The rest of the archive was more upbeat about statism. In textbook discourse, the postwar welfare state was a major political and social achievement, one that was later copied by other nations. Sked and Cook describe (1979, 45) the National Health Service as "an almost revolutionary social innovation since it improved the quality of life of most of the British people." Newspaper items published in the Labour Party-leaning *Daily Mirror* agreed with this view, as illustrated in calls for increasing pensions for workers (15 April 1980, letter) and giving resources to the Post Office (15 April 1980, letter; see also 15 February 1980, letter). Yet even

Figure 4.1 Top British identity categories in 1980 by frequency

the *Mirror* occasionally accepted that the welfare state had problems and needed to be pruned. "Public spending cuts are crucial to beating inflation and bringing about Britain's economic recovery," argued an editorial published on 15 April 1980.[2] An industrialist in Wilbur Smith's novel *Wild Justice* puts it slightly differently: "Could you imagine if we had a five-year wage freeze, and no industrial action during that time? It's them or us, Peter. We could get back to being one of the major industrial powers of the Western world. Great Britain! We could be that again."

For the prime minister, *reform* was a byword for privatizing state function and for shaking up the work-shy. "Human dignity and self-respect

are undermined when men and women are condemned to idleness. The
waste of a country's most precious assets – the talent and energy of its
people – makes it the bounden duty of Government to seek a real and
lasting cure," said Thatcher in her speech at the 1980 Conservative Party
conference in Brighton. From this perspective, unemployment, forced
or otherwise, was making Britain uncompetitive in the global economy,
practically for the first time in modern history. The panacea was simple:
more discipline and harder work.

Elsewhere, reformism stood for attempts to achieve ever-greater *fairness, justice*, and *civility*. The Victorian era, for example, was portrayed
in Hill's (1977) textbook as the contemporary kingdom's alter ago: unhealthy, exploitative, and unpleasant. The life of inmates in Wakefield,
the country's top high-security prison, is unnecessarily brutish because
of poor policy – something that Home Secretary Merlyn Rees could and
should change, an op-ed explained (*Daily Mirror*, 15 September 1980). A
similar penitentiary in *McVicar*, an exploration of crime and working-
class masculinity and that year's blockbuster commercial film, shows the
prisoners as having rights and power. When they riot over having to wear
new prison uniforms, the warden still tries to reason with them.

The Thatcher government's narrow definition of reform and reformism merely underscored the deep *partisan* divide in contemporary Britain. The pro-Conservative *Daily Express* thus saw the perceived turmoil
in the Labour Party following Thatcher's 1979 electoral victory as a major
opportunity for the Tories (15 October 1980, op-ed and letter). The *Daily
Mirror*, in contrast, seized on what it saw to be a reversal of Thatcher's
political fortunes in March, when she mishandled a strike called by York-
shire miners (15 March 1980, letter). Several years later this confrontation
would come to entail pit closures and the longest-running national industrial action since 1926. The sample of letters to the editor suggests that
the masses were deeply divided over Thatcher's reforms. Writing to the
Daily Express, one citizen urged the government to "buy back council
houses" as a way of aiding low-paid and unemployed workers (15 September 1980) – the precise opposite of the government's policy. As for
the new proposal for voluntary social work, one letter concluded it was
an "excellent idea," while another described it as something "straight out
of *Alice in Wonderland*" suggesting that only in a magical kingdom would

a government obligate unemployed individuals to engage in volunteer work as a way of demonstrating their worth (15 July 1980).

As in earlier years, Britain once again self-identified as *class-based*. Elite discourse normalized this as a fact of life everywhere, including in the countries of the Eastern bloc. In contrast, the working class thought the system was rigged against them, especially by "the City," as London's financial district is called. Judging by a pair of letters published in the *Daily Express* on 15 October 1980, students at elite public schools,[3] like Harrow School and Fettes College, were out of touch, and Prince Philip and the rest of "the privileged classes" were hypocritical. In *Wild Justice*, however, "fine aristocratic features" are always a plus. Peter Stride's teenage daughter is an "old-fashioned English porcelain beauty" with a "sweet Victorian face" and "the classical English skin of rose petals."[4] (Stride's palatial family home has an aristocratic-sounding name – Abbots Yew.)

In the right-of-centre elite discourse, *trade unionism* was as problematic as statism. In her Brighton Speech, Thatcher declared that her government was reforming "trade union law to remove the worst abuses of the closed shop." The opinion pages in the 15 February 1980 edition of the *Daily Express* were devoted to trade union leader Arthur Scargill and his response to a letter from a Welsh trade unionist who asked whether he could expect a job when the strikes ended. For the editors, Scargill's error was to allow for "force and undemocratic arguments [to win] the day." An opinion piece published in the *Express* several months later argued that the government's reform of the state-owned and cash-strapped British Rail would be successful were it not for the rail union: "Some people in the Labour and trades union movement regard nationalised industries as their own property, rather than public assets" (15 July). On the mass discourse side, judging by the letters at least, there was considerable support for the strikers – see the letters on the miner strike published on 15 January in the *Express* or those on the steel strike in the *Daily Mirror* from 15 April. In *Wild Justice*, in contrast, a strike at the British Leyland Motor Company is presented as a problem solvable only via strike-busting right-wing violence.

Economic weaknesses adversely affected Britain's natural strengths, the foremost of which were *capitalism*, *democracy*, and *orderliness*. The first category was understood as a system for creating the largest possible

economic space for both individual and national competition and therefore for social, economic, and even political progress. Some collateral
damage was inevitable of course. A letter to the editor published in the
Daily Mirror on 15 April 1980 expressed sadness about the tearing down
of Brighton's West Pier ("our piers are a national heritage") but, at the
same time, understood that "enough cash to save it could not be raised."
In Frederick Forsyth's novel *The Devil's Alternative*, one character explains counterterrorism as a function of capitalist necropolitics: "securing transoceanic tankers against terrorist attack was too expensive, hence
we pretended only securing airliners mattered."

Importantly, it was not always clear that democracy – a category that
seamlessly intersected with freedom and human rights – came before law
and order. The prison, as portrayed in the movie *McVicar*, or terrorism-
ridden Northern Ireland, was clearly understood as needing less democracy, not more. Consider also the section of *Wild Justice* where Stride is
court-martialled for killing a wounded terrorist leader in custody. There,
"wild justice" is portrayed as an antidote to the all-too-liberal British
state and society. In the Monty Python blockbuster *Life of Brian*, terrorists
are merely stupid: "We are the Judean People's Front crack suicide squad!
Suicide squad, attack!" screams the suicide squad leader, after which his
team members all stab themselves. "That showed 'em, huh?," he notes.
British orderliness was subject to exceptions as well. One example was
excessive public boozing, apparently a major cross-class pastime. "Hunting is a tradition for British gentlemen, like drinking and gambling," explains Wilbur in *Wild Justice*. No text in the archive for 1980 or any other
year argues for regulating these three activities.

Liberal identity was not a top category in 1980, but it clearly coloured
mass constructions of *patriotism*. *Life of Brian*, in which the eponymous
protagonist speaks to the crowd, captures the dominant feeling: "Look,
you've got it all wrong! You don't NEED to follow ME, you don't NEED to
follow ANYBODY! You've got to think for yourselves! You're ALL individuals!" In both *Wild Justice* and *Devil's Alternative*, the entire world appears
corrupt, with the fate of millions always subject to the machinations of
the powerful few.[5] Relatedly, both newspapers published letters from
citizens fed up with government policy on nuclear weapons. "By unilat-

eral disarmament we can start to reverse the race to destruction," suggested one citizen in the *Daily Express* (15 October 1980). Another, writing in the *Daily Mirror*, expressed anger: "In a TV interview about the possibility of a nuclear war, Home Secretary William Whitelaw remarked: 'Of course people will die.' Who the hell does he think he is – God? What right has any government to make such a decision?" (15 August 1980).

Another elite-mass gap existed in constructions of gender. In 1980, one of the phrases of the year was "Britain's first woman premier." Thatcher's iconic status had in fact been established several years earlier, when she became the first female leader of a major party in the free world (*Devil's Alternative*, where the fictional UK prime minister is a Thatcher-like character, uses the phrase "first woman premier," too). In the elite discourse, Thatcher's exceptionality was uses as proof that the UK was excessively *patriarchal* – again a top identity category. One newspaper opinion piece argued that "only when we have a true representation of women MPs will Westminster have a true connection with the nation – and Britain a real democracy" (*Daily Express*, 15 April 1980).[6] In the business pages, the same newspaper published an opinion piece that dismissed a female business leader as "a blatant feminist when it came to selling insurance" (15 October 1980) as well as a letter chiding the NHS for misallocating its funds – paying for abortions but not heart-swap and kidney transplant operations (15 February 1980).

Mass texts did not share such outrage. Both novels are excessively male-centric and articulate a social Darwinist world of competition involving powerful states and their tough-as-nails representatives – leaders, diplomats, spies, and military professionals. In *Wild Justice*, Stride scrutinizes all women as sexual objects. They do not seem to object: "It is very nice to have a man being masterful again, it makes me feel like a woman," powerful baroness Magda Altmann says to him. And Stride cannot stand his "shapeless" ex: "Give me a Bolshevik intellectual over a neurotic wife any day."[7] In *Devil's Alternative*, Munro discovers that one of the Kremlin's bureaucrats is his ex-lover and then easily proceeds to recruit her as a spy for the West (he later learns that he is himself a pawn). *Life of Brian's* construction of gender and sexuality is more complex since the movie at once mocks toxic masculinity ("Wait till Biggus Dickus hears of this!"

says Pontius Pilate) and the desire of one male character, Stan, to be a woman and a mother (the latter also spills over into mockery of feminism and transsexuality).

Though scepticism towards the ruling elites was common, it rarely bled into cynicism, much less into thinking that the governors had somehow lost touch with the governed. The masses in fact agreed with the elites that sources of British *influence* in the world included democracy, orderliness, "fine aristocratic features," *industriousness, scientific* ingenuity, and, of course, the military. As the extraordinary hero of Smith's *Wild Justice*, Stride is introduced as a man who hones his terrorism-fighting skills every day without a break. One night he practised shooting until after midnight, turning his pistol into an "extension of his hand – either hand, left or right." (This is an established Bond theme.) *Devil's Alternative* describes the British-made Nimrod as "about the best aircraft for submarine and shipping surveillance in the world." Another natural strength of the British nation was its long-standing commitment to *education* and scientific discovery. In *Wild Justice*, Stride accumulates books even if he has "no time to read," while the eponymous hero of *McVicar* is shown on his cell bed reading Alberto Moravia's *The Woman of Rome*. The excellence of British universities was always celebrated, not just that of the elite Oxbridge, whose ancient star continued to shine brightly even against the backdrop of the ever-rising suns in America (more on the US below), but also that of the many fine regional institutions who absorbed ever-higher numbers of high school students. The welcome the kingdom extended to international students and scholars was a plus too.

Britain was positive about *the monarchy*, in part because it was understood that the royal family stood for entertainment, not leadership. The relationship with *religion* was more ambiguous. Some elite texts, such as the Queen's Speech or history textbooks, regularly nodded to the country's Christian roots or values. Sked and Cook (1979, 98) note that "the racial policies … of the Afrikaaner nationalists … had proceeded, despite their profession of Christian principles." Overall, however, and especially in the mass-oriented sources, Christianity was seen as a thing of the past. So while in 1980 the Church was one of the largest voluntary organizations in the country, the year's most popular commercial film was *Life of Brian*, a satirical film about an eponymous man from Nazareth who is mistaken for a messiah and thus set on a life-ruining path.[8]

In the geographical imagination of this year's archive, "Britain" mostly meant "England." The nation's capital, beloved and despised at once, was undeniably "the City." Accordingly, all other places, whether British or global, appeared to be burdened by provincial politics, morality, and/or aesthetics. One of the main divisions in *McVicar*, for example, is between the prisoners, who mostly come from London, and the guards of a maximum-security prison in the northern city of Durham. In one scene, two cockneys talk loudly so that the guards can hear them. One of them, Terry Stokes, insists that the northerners are "fags":

Hey Billy, you heard the news? They've discovered another daisy chain in the Durham Light Infantry … Found an 'ole barrack load of 'em stuck up each other … Sunk, to the nuts they were. They're going to rename them y'know. The Durham Bumpers. Ah, do love an arsehole these Geordies!

(In another scene, the prisoners riot and then defiantly sing the ditty "Maybe it's because I'm a Londoner.")

On the opposite end from London was Scotland, whose education and gender relations needed "improving," according to the Queen's Speech. Wales was also backward, distinguished in 1970 by its two development agencies – one general, one for rural Wales (Queen's Speech). Northern Ireland was of course the worst of the three, marked as it was by terrorism and also "the horrors of urban terrorism" (Sked and Cook 1979, 311). It was also hopeless – "any solution to the problems of the province seemed as remote as ever" (364).

The *Irish*, not just the Irish Republican Army or Irish republicans, were threatening (e.g., *Devil's Alternative*). Consider the concerns over Prince Charles and his readiness for the throne should Queen Elizabeth abdicate. One person lamented the consequences of Charles's potential marriage to Diana Spencer because of its alleged impact on Northern Irish politics: "One would have thought that Northern Ireland had enough problems without the Protestants working themselves up over

something that may never happen – Prince Charles marrying a Catholic"
(*Daily Express*, 15 July 1980, letter). (In reality, Diana's Catholic identity
was unclear.)

Soviet, *US*, and *European* Others were all top five significant Other categories in 1980. The main foreign policy goal of the British state in 1980
was fending off the malignant influence of the Soviet Union, Britain's
political antithesis. That summer Moscow hosted "the KGB Olympics,"
which were boycotted by the Americans and in which censorship and espionage were rampant. This was repugnant: "As Lord Carrington pointed
out yesterday: 'The Soviet Union uses sport cynically to demonstrate the
"superiority" of the Soviet system and Soviet politics'" (*Daily Express*, 15
July 1980, letter). The prime minister agreed, expressing a mixture of dis-
gust and fear towards the Soviet Other: "Soviet Marxism is ideologically,
politically and morally bankrupt. But militarily the Soviet Union is a
powerful and growing threat" (Brighton Speech).

The masses agreed. *The Devil's Alternative*, the year's most outstanding
novel in commercial terms and set in what was then the future (summer
of 1982), is primarily about the Soviets. The novel begins with the story
of a catastrophic grain harvest. "Despite its monolithic appearance from
outside," Forsyth writes, Soviet Russia "has two Achilles heels. One is the
problem of feeding its 250 million people. The other is euphemistically
called 'the nationalities question.'" But there is a more immediate problem. Rudin, the moderate and seemingly Anglophile Soviet leader, is in
danger of being overthrown by a ruthless Politburo faction bent on going
to war in Europe as a way of diverting attention from the grain shortage
at home (Rudin also prefers Savile Row suits to Red Army uniforms and
yearns for Mayfair-styled city gardens).

The British were taught to worry about Marxism. This was not always
so. One textbook reminds the students that "Michael Foot, for instance,
could proclaim at the beginning of the 1945 Parliament that Great Britain
stood at the summit of her power and glory because she had 'something
unique to offer' – a middle way between Communism and Capitalism"
(Sked and Cook 1979, 55). By 1980, this middle had long disappeared. The
"truth" about the aforementioned union leader Scargill was "that he is
a revolutionary *Socialist*" (*Daily Express*, 15 February 1980, letter). Being
soft on terrorism had to do with the power of the "extreme left of British

Labour," suggested the other bestselling novel, *Wild Justice*. There, one
of the villains goes even further, arguing that the "survival of the Western
societies" was at stake: "Up to now we have had one hand tied behind
our backs, while the reds and the extreme left and the members of the
Third World have had both hands to fight with and a dagger in each one."

Britain's closest friend was once again the *US*. The special relationship
between Downing Street and the White House was understood as real
"based on military realities as well as on sentiment and diplomatic ex-
pediency" (Sked and Cook 1979, 106). In the *Devil's Alternative*, the US
president and the UK prime minister "knew each other well … Face-to-
face they used Christian names," while the the Anglo-American spy network is a "strange and guarded but ultimately vital alliance." The
asymmetry of the special relationship was a fact in both elite and mass
discourse. In *Wild Justice*, "Atlas Command" is an Anglo-American coun-
terterrorist organization known to no more than twenty people in the
world. Tactically led by Stride, the muscular British major-general of
Atlas's airborne Thor unit, the organization is in fact steered by a piano-
playing amateur philosopher in the Pentagon named Parker.

The British elites wanted more respect from the Americans. The Trident missile system, "our independent nuclear deterrent," was made possible through cooperation with the US and agreeing to "the stationing
of Cruise missiles in this country," explained Thatcher to the Tory party
audience in Brighton. The *Daily Mirror* had similar concerns: "President
Carter has a right to expect every help from the West in his struggle to
free the American hostages in Iran, but he mustn't expect blind obedi-
ence" (15 April 1980, letter). The US alliance indeed illuminated many aspects of Britain's international position. Although Britain understood
itself as sufficiently *well-armed*, for example, the country's decline and
economic woes caused constant foreign policy anxieties. "We have no
wish to seek a free ride at the expense of our Allies. We will play our full
part. We intend to maintain and, where possible, to improve our conventional forces so as to pull our weight in the Alliance" (Thatcher's
Brighton Speech).

The press took an abiding interest in all things American. A case in
point is the general election of November 1980 and the race between
Democrat Jimmy Carter and his Republican opponent Ronald Reagan.

The opinion pieces and letters to the editor expressed preferences for
the former or dislike of the latter (*Daily Mirror,* 15 August 1980, letter;
Daily Express, 15 August 1980, op-ed; *Daily Mirror,* 15 July 1980, op-ed).
Mass-level interest in the US was articulated in a *Daily Express* op-ed on
Sir Freddie Laker's "revolutionary air travel": "an incredibly cheap Sky-
train service [that] reduced the Atlantic to the size of a pond, suddenly
and dramatically making the United States accessible to virtually everybody [and] making it increasingly possible for all to do a Columbus and
make their own personal voyage of discovery to the New World" (15 August 1980).

The US was both similar and different. Frequently invoked similarities
included not only freedom and democracy but also patriarchy ("The
only woman given a chance of selection is former Ambassador to Britain
Anne Armstrong," said the *Daily Mirror*'s 15 July 1980 reflection on the
Democratic Party presidential primaries). The differences were many,
but they were perhaps most obvious in the area of culture. Following
John Lennon's tragic death in New York in December, a letter expressed
a fear that Reagan, now the incoming president, would do nothing to
change America's strange gun laws (*Daily Express,* 15 December 1980).
Devil's Alternative portrays Americans as too materialistic and too relig-
ious at once. In the author's words, "the spiraling increase in US oil consumption [is] based on the ordinary American's conviction of his
God-given right to rape the globe's resources for his own comforts." (The
US is also too Irish, for that matter).

Britain's relationship with Europe was more complex. For one, there
was a major difference in valence between the friendly but militarily weak
Western Europe and EC, on the one hand, and the threatening Europe
that lay beyond the Iron Curtain, on the other. Southern Europe was in
the middle of the continuum, interesting for its climate but backwards
in terms of politics and the economy. Within Europe, *France* was the most
significant Other in the archive, not Germany, as in previous years. A
textbook calls eighteenth-century France "the most civilised country in
the world" (Sked and Cook 1979, 202–3) before it turned into a militaristic
behemoth bent on destroying Britain. Twentieth-century France was a
NATO ally and, within the EC, both a partner and a rival.

Britain felt more European than before – at least in the elite discourse. Sked and Cook (1979, 169) note that, in the 1960s, "Britain was still regarded by the British as the leading power in Europe and there was little expectation even in official circles that the Common Market would amount to very much." In 1980, however, the UK prime minister was welcoming Greece's accession to full EC membership (see Thatcher's Brighton Speech). Yet Britain did not see itself as being *of* Europe. One reason for this was that Europe was simply too red and too soft. Here is Forsyth, imagining a future clash with the Soviets in *Devil's Alternative*:

> The military thrust would avoid the Italian and Iberian peninsulas, whose governments, all partners with the Euro-Communists in office, would be ordered by the Soviet Ambassador to stay out of the fight or perish by joining in. Within half a decade later, they would fall like ripe plums, anyway. Likewise Greece, Turkey, and Yugoslavia. Switzerland would be avoided, Austria used only as a through-route. Both would later be islands in a Soviet sea, and would not last long.

And here is Smith, through the words of his hero in *Wild Justice*: "A millionaire Italian living in his own country had to be the earth's most endangered species after the blue whale, Peter thought wryly." In other words, not every country was lucky enough to have low taxes like the British. A passage in *Devil's Alternative* about the *Amoco Cadiz* affair, a big 1978 oil spill, speaks of British superiority towards the Europeans: "The French refused to accept our help, even though we had better emulsifiers and better delivery systems than they did. Their fishermen paid bitterly for that particular stupidity."

British society was far more Western than European. From Thatcher's Brighton Speech: "The restoration of Britain's place in the world and of the West's confidence in its own destiny are two aspects of the same process." *Devil's Alternative* defined the West roughly as NATO plus capitalism: "You are in Turkey. You are in the West. You made it," says one of the protagonists. "The cars are Austins and Morrises, imported from England … Peugeots from France and Volkswagens from West Germany. The

words on the billboards are in Turkish. The advertisement over there is
for Coca-Cola." Maintaining Western unity was understood as para-
mount in the fact of the Soviet and other threats: "We simply cannot af-
ford great fissures in the Western Alliance over Iran, or over Afghanistan"
(*Daily Express*, 15 April 1980, letter).

Britain defined its modernity and Westernness in opposition to the
developing world, a.k.a. the South, which was seen as authoritarian and
poorly governed. From the Queen's Speech: "Serious economic problems … affect both developed and developing countries and will continue to work with other countries and international organisations in
seeking to alleviate them." Like in previous years, the same speech mentioned the Commonwealth and the UN in the same sentence, suggesting that the British elites were at ease with their country's *post-imperial*
identity (the Commonwealth, after all, was a voluntary association of
nations with shared interests, like the UN). The textbooks showed
awareness of imperial excesses, of tortuous aspects of decolonization,
as well as of *some* present-day consequences of empire. "Commonwealth immigration into Britain increased dramatically after the war,"
explain Sked and Cook (1979, 200, 284), and already in the 1970s there
were calls for "limits on immigration, culminating in the panic moves
to slam the door on the Kenya Asians," especially among the Conservatives and their supporters.

The masses were well aware of the changing demographics as well as
of the darker side of their kingdom's history. A letter in the *Daily Express*
from 15 April 1980 asked the British to pause over their own complicity
in Palestine's ongoing woes. *Wild Justice* makes it clear that the British
state routinely "discarded the right of habeas corpus," whether in the
earlier counterterrorism campaigns in Cyprus or Palestine or "now" in
the H block, the infamous section a Belfast prison built recently to house
Irish Republican Army terrorists. Importantly, the novel is not necessarily a critique. As Stride's corrupt brother puts it: "Those damned shop
stewards up in Westminster may have thrown the empire away, but we
still have our responsibilities." One of those responsibilities was to remind the natives about the good things the Empire left behind, a point
vividly illustrated in *Life of Brian*'s "What have the Romans ever done
for us?" scene.[9]

Still Victorious

Analysis presented in the preceding section suggests that British society agreed on a number of issues. First, apart from the Soviet Union, the British feared the Irish and Irish Revolutionary Army terrorists in particular. Second, Britain was a strong supporter of the UN Charter's vision of sustainable peace and common security, key principles of which are the right to security of all states and their peoples, and the primacy of conflict prevention and the peaceful resolution of disputes. Britain was simultaneously a strong supporter of the US-led Western alliance, starting with NATO but also including European integration, and an equally strong opponent of the Soviet Empire. The country understood itself as a leader of, and the model for, the still relevant Commonwealth.

Beyond this wide area of significant elite-mass disagreement, there were also two opposing Britains in 1980: Muddling Through – for Modern Britain was now simply muddling through[10] – and New Britain.[11] The disagreement between them was primarily about the political economy and, specifically, the response to slowing growth and rising inflation. Representing majority opinion among both the elites and the masses, Muddling Through stood for small modifications to the status quo – Britain was not doing well but neither was the rest of the West. Whether from the vantage point of the press or commercial films, the British were now much more sceptical about scientific and technological progress, the expansion of production, and the ability of government to respond to social and economic problems rationally. On top of the economy, Muddling Through was dissatisfied with the nation's overall decline, class and gender hierarchies, and corruption of the ruling elites as well as unfairness and injustice. Some of these identifications were not seen as problems to be solved but, rather, as challenges to be mitigated. Others were not even challenges. In the mass discourse, for example, sexism and racism were normal rather than abnormal. Finally, Muddling Through was proud of Britain's democratic and trade unionist traditions as well as its education system.

New Britain argued for the abandonment of Keynesian orthodoxy in economics. Other targets were immigration, statism, and socialism, which in this discourse were configured as twin atavisms of a bygone era.

New Britain defined the British people as reformist, hard-working, capitalist, strong, free, orderly, and competitive. Although the debate about
the wisdom of consolidating the market imperative at home was vigorous, it did not actually translate into opposing foreign policy stances.
Whatever their assessment of the causes of decline, both discourses saw
the nation as a world leader on many dimensions. Analysis notably failed
to identify the presence of a third discourse. If some sort of a socialist
discourse existed in the UK at the time, this had to be within Labour itself
– Labour's "Tribune group," perhaps – rather than in either elite or mass
discourse at large.[12]

The 1981 white paper on defence reflected aspects of both Muddling
Through and New Britain. Officially titled *The Way Forward*, but pop-
ularly referred to as the Nott review, after the secretary of state for defence, John Nott, this document attempted to reassess the commitment-
capabilities gap faced by the Armed Forces in light of government
turnover, the worsening financial situation, and the Soviet invasion of
Afghanistan in 1979 (Chalmers 1985, 142–7). Yet, the review did not
change the old defence roles: it only reordered the spending priorities.
This was in line with some earlier white papers and with the basics of
Modern Britain discourses discussed in preceding chapters.[13]

Looking at the actual foreign policies that followed the Nott review,
however, we see a much stronger imprint of Thatcher and of the New
Britain discourse that she embodied. Let us begin with the procurement
of the US Trident system, a fleet of submarines that were to form the
backbone of the UK's semi-independent nuclear deterrent. At this point
in history, there was nothing particularly strange about buying American.[14] The Polaris missile system, discussed in chapter 2, had since the
1960s evolved into an entirely submarine-launched nuclear deterrent.
Trident built on this evolution, and Thatcher declared her government's
intent to purchase the system on 15 July 1980. Nott himself supported
the secret deal, as did Lord Carrington, Thatcher's foreign secretary. The
decision created considerable political risk. Once some of the secrecy
surrounding the deal was lifted thanks to leaks in the US press later that
year, Britain saw both the beginning of the famous Greenham Common
Women's Peace Camp and a 250,000-strong national Campaign for Nuclear Disarmament rally. Undeterred, the Thatcher government reaf-

firmed the Trident decision in the 1981 white paper, and then, in the subsequent year, placed an order for four submarines. Labour responded
with a campaign to cancel the purchase and also to unilaterally denu-
clearize the country. These promises, put in manifestos for the 1983 and
1987 elections, proved to be an electoral kiss of death (Freedman 1999,
132; see also Vickers 2011, chap. 5). The prime minister's policy prevailed,
and the UK eventually received the submarines – all four in the 1990s.

Paul Beaumont's (2014) discourse analysis of the Trident debate puts
questions of British identity at the analytical forefront. Labour's argument that the new system at once "threatened UK security and wasted
money" was at first shared by more than a few Tory MPs and bureaucrats
(Beaumont 2014, 91). In February 1981, Nott explained to Thatcher that
Trident had less support than expected: only a third of Tory MPs were
for it, and the cabinet was no different. Top military brass were likewise
divided (Travis 2011). According to Beaumont, Thatcher won this battle
through employing four main interrelated frames. The first involved re-
moving the ethical responsibility of aiming for a nuclear weapons-free
world and marginalizing the anti-nuclear movement in general as utopian and naïve by claiming that she was behaving responsibly: by sustaining nuclear deterrence her government was being responsible, while
Labour leaders were being dilettantes. The second frame involved emphasizing the urgency of the Soviet threat: because the Soviets were arming at a faster rate than would a purely defensive state, Britain needed
Trident in order to defend itself and its allies. The third frame involved
criminalizing Soviet behaviour: for example, the Soviets' nuclear-build
up was a means of "blackmailing" Europe. The fourth frame involved es-
tablishing Britain's status within NATO: securing Trident at once secured
Britain and its privileged position in the alliance hierarchy.

Thatcher's frames drew on uncontestable aspects of British identity
as well as on New Britain. As before, British society had strong Atlanticist
leanings – though not as strong as those of the prime minister herself
(Haseler 2012, 103). Also strong was British techno-nationalism: if Britain
was one of the leading, technologically advanced states in the West, a protector of Europe against the Soviets, then it made sense for its government to acquire Trident. Last, the French Other played a familiar role of
being close but inferior to the UK. In Carrington's words: "Failure to

acquire Trident would have left the French as the only nuclear power in Europe. This would be intolerable" (Travis 2011). Together, these reasons meant Labour's policy of unilateral nuclear disarmament was intolerable, too. (In 1987, the Thatcher re-election campaign poster showed a surrendering British soldier with his hands in the air and the slogan "Labour's Policy on Arms.")

Gender, meaning the configurations of masculinity and femininity, doubtless played a role in the Trident debate as well. As Nick Ritchie argues, Britain's obsession with its "own" nuclear deterrent cannot be fully understood without an appreciation of the role of gendered power in international relations. If having nuclear weapons signals virility, strength, autonomy, and rationality, then nuclear disarmament, advocated by Labour, means the opposite (Ritchie 2012, 88–9). The plausibility of this thesis is demonstrated in the identity topography above, given that it posits masculinity as a fundamental cross-discourse tenet of British identity.

In addition to working assiduously to solidify the transatlantic alliance, Thatcher made several politically risky moves in defence. One was to strengthen Britain's continental contribution to NATO at the expense of the Royal Navy, which was slated to take more than half of the planned budget cuts. This decision can be seen as consistent with British identity, given its direct and indirect obsession with the Soviet threat, NATO, and nuclear weapons. However, just six months later, Britain found a good reason to obsess about the Royal Navy too.

The Falklands War is another well-worn case study in the scholarship on British foreign policy. Weeks before the election that brought Thatcher to power in April 1979, the outgoing British ambassador to Paris, Sir Nicholas Henderson, sent a candid memo to the Foreign Office in which he bewailed a "poor and unproud" Britain and its precipitous decline relative to France and Germany. The memo was subsequently leaked to the press, and the ambassador became a household name during the electoral campaign, especially among those keen to attack Labour's foreign policy record (Henderson 1979). What upset the elite at the time was not so much the argument about relative decline but, rather, the notion that Britain had lost its patriotism and pride.

Rather than accepting Henderson's imminent retirement – the despatch was meant to be a farewell memo to his colleagues – Thatcher installed him as ambassador to Washington, which is where he would participate in the defining crisis of British foreign policy in the 1980s: the Falklands War. A small British colony located off the coast of Argentina, where the islands are known as the Malvinas, this remnant of the old Empire had for years been subject to a diplomatic impasse between Buenos Aires and London. Analyses in chapters 1 though 3 suggest that most Britons likely had some inkling that the islands existed and were somehow British but without knowing how or why. As for British strategists, they viewed it as a nuisance, not a threat – the name "Falkland Islands" appears only once in the 1981 Nott review, the same number of times as Belize, which gained independence in September that year, and Hong Kong. But after an elaborate cede-and-lease-back plan fell through, Argentina brazenly moved on 2 April 1982 to occupy the islands. The action astonished the world. So did the subsequent British reaction. Undeterred by ten thousand Argentine soldiers, but with overt and covert support from European and American allies, the Thatcher government dispatched a counter-invasion force that managed to push the invaders back.

The spectacular, swift reinvasion of the faraway, almost forgotten outpost built upon the patriotic, masculine fervour and the idea that responding to violence with violence was a manly thing to do. Recall also that the memories of the Suez debacle were still fresh for many decision makers and most voters. In her victory speech at a Conservative rally at Cheltenham on 3 July 1982, Thatcher explicitly countered Suez with analogies to the Second World War, stressing the kingdom's unity and the strength of its men:

> The lesson of the Falklands is that Britain has not changed and this nation still has those sterling qualities which shine though our history. This generation can match their fathers and grandfathers in ability, in courage, and in resolution. We have not changed. When the demands of war and the dangers to our own people call us to arms – then we British are as we have always been.[15]

Labour's own sabre-rattling could be seen in this context, especially if we accept that the meanings of partisanship and declinism would have shifted during the war. Initially, however, the baseline discourse, Muddling Through, supported strong diplomatic reaction but not necessarily a military one. New Britain, in contrast, wanted war, almost treating it as a vitamin shot for an ailing patient, not unlike the radical interventions in the economy that Thatcher advocated. Either way, the moment reversed much of the decline discourse as far as British foreign policy was concerned (Jackson 2007).

For Hadfield-Amkhan, Englishness and Britishness both played a role in the reinvasion, the latter more directly because it offered more helpful constructions of sovereignty, democracy, legality, and what she calls "islandness" – the configuration of the disputed islands as "a microcosm of British demography and territory" (Hadfield-Amkhan 2010, 146). That Conservative policies were consistent with this iteration of Britishness was prima facie evident from the popularity of the war as well as from Thatcher's landslide victory in the 1983 election (159).[16] Those who then believed that Britain was a great power, entitled to act independently to safeguard its core national interests, were vindicated (not least because Argentina was a significant power in South America, second only to Brazil). Those who mocked this view, citing the economic and geopolitical realities of the Cold War era, were themselves mocked. (Ironically, the success of the Falklands campaign later helped "realists" in the Foreign Office to negotiate with Communist China the "retrocession" of Hong Kong.)

Beyond Hadfield-Amkhan's study, there are several more analyses of the links between the discursive strategies used by the Thatcher government and the media, on the one hand, and discourses of British identity, on the other (Barnett 1982; Dillon 1989; Aulich 1992; Femenia 1996; Henderson 1996; Foster 1997; Parr 2014). Based on this literature, we can say that the leadership constructed four key frames. The first was the idea of "greatness," which was almost always bolstered by references to Churchill and Britain "standing alone" in 1940 (Barnett 1982, 55–6, 84). The second was the claim of defence of morality and the rule of law in the international community. In this frame, the conflict was structured as a clash between the evil Argentines – on 7 April 1982, Secretary of State for Foreign and Commonwealth Affairs Francis Pym spoke of "their rape of the islands" – and the good Britons. The latter claim was bolstered by references to the Second World War as well as by the UK's history of "helping" its colonies to independence. As Thatcher put it on 14 April 1982: "We have a long and proud history of recognizing the right of others to determine their own destiny. Indeed, in that respect we have an experience unrivalled by any other nation in the world."[17] The third frame was the notion that British men – not just those in military service – have to be strong, disciplined, and violently patriotic (Foster 1997, 241). All three frames resonate with my reconstruction of Britishness: greatness, justice/fairness, law and order, and (militarized) gender inequality were salient identity categories in 1980. The one frame that the literature identifies but that is missing from my topography is "pastoral Britain," a fantasy land with no immigration and no post-industrial upheaval (248).

While the leadership in London insisted that the UK was once again "standing alone" against overseas miscreants, in reality the British war effort critically relied on American help. To begin with, Ambassador Henderson's public relations campaign in Washington was decisive in securing American support in intelligence and logistics for Britain's war effort, which, in fact, proved decisive. Washington went to great lengths to support Britain's military effort, at first covertly and then overtly, from late April until the end of the hostilities in June, when it moved to freeze all military exports and loans to Argentina. This is indeed why the Falklands episode is sometimes seen as a mirror image of the Suez Crisis (Louise Richardson [1996], cited in McCourt 2014a, 163). This time, however, there was no Traditionalism and no Socialism to problematize dependence on Washington. (This arguably changed later in the 1980s, with the rising power of the Greenham Common Women's Peace Camp and similar anti-militarist and feminist protests in the UK.)

According to McCourt (2014a, chap. 5), Britain's decision to try to retake the islands was a function of its emergent role: that of "residual great power." As before, it was the US and, to a lesser extent, Britain's Commonwealth and European allies who made crucial contributions to this role construction. But McCourt's theoretical joust with identity-based readings of foreign policy notwithstanding, his interpretation is essentially complementary to the one offered here. For one, it appears that *both* the national identity *and* role-formation processes obliged the British government to respond militarily to Argentine aggression. In this context, we can draw another parallel with Suez, given that the identity topography at the time likewise suggested swift and decisive counteraction to "foreign aggression." This time, however, British leaders had a much stronger case internationally. As Labour's Denis Healey put it in the House of Commons on 7 April 1982: "The argument in Suez was about property rights – that in the Falkland Islands is about human rights" (Quoted in McCourt 2014a, 157).

Both identity- and role-based perspectives could shed light on UK reaction to the US invasion of Grenada in 1983. President Ronald Reagan justified the action as necessary to protect American citizens on the Caribbean island of Grenada, many of whom were students at a medical school, against Grenada's new Marxist government. What he did not do was consult with the UK, Grenada's fellow Commonwealth member and former colonial master. However, Reagan famously called Thatcher to apologize, and the tiff was straightened out. Indeed, the Grenada invasion was problematic for many in the UK, not as a manifestation of US militarism and imperialism but, rather, of US exceptionalism – the British deserved much, *much* better from their American ally.

When it comes to relations with Europe, a typical issue at the time was the struggle for a budget rebate from Brussels, a.k.a. the Thatcher rebate.[18] Shortly after being elected prime minister, Thatcher demanded that the EC give Britain a "correction" to rebalance British budgetary contributions. Her argument was based on the idea of fairness. Although one of the least well-off member state on many measures, Britain was one of the largest net contributors to the EC budget. The reasons were structural. Other member states had larger agricultural sectors, which made them eligible for the EC's lavish agricultural subsidies, yet most of them raised less revenue in value-added taxes and imported less from countries outside the EC.

The Thatcher government won this battle through a combination of dogged determination and threats to cease payments altogether. It first turned down a rebate offer of £350 million and then persisted through five years of negotiations to secure a much better deal for Britain at the Fontainebleu summit in 1984. Crucially, the EC agreed to raise the amount of the rebate in accordance with the future growth of its budget – an annual reduction that in any given year is equivalent to 66 per cent of Britain's net contribution in the preceding year. The rebate deal was warmly welcomed in Britain, with Thatcher using this as political capital for domestic triumphalism and for committing her government to moving European integration forward, the occasion for this being the British presidency of the EC in 1986. (Years later, the Thatcher rebate was constructed as a Eurosceptic victory over the EC/EU.)

As we see in the following chapters, the struggle also prolonged Britain's "trench warfare" with the EC for years and even decades (McCourt 2014a, chap. 5). Alternative policies were no doubt plausible at the time. For one, the Thatcher government could have accepted the initial offer in exchange for concessions in other policy areas, much as did other member states in similar situations. It could have also spent its political capital to push for more equitable budgetary mechanisms, thus helping strengthen rather than weaken the EC. Yet neither option fit the dominant discourses of British identity. According to Muddling Through, Britain stood not only for what was fair but also for the protection of British workers. As for New Britain, it took pride in Britain's insularity. And if Europe was the Other, then Britain had no reason to "play Bountiful to the Community," as Thatcher once put it before embarking on her rebate fight with Brussels (McCourt 2014a, 91). The fact that these exceptionalist ideas were as commonsensical in 1980 as they were in earlier years helps us understand the particular realities within which Britain's EU policy was formulated, enacted, and justified in this period. In other words, much like the reinvasion of the Falklands Islands, Thatcher's hard push for a rebate strongly resonated with what British society instinctively thought was right.

5

The West Has Won, But ...

In the preceding chapter, I open with a story of British insecurity. For a society that felt it had no lesson to learn from anybody, 1980 was a particularly grim year. The year 1990, the opening subject of this chapter, was much better. A series of uprisings in Eastern Europe that brought down the Berlin Wall in November 1989 and subsequently destroyed the Soviet Union proved once and for all that Britain and the West had the optimal political and economic model. And whereas earlier in the decade economic decline appeared unstoppable, in 1990 the economy compared favourably with those of other top industrial countries.

Nevertheless, many Britains viewed the kingdom as embroiled in a state of continued crisis. They pointed fingers to three realities in particular: the Troubles in Northern Ireland (then the longest-running civil war in Europe), social inequality, and the high concentration of power in the hands of the executive and Margaret Thatcher in particular. The surveyed mass-level texts indicate no shortage of resistance to Thatcher's and Thatcherist endeavours to deregulate, or privatize, the economy and, in turn, remodel British society away from the collectivism and socialism of previous Labour governments. These were no hallucinations: Thatcher's government did carry through more reforms than any government since Clement Attlee's.

In terms of an identity topography, we can see multiple discourses: the latest version of "Modern Britain" at the centre, with its "Aspirational" and "Aversive" discourses, plus an equally central contest between "Thatcherite" and "anti-Thatcherite" responses to the deep economic malaise that enveloped the country. Yet, beyond said contestations, the governors and the governed agreed about many things. One important intersubjective belief was that outsiders were wrong to assume that the British were culturally similar to their European neighbours or to their American allies – the truth was that the British were unique.

Open divisions in British society over politics and the economy did not directly translate into British foreign policy debates. A conceptual agreement held that Britain had the status of a great power, a claim eminently demonstrable by the nation's many contributions to the vanquishing of the once-mighty Soviet Empire. In addition to looking back to the glories of the past, all discourses of British identity also posited that Britain should continue to extend robust and reliable support to the US, including in responding to Saddam Hussein's revisionism in the Gulf – Iraq's annexation of Kuwait in 1990 – and other deadly and dangerous parts of the international politics game. The premise of considerable value differences between the UK and Europe, which this analysis indicates was central to the contemporary British *doxa*, similarly helps explain why Britain remained less than enthusiastic about the Maastricht stage in the European integration project. Where this topography falls short is in predicting the British stance on Bosnia under John Major, Thatcher's successor at 10 Downing Street.

1990: "Britain Is Supposed to Be a Democracy"

As in the previous chapters, we begin by depicting top identity categories as a word cloud, in Figure 5.1.[1] This time the leading category by frequency is *democratic*. One reason for this was Thatcher. Regarded as the most powerful prime minister since Churchill, Thatcher was understood in 1990 to have worsened a number of Britain's long-standing problems – sclerotic economic growth, unhealthy labour relations, class stratification – while also creating new ones, namely, by threatening the freedom of the press and other basic liberties on which British democracy was founded.

The new prime minister, John Major, seemed less authoritarian, if only because he saw democracy as symbiotic with *capitalism*, Britain's other core value. In his first speech of the year on 4 December 1990 he comments:

When I came into the Party we had set ourselves the goal of a property-owning democracy. We wanted people to own their own homes. Now two thirds of families do. In the 1980s we worked for the capital-owning democracy – more building society accounts, more shares, more personal pensions.

In the same passage we also see that Britain aspired to be *family-oriented*. This was not simply Tory rhetoric. As in the previous years discussed, owning a home was a key aspect of the British dream in 1990 – a core British conception of good life.

What clashed with this conception was the upbeat spin the prime minister gave to the policy (rhetoric) of his predecessor, for the rest of the archive explicitly configured *Thatcherism* as a threat to democracy.[2] Consider a flurry of letters to the editor published in the *Daily Mirror* on 15 March 1990, angrily responding to the controversial Community Charge, the new flat-rate per capita tax – a.k.a. the poll tax – to be collected by local councils. One: "Dictator Thatcher should remember that he or she whom the electorate vote in they can just as easily vote out." Two, from which we borrow the title of this report: "Britain is supposed to be a democracy. If it was we'd be able to vote on this tax. I firmly believe that most people in this country do not want the poll tax in its present form. We should ask for a referendum."[3] Three: "Does Mrs. Thatcher think we are all as stupid as she is? She says she thinks the poll tax is fair. Who for?" Four: "Thatcher the Snatcher is a very good name for someone who should be ashamed. She gives to the rich and robs from the poor." Five: "The Tory government is determined to make the poor of Britain pay more while the rich pay less." In its 15 November issue, the *Daily Mirror* once again gave space to concerns about the nation's democracy, this time on the editorial page: "At the moment only Tory MPs have a vote in deciding who should be their leader and therefore our Prime Minister. Our message to them is simple and for that reason very short. We expect them on the day to do their duty. And that duty is to put Britain first." As these reactions suggest, Britain self-defined as a *free* country: free to speak its mind, not simply a country of free enterprise (*Sun*, 15 May 1990, op-ed).

Figure 5.1 Top British identity categories in 1990 by frequency

Anti-Thatcher feelings were widespread elsewhere in the archive. Consider the textbooks: in 1990, as before, British capitalism and democracy were commonly evaluated in relation to *statism*, *socialism*, and *partisanship*. For historians Kavanagh and Morris, the authors of one of the history textbooks surveyed, "the postwar consensus" had wide and deep roots, going back to the era before the Second World War: "This is true of the National Health Service, [economist William] Beveridge's reform of welfare, and the public corporation form of nationalization which built on Herbert Morrison's model of the London Passenger Transport

Board" (Kavanagh and Morris 1989, 16). May's textbook agreed. "Buts-kellism" – the well-known phrase coined in a 1954 issue of the *Economist* conveyed an essential similarity in *economic* policies between the then Tory chancellor of the exchequer (Rab Butler) and his Labour prede-cessor (Hugh Gaitskell) – held across the board: "From 1951 onwards there was no major issue which produced a fundamental cleavage be-tween the official policy of the Conservatives and that of the Labour Party" (May 1987, 393). Then came Thatcher and her series of lacerating cuts to social programs, with which she sought to "kill off socialism" or, rather, the Labour Party because socialism never really existed in Britain (Kavanagh and Morris 1989, 123; May 1987, 304, 393–4). This was a com-mon refrain across surveyed texts: British life used to be much better with Keynesian demand management and a strong, interventionist state.

In the event, the Thatcher years caused damage to both parties. Re-flecting on "the sheer number of splits" in the Conservative government, columnist Alastair Campbell wrote this in the 15 October 1990 edition of the *Daily Mirror*: "It used to be Labour that hung out its dirty linen in public." A month later, the same newspaper concluded that Thatcher had succeeded in damaging, if not destroying, *trade unionism* as well: "Her biggest achievement was to destroy excessive trade union power."[4] A long-lasting recession and high unemployment – here coded under the rubric *economically depressed* – were made worse by Thatcher's policies, which resulted in increasingly heavy mortgages. This is from a comment piece published in the *Daily Mirror* in February 1990: "Mrs Thatcher won the 1979 election promising to make it easier and cheaper to buy a home, instead she made it harder and dearer. The dream of a property-owning democracy has become a nightmare." The per centage of good manufac-turing jobs was perceived as falling due to technological change as well as to the internationalization of production and finance.

Thatcher's "conviction politics" were accepted in the domain of law and *order*, a development that was keenly perceived by Hall and Hallsian analysts from the very beginning. This is one reason the Queen's Speech could promise "resolute anti-terrorism" in Northern Ireland. The other reason was that *Ireland*, north and south alike, was again a significant Other for a nation centred in England. (For an exception to prove the rule, see the description of England in May [1987, 313–14].) London was likewise still the nation's heart, albeit less attractive than before. In *The Krays*, that year's blockbuster, the capital city is a gangster paradise, whereas in *The Negotiator* it is the gloomy preserve of a secretive, corrupt elite, whose everyday needs have little in common with those of ordinary people.

Ranked second by frequency is a compound identity category *patriarchy/sexism*. Leadership speeches and most op-eds duly identified Britain as a place of equality between the sexes as well as the "will and determination of one woman" (Major's Speech). The rest of the archive disagreed. The textbooks were explicit about Britain's patriarchal Self. The May (1987, 232) textbook notes that the changes began in the First World War: "Many people were surprised at the heavy work which women could accomplish, although this was due partly to an ignorance of the nature of much pre-war women's work." Yet, according to May, because of the "one-sidedness" of gender politics in Parliament, in British society, and in the rest of the Western world, progress was not straightforward.

The fictional sources are divided. While the two novels cherish the status quo, the two movies offer multiple critiques of patriarchy from a female position. In Frederick Forsyth's novel *The Negotiator*, among forty key characters, only two are female – one is Thatcher and the other is an FBI agent, Sam Somerville, who is professional but also gorgeous and a "good cook." Wilbur Smith's bestseller *A Time to Die* has a lot of time for misogyny and the subjugation of women. Claudia Monterro, a naïve American, to Sean Courtney: "I'm only brave when you're here."

The Krays, which is a movie about a matriarchal, working-class criminal family in the East End of London during the 1950s and 1960s, has several memorable critiques of patriarchy. In one, the twins' mother Violet and her sister Rose agree that "men are born children and stay children"; in another, the two women talk about life and death in working-class London during the Second World War: "Men! Mum's right. They stay kids all their fucking lives. And they end up heroes – or monsters. Either way they win. Women have to grow up. If they stay children, they become victims."

Shirley Valentine sends the same message. The opening scenes centre on the boredom and gloom of female domesticity in contemporary Liverpool life: Shirley is an empty-nester housewife who likes to drink and talk to the kitchen wall, lamenting a past that appeared to promise her a more romantic life. In one scene, Shirley's husband becomes violent after learning about an unauthorized change in his habitual Thursday steak-and-chips dinner menu. This pushes Shirley over the edge, and so she departs on a two-week holiday to Greece – a lottery win – with an old girlfriend, Jane. This is a dialogue with a neighbour, Millandra, in which Shirley yells through her window:

> Millandra: Greece, at your age, you and that Jane? It's obscene!
> Shirley: That's right, Millandra, I'm going to Greece for the sex! Sex for breakfast! Sex for dinner! Sex for tea! And sex for supper!
> Random delivery man: Sounds like a fantastic diet, love!
> Shirley: It is, have you never heard of it? It's called the F plan!

In Greece, Shirley does end up having sex with a mustache-sporting local restaurant owner, Costas. Eventually, she returns to her husband, in what seems to be a reversal of power relations: "I know. I used to be The Mother. I used to be The Wife. But now I'm Shirley Valentine again. Would you like to join me for a drink?"

In addition to scrutinizing the idea of women as housewives and mothers, in charge of the household budget, both movies scrutinize marriage using the language of war. For Violet, "a house is a bloody battleground all on its own," and for Shirley, "marriage is like the Middle East – there's no solution."

The entrenched *class* system is another painful manifestation of the UK's slow *progress* towards *fairness and justice*. The Queen's Speech intimated that Britain continuously worked on justice, and not just for its people: "A Bill will again be brought before you to give our courts the jurisdiction to try alleged war criminals." Both newspaper samples had no shortage of justice system stories, some of which had direct implications for what it meant to be British. An example is the sentencing on 13 December 1990 of Russell Bishop in Brighton for child molestation and abduction but not for the Babes in the Wood murders, which appeared to either prompt or index a nation-wide debate on whether double jeopardy and/or capital punishment were right from Britain (*Sun*, 15 December 1990, two op-eds).

Fictional sources, in contrast, were more likely to see life as unfair in general. The world of *A Time to Die* is basically socially Darwinist: African Marxist dictators versus Western corporations versus European settlers versus the poor. In *The Negotiator*, Cold War realpolitik is similarly brutal: the Soviets are about to invade Iran and the US oil-military-industrial complex is sabotaging a liberal president's arms reduction treaty with the Soviets. Same for *The Krays*: "When people are afraid of you, you can do anything," says one brother to another.

Present-day Britain was infinitely more equal than Edwardian Britain, but the best Britain was still in the future, not least because of Thatcher's policies. May's textbook suggests that the rise of the welfare state, Labour, and trade unions meant that the working class was a more meaningful category in 1990 than in 1800. Class *egalitarianism*, furthermore, arose out of the First World War: "A realisation by ordinary men and women that their co-operation was essential to the well-being of the country contributed towards a major social change – the decline of deference and the spread of a mood of egalitarianism" (May 1987, 321). Kavanagh and Morris (1989, 93) agreed that Labour was the more egalitarian of the two parties: "Labour was committed in a way that Conservatives were not to racial equality, internationalism, and 'the brotherhood of man,' which meant enthusiastic acceptance of a multiracial, internationalist Commonwealth and also of the United Nations."

The kingdom was defined as at once *powerful/influential* and *declining*. To begin with, the military burden of the Cold War had just paid off in a big way, adding further credit to claims of historical, moral, and technological superiority. Furthermore, Britain was a *modern, developed, and well-educated* country – obvious facts in the context of comparisons with the countries of the crumbling Eastern bloc or of the Third World, to say nothing of Britain's own history of violence against the poor, against women and children, and against colonized peoples. The British state was also overly *bureaucratic*, and there was also an elite-mass divide

on *patriotism*. In his first speech, Prime Minister Major said he wanted
to see only one kind of savings in the economy: "I want those savings to
be British."

Britain's struggles with modernity also manifested themselves through
the rise of mindless *consumerism* and obsession over *image* and style.
This was in evidence in the letters sample, in the movies, and in the novels
– the mass side of our archive. In *The Krays*, the sadistic gangster twins,
Ronald and Reginald Kray, grow up to become Savile Row suit-wearing
national celebrities – a measure of success but also a compromise with
their masculinity. In the Smith novel, Claudia is repeatedly represented
as strange for being anti-materialistic.

The textbooks treated the British Empire as a folly, both economic and
moral, finding comfort in the seemingly *post-imperial* present that began
around 1970. According to Kavanagh and Morris (1989, 104), "The questioning of the viability of the Commonwealth coincided with the sudden
decline in confidence referred to elsewhere about Britain's prospects as
a great power, both politically and economically." For May (1987, 193),
who cited Lenin approvingly, imperial conquests benefitted only capitalists: "The white dominions – Canada, Australia and South Africa –
were the favoured market, and by 1913 37 per cent of Britain's overseas
investments were there, with a further 10 per cent in India bringing the
Empire's share to almost half." This did not make a difference to the poor
at home:

> Dreadnought battleships were, of course, necessary for the main-
> tenance of imperial glory. And here lay a second contrast, that the
> nation which was bearing "the white man's burden" in the colonies,
> turned a blind eye to the problems at home. Winston Churchill de-
> clared, "I see little glory in an Empire which can rule the waves and
> is unable to flush its own sewers." (393)

The Smith novel agreed that the Empire was no more but did not necessarily agree that this was always a good thing or that the old imperial structures did not matter. An early description of a meeting between Sean, a
local white settler and the main protagonist, and the two Americans, Ric-

cardo and Claudia Monterro, on a hunting safari sets a nostalgic tone: "There were twenty servants to care for three of them, all so sybaritic and colonial and exploitative. This was 1988, for God's sake, and the empire was long gone, but the whisky was delicious."

Though the Empire was long gone, Britain was still an exceptionally *well-armed* country – perhaps a little too well armed now that the prospect of a nuclear Armageddon had subsided. According to Kavanagh and Morris (1989, 94–5): "The breakdown of the wartime alliance with the USSR led to the maintenance of high levels of defence expenditure and conscription. Britain's defence expenditure in 1952 was higher in per capita terms than that of the United States." Britain's *diplomatic* identity was similarly strong, with multiple references to the skill and professionalism of the Foreign and Commonwealth Office and the supporting agencies.

In the archive, *America* emerges as Britain's most significant Other, comparable in frequency only to *Europe* (a.k.a. the EEC, the Common Market, Brussels) as a stand-alone category, and far more significant than either *France* or *Germany*. The implication was that Britain was decidedly *Western*, which meant capitalist, democratic, manly, materialistic, and at least culturally Christian: "Now the Ministry of Defence want to ban carols for our lads in the Gulf because they'll offend the Saudis. The bureaucrat loonies should tell the Saudis that we allow mosques in our country and we'd appreciate a small gesture in return" (*Daily Mirror*, November 1990, letter).

In the textbooks, newspapers, and novels, British elites are consistently configured as pro-American. "The bulk of the Labour Party – and almost all Conservatives – viewed US militaristic and economic assistance with enthusiasm," note Kavanagh and Morris (1989, 95). May (1987), in his textbook, explains British decline relative to the US as inevitable in the light of size, war, and cultural political economy: the inefficient use of capital, lower productivity, the short-termism of British managers, traditionalism (a.k.a. the relative lack of "social depth of demand"), and the pervasiveness of "gentleman's agreements" as opposed to formal rules. So, while not a model per se, the US was crushingly competent in the technologies that were shaping Britain.

The letters to the editor sample shows a high degree of interest in, and knowledge of, American mass culture. In the *Daily Mirror*, for example, readers variously could learn about the American origins of the phrase "at the drop of a hat" (August), talk about the merits of American comedians Joan Rivers (June) or Brooke Shields and Bob Hope (December), or, in the *Sun*, wonder about the similarities and differences in British versus American popular music (January). In *The Krays*, Ronald invokes two Wild West characters, Colonel Custer and Geronimo, as "proper men."

Much like the elite characters in *The Negotiator*, the masses were supposed to see themselves as more substantial than the Americans. According to May (1987, 83), men living in a "working-class area of Manchester, before the First World War" lived by a moral code that praised stoicism and "derided the glutton, the American and the French." The same author is also critical of the American alliance. In discussing lend-lease, he thus wants the reader to know that the Americans were not being altruistic; rather, this historically important agreement "was a mixture of friendly generosity and hard-as-nails business dealing" (370). He adds that America posed problems for Britain's foreign policy:

> Britain's attitude to Europe at the end of the Second World War was haughty, and reflected feelings that were themselves a compound of sentimental attachment to the Commonwealth and a desire to foster the "special relationship" which it was thought existed with the United States. (402)

In other words, Americanism muddied the waters for British policy-makers, rendering them incompetent with regard to resolving the dilemmas and trilemmas emanating from Churchill's three circles.

Much as before, in 1990 white skin conferred status but was itself subject to hierarchy. Among the Europeans, the British were on top for obvious reasons: "At the end of the war Britain was the only imperial and West European state with the status of a world power" (Kavanagh and Morris 1989, 5). This is also evident in the Smith novel, at least from the perspective of the protagonist, Sean, who compares the British and Portuguese Empires in Africa thus:

"Your average Indian or African living today in a former British colony is a damned sight worse off now than he was then. Certainly that goes one hundred times more for your average black man living in Mozambique."

"At least they're free," Claudia cut in.

Sean laughed. "This is freedom? An economy managed under the well-known socialist principles of chaos and ruination which has resulted in a negative growth rate of up to ten per cent per annum for every year since the Portuguese withdrawal ... The only worse countries in the world are Afghanistan and Angola, but as you say, at least they are free. In America, where everybody eats three huge meals a day, freedom may be a big deal, but in Africa a full belly counts for a hell of a lot more."

Despite much talk of former British colonies, the Commonwealth was not made to matter at all.

Europe was defined by the existence of sharp cultural and political differences. In *Shirley Valentine*, the heroine offers to work for her lover in Greece by making "eggs and chips" for British tourists who come to his seaside café but cannot deal with Greek food. And if you read the *Sun*, you would know that France was an interesting destination for British pensioners, some of whom were in fact interested in buying rural French homes (June 1990, op-ed) and also that the French government was neither a close friend nor a trustworthy ally of Britain. A letter published in the August 1990 issue of the *Daily Mirror* had this to say:

It's typical of the underhand French to hang back from the Iraqi confrontation – especially since the British are involved. We received no thanks for freeing France in 1944 and we have little to thank them for over the Falklands War, in which French missiles took many British lives. French self-interest is again served by keeping out of the Gulf trouble, since they supply Iraq with weapons.

Another problem with France was that its politics was veering too far left: "The British political experience differs markedly from that of its nearest neighbour, France, where a powerful Communist Party was for a long period able to challenge the underlying premises of state foreign policy" (Kavanagh and Morris 1989, 91).

Like in the equivalent British identity reports for 1950 to 1980, the German Other looms large, mostly via the war. A few minutes into the movie *The Krays*, for example, we see the boys and their mum in a bomb shelter and the rubble on the streets left behind by the Blitz – a testament to the tough life of East Londoners. Contemporary Germany, as seen in *The Negotiator*, is a different place: threatened by red terrorism and a little too enamoured with civil rights.

Beyond the Atlantic, the most significant Other in the 1990 archive was *South Africa*. The relationship was configured narrowly: our *anti-racist* state and society versus their racist government. In contrast to what we see in chapter 3, this time the prime minister did not show understanding for the former colony but, rather, called for a "policy of encouragement … to create through peaceful means a democratic non-racial society" (Queen's Speech). The masses supported this policy but did not necessarily think it would actually work. The *Sun* showed interest in the life and politics of Nelson Mandela but expressed scepticism about his ability to unite the country after the end of apartheid (February, March 1990 editorial). Over in the *Daily Mirror*, a TV columnist praised a "non-preachy BBC film about the accidental death of a corrupt mayor in South Africa." Non-preachy meant this: "How brave to show acts of black harshness—a 'necklacing' with a burning tyre and the pushing of soap powder and oil down the throats of black women who'd bought from white shops" (December 1990).

The works of fiction were far more sceptical about sanctions than was the BBC. In *A Time to Die*, Sean, a professional hunter and former Rhodesian army colonel, does not think a free, democratic South Africa is possible either, as revealed in a number of his dialogues with Claudia. Later in the novel, Claudia is abducted and tortured by a local warlord, General China. This experience leads her to agree with some of Sean's points, partly because they mirror the general's views: "In Africa, there are no good guys and no bad guys, there are simply winners and losers." *The Negotiator* portrays the world in similar dog-eat-dog terms, with its share of torturers (the female character, Sam, is tortured in this novel too), terrorists, child pornographers, and racists.

It is only in these two Cold War thrillers that the Soviet Other appears as significant: Soviets are drunk and racist in *A Time to Die*, and scheming and powerful in *The Negotiator*. But Soviet is not a top category in 1990. For instance, the two leadership speeches do not mention the old enemy at all, only that the government "will take forward work on restructuring our forces to reflect the welcome changes in Europe" (Queen's Speech).

New Orders

The nation that emerged in the preceding section was no longer "muddling through" but once again "modern." As always, Modern Britain wanted more and better things for itself: more freedom, more influence, more order, more social progress – the contours of an Aspirational Britain. We can likewise assemble a cluster of Aversive Britain: a country that yearned to be less racist, less patriarchal, less partisan, less classist, less fake, less consumerist, and so on. Importantly, some of these categories were subject to the elite-mass divide. Anti-racism, for example, was seen as a normal aspiration in a society that was at once liberal and cosmopolitan. However, with some exceptions – the anti-apartheid movement, for example – anti-racism appeared to be an elite preoccupation, with the masses having other things to worry about first, namely, the poor state of the economy. The masses seemed more relaxed about heteropatriarchy and consumerism as well.

Two more discourses of British identity emerge as well. The years of the Thatcher government and Thatcherite reforms affected in numerous ways how the British viewed the world and their place in it in 1990 – that is, as capitalist, patriotic, family-oriented, and anti-bureaucratic. They belonged to one of the world's wealthiest nations, with a quality of life to match, and were ready to trade to capitalize on the end of the Cold War. This discourse, which we can call Thatcherite, was strong only among the elite and generally Tory-leaning.

The oppositional "Anti-Thatcherite" discourse can be found at both elite and mass levels. As its name implies, its target was the prime minister and the hierarchical politics she represented. Emphasizing democracy and fairness/justice, this discourse had a lot of time for trade unions and

postwar statism and even for socialism (though less as a political program and more as an alarm bell to awaken people from their resignation
and polite deference to Britain's political class). This time, Anti-Thatcherism held, the problem was not merely with Britain but also with the
free world in the sense that no Western social democracy appeared to be
able to deal with the growing power of multinational corporations and
transnational capital.

In addition to struggling to adjust to capitalism's victory in the Cold
War, anti-Thatcherite Britain struggled for institutional representation.
Claiming to represent all citizens, parts of the Labour Party were now
turning to a middle way between capitalism and socialism, while others
parts clung to the past to remind itself of the inadequacies of the present.
(Eventually Labour transformed itself into "New Labour," at first hesi-
tantly, under the leadership of Neil Kinnock and his successor John
Smith, then, after 1997, far more comprehensively under the premiership
of Tony Blair.)

Importantly, none of the discourses had a problem either with an
English-dominated kingdom or with the fact that all roads led to London. Contestation was mostly absent from foreign affairs as well. Everyone agreed that the UK was at once diplomatic and militarily strong.
Western and post-imperial identities were not questioned, and neither
was the fact that the country could be both modern and developed as
well as monarchic and traditional. The US was very important and close,
followed by the ancient European rivals-turned-friends France and Germany. Apartheid South Africa, the conflict-prone Gulf, and even sec-
tarian Northern Ireland were represented as anti-Britains. As such, they
were also understood to be subject to British power. The Saudis, as we
saw earlier in the *Daily Mirror*, were in need of reform because they
proved themselves religiously intolerant, unlike the British, who tolerated mosques in their own country.

Looking at foreign policy in objectivist terms, we see that Britain was
entering the new post-Cold War era as a shadow of it former self – a point
Wallace made forcefully in his 1991 article by looking at the state of manufacturing, the pound, the nuclear program, the automobile, aerospace
and computer industries, and the merchant fleet (see Wallace 1991, 74).
Yet we also see the presence of a familiar consensus. A study of elite

opinion on British foreign policy conducted between May and August 1990 by David Sanders and Geoffrey Edwards confirms this observation. Whitehall, Westminster, and Fleet Street leaders were committed to Brussels-based institutions, to France and Germany, "in both defence and economic matters," and to the US in all areas except in its "dollar policy and its unwillingness to control its trade and budget deficits" (Sanders and Edwards 1994, 438). Instead of attention towards the Commonwealth, however, Sanders and Edwards find compassion towards the peoples of the former Soviet Empire. These orientations were in line with the above reconstruction of British identity, regardless of the balance of discursive power between and among Modern Britain, Thatcherism, and anti-Thatcherism.

The same can be said about Britain's Gulf War. In the archive for 1990, Saddam Hussein is a threatening figure, even if Iraq, like the rest of the Middle East, is no longer configured as a former colony that again needed British help. Indeed, what we observe is the dissipating salience of the Middle East relative to earlier identity topographies.[5] Furthermore, Britain was bound to follow America in building a new world order. The collapse of the Soviet Union had given the US the status of "sole superpower," thus enabling Washington to more aggressively confront dictators it did not like. In a letter to the editor of the *Sun* published on 15 December that year in relation to the Gulf War, a man from Lincolnshire put it thus: "When American Secretary of State James Baker and President Bush start talks with Saddam Hussein, our Foreign Secretary Douglas Hurd should also take part," because "the lives of our soldiers are at stake, too."

In the event, Britain distinguished itself both diplomatically and militarily, demonstrating once again that it still cuts a significant figure in the world. Not only did it help the US build a large international coalition against Hussein's Iraq but it also made an oversized combat contribution: fifty thousand soldiers, the largest contingent of any European state.[6] In the subsequent confrontations in the air and on land, British troops and Royal Air Force fighter jets engaged in high-risk missions and suffered about 10 per cent of coalition losses in the process. This outcome, too, is consistent with my topography of British identity. Backed by a series of United Nations Security Council resolutions condemning Hussein's annexation of Kuwait, including Resolution 678, which authorized the war, the government's policy was congruent with a number of categories clustered in both Modern Britain and Thatcherism: diplomatic, militaristic, influential (powerful), freedom- and order-loving, and supportive of the US-led West. In other words, the government's assertion of duty and moral prerogative appealed to Britain's common sense. (In the absence of UN resolutions authorizing the intervention, a war against Hussein would have been harder to justify – a counterfactual explored in the next chapter.)

The Conservative government received strong support in the House of Commons throughout the crisis – from the moment Thatcher recalled Parliament on 6 September 1990, a month *after* she began deploying troops to the Middle East, to Major's generous decision to invite the first substantive debate on the war on 21 January 1991, five days *after* the first bombs were dropped on the Iraqi troops. Labour leader Neil Kinnock and his shadow foreign secretary, Gerald Kaufman, saw the matter as clear-cut, largely because the UN continued to press Hussein to withdraw from Kuwait.[7] Paddy Ashdown's Liberal Democrats made similar arguments, albeit with more enthusiasm for the military option.

A group of around fifty MPs did resist the intended course of action. Labour left, led by Benn, argued for a peaceful settlement via diplomatic means.[8] Others, such as Labour's Healey (he of the Healey review) and occasionally Edward Heath, the former Tory prime minister, asked for more time to be given to sanctions against Baghdad. When the bombing campaign began, a small-scale Labour rebellion took place, as did a few resignations (Vickers 2011, 147–9; Pythian 2007, chap. 6). In other words, among the elected politicians, only a minority wanted the UK to abandon pretensions to world power.

Similar near consensus characterized the British media as well. Among the dailies, only the *Guardian* argued for giving sanctions another chance – partly because of a general anti-war stance and partly because the Iraqis held a number of British hostages in Kuwait. However, once the government announced the invasion, the *Guardian*'s editors came to support the troops as enthusiastically as did those of the *Times*, the nation's conservative newspaper of record, or, for that matter, the mass market *Daily*

Mirror (Willcox 2005, 98–9). Basically, *all* newspapers revelled in the fact
that the British forces were fighting right alongside the Americans in the
air and on the ground. (On television, BBC and ITN played a somewhat
different role given that they sent crews to Iraq to examine evidence of
collateral damage caused by coalition bombs, for which they were
slapped with the label of "unpatriotic" at home.)

In contrast to the Gulf War, the scope of the King and Rifkind defence
papers as well as Britain's position on the Bosnian war are both at considerable odds with the reconstruction of Britishness presented above.
In July 1990, Secretary of State for Defence Tom King took stock of the
new strategic environment with a document called "Options for Change"
(Dorman 2001, 20–2; Rees 2001, 43). The best option was said to be a
smaller force within the next few years, including a significant reduction
in personnel across all three services, supported by the nuclear deterrent,
as before. That same summer Hussein's Iraq invaded Kuwait, prompting
another look at King's document and the reasoning behind the growing
policy discourse on "peace dividend." Defence officials publicly compared
"Options for Change" to the Nott review, which, for all its hard work at
closing various gaps, was still remembered in light of the Falklands campaign.[9] The violent death of Yugoslavia from 1991 onwards and the request for a British contribution to UN peacekeeping there strengthened
the case for revisiting "Options for Change" as well. The Major government took all of these developments into consideration when it produced
"Front Line First: The Defence Costs Study" in 1994 (Dorman 2001, 22).
As per the title, the emphasis was on costs and how to reduce them by
2000, which the document proposed to accomplish by foregrounding
"jointery," or joint force operations, and by discontinuing the conven-
tionally powered submarines in favour of adding more capabilities to the
nuclear-powered ones.

The identity topography correctly predicts the way the two defence
documents mapped the world: a strong focus on the Euro-Atlantic area,
with only minimal acknowledgment, in the 1990 paper, of dependencies
and bases in Hong Kong, Belize, Gibraltar, Cyprus, and the Falkland
Islands. That said, the more technical aspects of the defence reviews
do not fit the dominant discourse. First, their proposed solutions were

excessively Thatcherist in character: improving tooth-to-tail ratio, rationalizing, and, whenever possible, privatizing. Second, while all discourses of identity agreed that Britain was "post-imperial" and that it should seek positive outcomes via diplomacy rather than by spilling blood, they nevertheless articulated a vision of a still-powerful country, one with no shortage of influence, both military and diplomatic. (The novels in particular insisted that British power stretched across the continents, covering all of the territories of the British Empire and beyond.) One reason for this misfit is arguably institutional: the Ministry of Defence and the Foreign and Commonwealth Office had very different ideas about what role and types of Armed Forces were needed in the post-Cold War period.[10]

Britain's Bosnia policy is likewise puzzling from this perspective. For one, Whitehall claimed and maintained a strong diplomatic role for itself during the war – namely, via Lord Carrington and David Owen, two former foreign secretaries (one Tory, one Labour), who were both central to the joint EC-UN peace process for the Balkan country. However, Britain all but broke ranks with its allies in resisting military action (not counting UNPROFOR peacekeeping). Foreign Secretary Hurd and Defence Secretary Rifkin were the key players: they denied not only any parallels between Hussein and Serbia's Slobodan Milošević but also that Bosnian Serb forces were carrying out a genocide. With this, they effectively denied the "strike-and-lift" policy advocated by Washington. "Lift" was a reference to the lifting of the arms embargo so that the Sarajevo government could defend its people. Hurd's response, to borrow a phrase from his memoirs, was, why "level the killing field"? (quoted in McCourt 2013, 251). For a number of critics, this stance was essentially un-British. Simms (2001, 4) puts it thus:

As Douglas Hurd observed on New Year's Day 1992, in a formulation which was later to take on a life of its own: "In recent years Britain has punched above her weight in the world. We intend to keep it that way." It was therefore a considerable irony that Britain spent virtually the whole of the Bosnian crisis punching much below her actual weight, and preventing heavier-weights from connecting with a vastly overrated adversary. Britain could have been a contender, if only she had wanted to be.[11]

Yet the fact is that Westminster mostly accepted the policy of inaction. As Simms points out, Bosnia received little substantive debate in the House of Commons between 1992 and mid-1995, but, when it did, it was to affirm that the crisis was not Britain's business. Conservative MPS all supported the policy of inaction save for Sir Patrick Cormack. Labour, led first by John Smith and then after 1995 by Blair, was more divided, thanks to a doughty minority consisting of Peter Mandelson, Peter Hain, Clare Short, Kate Hoey, and others who could not be indifferent to massacres and ethnic cleansing (Simms 2001, 275–6). Liberal Democrats, including Ashdown and Sir Russell Johnston, were critics as well, calling for a more courageous policy ("Is this who we want to be?"). As for the British media, save for a few notable exceptions, it "remained confused, ill-informed, and in the grip of Whitehall 'spin'" (Simms 2001, 300). But while some "issue capture" did play a role this event, its outcome nevertheless constitutes a puzzle: a moral leader of the world refused to act as a saviour and protector.

McCourt's and Hansen's findings are similar. McCourt notes that Major's foot-dragging on Bosnia was essentially costless politically. Referring to Labour's Andrew Faulds and Conservative Tom King, both of whom were critics, he finds that, for "every Faulds and King, there was a Tony Benn and Edward Heath arguing as passionately against the use of force" (McCourt 2013, 250). For Hansen, the entire debate came down to two main positions: the Balkan discourse, according to which the war in Bosnia had to do with "ancient hatreds," and the humanitarian responsibility discourse, which modified the former with an argument that the West ought to help the victims where possible.[12] Like Simms, Hansen finds more diversity and discontinuities in the media than in the House of Commons, where the vast majority of MPS, Conservative and Labour alike, consistently tended towards the core Balkan discourse. What is more, they continued to parrot the Balkanist line even after the NATO air strikes of 1995. Rifkind's response to Robin Cook, Labour's new shadow foreign minister, on 22 November 1995 that year is telling: "The prime responsibility for the time that it has taken for the war to come to a conclusion must lie with the combatants" (Hansen 2006, 132).

The interpretation of the war indeed shifted in the last six months of 1995. For McCourt (2013, 248–9), this shift is a testament to the power of Atlanticism, which he defines as a cross-partisan tendency to support US foreign policy goals, including military interventions, as well as US-centred security institutions, such as NATO, over all others. From this perspective, British policy-makers merely followed the US lead: when Washington changed its Bosnia policy in July 1995 after what we today call the Srebrenica genocide, so did London. What remains puzzling, however, is that British policy-makers went out of their way to undermine *any* initiative to help the government in Sarajevo with any military means, including the lifting of the arms embargo. My answer would be that the available discourses of British identity supported different policies: the peace process, humanitarian aid delivery, the arming of the Bosnian government, and air strikes. They also supported American leadership: if Washington went to war, especially a humanitarian one, then London should not be far behind. What we are left with, then, is the exercise of the political agency of "realists" such as Hurd and Rifkind and their many "anti-militarist" supporters in Westminster. While Bosnia was never going to be understood as "Britain's business," as would a former colony, the fact is that many British politicians went out of their way to give the Serb side the benefit of every doubt. This often required considerable creativity. The next time Milošević misbehaved, in Kosovo, the UK's policy response was much more straightforward.

The last event of interest to this chapter is Britain's policy on European integration in the 1990s. Immediate historical context is important: by all accounts, the pulse of the British debate on European integration was radically transformed by events surrounding two speeches in September 1988. Jacques Delors, the president of the European Commission, first spoke to the Trades Union Congress, arguing that Britain's labour movement should support the commission's model of "guaranteed social rights." Thatcher's Bruges Speech rejected Delors's call, all but equating the European Commission-led supernationalism to socialism.[13]

Some cultural historians would say that anti-Brussels politics filled a void left by the disappearance of the previous quintessential Others: the

Soviet Union and the delegitimation of overt anti-black and anti-brown racism.[14] Based on my analysis above, this thesis appears at least plausible. Though the British economy and British military capabilities were both firmly focused on the Continent even before the end of the Cold War, the UK government had deeply commonsensical reasons to continue to keep Britain on the sidelines in the European integration project. At the time of the Gulf crisis, for example, Thatcher decided to strenuously oppose British membership in the European Exchange Rate Mechanism, thus putting into a motion a chain of events that led her to lose her prime ministership to Major later that year.

The same crisis had another, much larger effect: increasing dissatisfaction with the Maastricht Treaty, a.k.a. the Treaty on European Union, on the political right. The treaty was a direct outcome of the end of the Cold War and German (re)unification, which together emboldened political leaders in Berlin, Paris, and elsewhere on the Continent to push reforms that gave shape to the EU, as the European integration project is known today. Signed on 7 February 1992, the treaty entered into force on 1 November 1993, setting the stage for a central banking system and a common currency, the euro; for greater coordination in a number of policy areas, including foreign and security policies, the environment, and social policy; and for EU citizenship. Britain, which was in fact forced out of the European Exchange Rate Mechanism in September 1992, received important concessions via the treaty, including the single currency opt-out.

Much like the 1975 referendum on EEC membership, but more intensely, Maastricht generated convulsions in British politics, with bouts of claims and counterclaims regarding the meanings of sovereignty, free trade, and economic and social liberalism. (The main long-term outcome of this process was the "maturing" of Euroscepticism in the UK, not simply in the Conservative Party but, more important, in the press and the public sphere writ large.) As with the referendum debate, both Gibbins (2014, chap. 3) and Todd (2016, chap. 4) provide extensive discourse analyses of the Maastricht debate by looking at key sources of elite discourse. Gibbins looks at the election manifestos, memoirs, biographies, and House of Commons debates, specifically the one from 20 May 1993, when forty-six Conservatives rebelled against Major and his support for the treaty. Todd covers similar ground, from May 1992 to July 1993. His corpus includes parliamentary debates on the ratification of the Maastricht Treaty – the European Communities (Amendment) Act, 1993, and the subsequent debates on the Social Protocol, which are a key site in the Maastricht "rebellion" (a division that reverberated right through Brexit) – as well as the editorials in the *Times* and the *Daily Mail*.

Gibbins discovers the circulation of four discrete British Selves – a liberalizing European nation-state, a reformist role model, a global European authority, and a sovereign civic body –bringing together diverse identity categories, from Peaceful/Prosperous and European to Self-governing and Essentialist (meaning uniquely independent). Of the four Selves, the first three can be said to fit my topography of Britishness in 1990 well in the sense that they are entirely in line with either Modern Britain or with Thatcherism. One interpretation is that the government won in supporting Maastricht because both the elites and the masses failed to see any necessary "contradiction between upholding the sanctity of the nation-state while simultaneously forging new markets and patterns of trade" (Gibbins 2014, 124). The fourth Self identified by Gibbins, a sovereign civic body, is in line only with what this chapter calls the Thatcherist discourse. In this view, Europe is a potentially threatening Other because of a number of anti-British features, including Franco-German hegemony, supranationalism, and socialism (125).

Todd's (2016) discourse analysis of the Maastricht Treaty debate reconstructs three themes that show either direct or indirect linkages with his thematic reconstruction of the 1975 referendum debate "Centralisation, Federalisation, and Subsidiarity"; "Economic and Monetary Union"; and "Sovereignty and Democracy." Of these three, the last one was the most important in general and also, paralleling Gibbins, in specific constructions of the Self threatened by an anti-democratic European Other (80). As before, the overall tone was negative: "Historical allusions to invasion, worries about loss of sovereignty, and implicit and explicit threats to national identity and the self (both individual and collective) feature throughout" (110). Negativity likewise features in the one discursive discontinuity between 1975 and the 1992–93 debates: the representation of the EC/EU as unelected and unaccountable (108). All this supports the argument that the pro-EC/EU politicians never managed to sell "Europe" as anything other than an economic project (Daddow 2015b).

A look at the positions of the main parties is likewise instructive. Whereas in the 1980s Labour was staunchly against EC membership, in the 1990s it reversed this role, such that its leader, John Smith, came out in support of Maastricht, albeit conditional to future improvements in the treaty's "social chapter." The Conservatives, in contrast, travelled from being as pro-European as the Liberal Democrats in the 1960s and 1970s to being deeply divided internally (Todd 2016, 110–11). Maastricht showed this clearly, as a group of rebels defied the party line to vote against the said social chapter and so cause a confidence vote against the prime minister, which he managed to win in July 1993, thus ensuring the success of the treaty. Prima facie, these political tensions map onto my analysis of Britain in 1990, in which Modern Britain appeared to be either content with itself or in continuous search of self-improvement (or in fact both). That being said, Thatcherism was still strong enough to put Britain's ambiguity towards Brussels into even sharper relief and so open up a path for Major's eventual downfall over the European issue.

As a broad-brush explanation of British foreign policy, my reconstruction of Britishness does well with respect to the Gulf War and European integration, and less well with respect to the content of the two defence reviews and Britain's Bosnia policy. But the first two events were so consequential that I return to both in the next chapter. The Gulf War led to Iraq's retreat from Kuwait, but Hussein was removed from power only in 2003 in an event that would become known as Britain's greatest foreign policy blunder since at least Suez.

As for the Maastricht debate, rather than settling the Europe question in the Conservative Party or in UK politics more generally, it in fact deepened the tensions. Five years after the ratification of the treaty, the ambiguities persisted such that Britain would say yes to the idea of EU defence in 1998, via the Saint-Malo Declaration with France, and no to the euro in 2003.

6

A Bridge, of Sorts

In this chapter, I end the story of Britain. The year 2000, a.k.a. "the turn of the new millennium," prompted reflection about the nation's postwar, post-imperial transformation, as did the two "new" constitutional issues: the referenda on regional devolution in Scotland and Wales, which paved the way for the (re)establishment of assemblies in these regions in 1999, and the UK's relationship with the EU, now expressed as a debate on whether or not to join the single currency – the euro. Foreign policy likewise prompted some reflection on what it mean to be British as the Armed Forces had just completed a major military intervention in Kosovo under NATO and were now fighting again, in Sierra Leone. All this meant that all eyes were also fixed on the "New Labour" government under Tony Blair. In power since 1997, Blair stood for both change and continuity, depending on the context. Yes, his government was modernizing Britain by spending on education, health, transport, and, it seemed, by leading Britain into Europe. But New Labour also stayed the course on the macroeconomy, which meant that he continued Thatcher-era policies of privatization, low budget deficits, and low pay rises, arguing that these fostered greater personal initiative and individual responsibility.

As in the previous five chapters, the Britain of the present chapter did not speak with one voice. The predominant discourse can be called "Adaptable Britain." Similar to the Modern Britain discourse we encountered earlier, this discourse emphasized being or becoming modern, dynamic, united, democratic, just, fair, open, and postcolonial. But Adaptable Britain was also multicultural, multinational, and ever more gender equal. "Nostalgic Britain" is the name of the main challenger discourse. Viewing many of Blair's reforms as woolly futurism, this dis-. course resented the inegalitarian outcomes of the new macroeconomic consensus and celebrated a British nation that was once united in itself and also proudly separate from the Continent. Importantly, millennial Britain was for the first time criss-crossed by subnational identity discourses. Of these, Scottish identity was by far the most prominent – to the point that it challenged both Adaptable Britain and Nostalgic Britain as hopelessly English-dominated.

My goal in in this chapter is to explore the ramification of this identity topography for the "big" foreign policy choices of the early 2000s. Adaptable Britain accepted that competition was fierce in an ever-changing global economy, while at the same time arguing, as Blair did, that decline had been reversed. Nostalgic Britain disagreed, but without necessarily calling for a change of direction. Instead, it articulated a sense of defiance towards the outside world, starting with Europe. In the end, it appears that Blair actually overestimated Britain's "adaptability." His first mistake was to say yes – three times – to American-led wars. The first and second, against the Taliban in Afghanistan and "on terror" more broadly, were no-brainers for a kingdom that had long thought of itself as one of the world's moral leaders. However, the Blair government struggled to make the case for the third war, the one against Saddam Hussein's Iraq. The prime minister, who saw Britain as a transatlantic "bridge," decided to support US president George W. Bush and, at the same time, attempted to get the UN and the key European allies, France and Germany, on board. This earned Blair a series of humorous and unedifying monikers: "Bush's poodle," "the accidental American," "America's roving ambassador," and "US foreign minister." This did not sit well with the dominant idea of Britishness even at the time, much less later, when the war on terror and the occupation of Iraq both went south. Multiple inquiries into what went wrong in Iraq took place afterwards, and their echoes continue to reverberate to this day. The second mistake concerns the next stage of the European integration process, the euro. Unlike Blair and a segment of the ruling elite, civil society as a whole was simply not interested in the new currency experiment.

2000: "Britain Is No Longer in Decline"

Figure 6.1 summarizes the top forty categories by frequency (roughly a third of all categories recorded by the coders).[1] *Solidary*, a composite identity category that variously refers to the need for unity amidst diversity, came out on top. Text upon text asked how "we" could remain ourselves over class and subnational divisions, while also responding to devolution and fast-changing transformations in the European and global economies.

The characterization of Britain as significantly *classed* is consistent with all previous chapters. In *Chicken Run*, a children and family claymation film, Mr and Mrs Tweedy, the human antagonists, encompass themes of class, as well as of gender and modernity, with considerable ambivalence. Mr Tweedy has a Cockney accent and is represented as being subordinated to and emasculated by his unfeminine but articulate upper-middle-class-sounding wife, Mrs Tweedy. *Multinational*, in contrast, was new. Whereas before Britain appeared to be an English nation-state containing assorted minorities, now we see regular acknowledgment of the UK's plural national identities, with the English, the Irish, the Scots, and the Welsh all maintaining legitimate distinctions. Yet, as we see below, some voices dismissed this "awesome foursome" as theoretical, given that almost nine out of ten Britons were English.

The *modern* identity, a third-ranked category overall, was invoked explicitly. "To fail to modernize would be fundamentally to fail Britain. But we modernize according to our core values as a country," said Blair in his Britain Speech. Then he painted the Conservatives as part of the past: "The first category of criticism is a traditional Tory one – based on the claim that the pre-devolution, pre-reformed House of Lords, political institutions have been a uniquely important part of British national identity."

References to class *elitism* sometimes signalled contradiction or tension vis-à-vis the UK's *democratic* identity as well as the nation's view of itself as *just* or at least as tending towards a just society. Indeed, Britain cultivated a culture of *reformism*. The prime minister saw democracy as always changing for the better: "In the 19th century, in response to tumultuous economic and social change, we reformed the suffrage not

Figure 6.1 Top British identity categories in 2000 by frequency

once but three times" (Brighton Speech). The economic renewal inspired confidence as well: UK companies were once again the largest in Europe and much more competitive than they had been before.

That *capitalism* created economic insecurity in addition to "opportunities" for individual capacity for self-fulfilment was accepted as a fact of life. The most radical critique of the free market philosophy comes from *Chicken Run*. Technically a children's movie about animals and a parody of popular Second World War dramas about escaping enemy prison camps, this is in fact a story of female-driven resistance to capitalism. The heroine of the movie is Ginger, a tough and ingenious hen who leads her entire coop to freedom – a self-managed commune operating under the principles of natural economy. In contrast, the budding human capitalists, the Tweedys, are concerned that the chickens are "organized," referencing labour and *unionism*. (Immediately after this word is mentioned, the scene cuts to the hens having a meeting reminiscent of clandestine efforts to unionize or take strike action.)

Corruption once again does not appear as a top category. Although justice was occasionally seen as being at odds with the persistence of class hierarchies, and several texts criticized the political leadership for mobilizing to defend the existing power structure, Britain did not see itself as corrupt beyond repair or even as unusual for its divisions between the haves and have-nots. The masses in particular knew that social mobility was not impossible so long as you had the right connections. In one of the year's two Harry Potter bestsellers by author J.K. Rowling, Draco Malfoy explains this to the eponymous protagonist. "You'll soon find out some wizarding families are much better than others, Potter. You don't want to go making friends with the wrong sort. I can help you there," he says in *Harry Potter and the Philosopher's Stone*.

The British state and its people were, or were supposed to be, *scientific* and *rational*. According to one textbook: "Science has provided answers to many of the great mysteries of life, to which religion at one time seemed to have the only key. A generally better standard of living has softened the sharp need for a spiritual message which once led people to walk miles to hear Wesley preach" (Culpin and Turner 1997, 224). One of the embodiments of scientific rationality was the National Health Service, which now needed more work:

> Good health care in a modern society does not come cheap. Yet we have tried to get it on the cheap for too long and tens of thousands of Britons are paying the price with their lives. It is beyond belief that our political leaders don't cringe with shame to see this country bottom of the league tables for cancer and heart treatment. (*Daily Mirror*, 15 February 2000)

Modernity invoked *industry*, and industry invoked *prosperity* for all. In *Chicken Run*, Mr Tweedy quickly loses an argument to Mrs Tweedy, who is set on taking "Tweedy's farm out of the Dark Ages and into full-scale automated production." The *Sun* likened prosperity not so much to automation but to Britain's departure from an EU institution, the so-called European Exchange Rate Mechanism: "Britain has prospered splendidly from the moment we were hurled out of the Exchange Rate Mechanism on Black Wednesday 1992. According to respected economist Maurice Fitzpatrick, of accountants Chantrey Vellacott, we have enjoyed NINE successive years of growth" (*Sun*, 15 April 2000). (Triumphalism aside, the tabloid had a point, or, rather, two points: one, the British economy was performing better than it had for a generation; two, recovery from the last recession was earlier and more energetic in the UK than in the countries that remained inside the system.)

Importantly, in 2000, the textbooks also addressed decolonization in detail, configuring modern Britain as necessarily *post-imperial*. Modern Britain was likewise *both cosmopolitan and multicultural*, a twin identification that did not appear in previous years (and also one that was surprisingly rarely related to post-imperial). A letter in the *Daily Mirror* (15 May 2000) from a reader in Birmingham schools a famous comedian: "Jim Davidson goes on about how great we British are, as if it's some kind of personal achievement. But I hate racial superiority when it's described, quite wrongly, as being patriotic. No one chooses where to be born, or what colour they will be."

Elite-level texts agreed, but they also pushed an idealized image of the multicultural good life – a "potent mix of cultures and traditions which have flowed together to make us what we are today" (Blair's Britain Speech). In this view, Britons were supposed to view themselves not as former imperialists, English-dominated, or as distinctively "white," but as a multicultural haven erected at the confluence of trade and tolerance.

Beyond such metaphors, it was not clear exactly who or what went into said mixed cultures and traditions. Some texts kept Britain's multi-culture reduced to four nations, while others expanded it to include minority and immigrant groups labelled "black," "Asian," and "Muslim" – a signal that race was viewed as a minority issue only. Still other voices expressed deep worries about such government-managed diversity. Among the elites, "liberals" insisted that distinctions that matter came down to class regardless of labels used (white/non-white, rich/poor, north/south, and urban/rural), while those on "the left" professed an indifference towards all collective identities, suggesting that the differences that matter most in the modern world are those between individuals. Then there was an impatience with ungrateful *Refugees*, a significant Other in 2000. An editorial in the *Sun* from 15 February:

> There's gratitude for you. Seventy-three of the hijacked Afghans arrive home and immediately lay into "infidel" Britain. The weather was depressing and the food was awful, they declare, asking: How could we stay? The 74 Afghans who are being put up at the taxpayers' expense in a college in Gloucestershire don't seem to have any problems with the food, the weather, the fags or the handouts. Shame THEY don't feel homesick.

Britain's *orderliness* connected to both modernity and tradition. In the former case, being orderly is a theoretical feature of a post-industrial society; in the latter, being orderly denoted strong rule of law, efficiency, and respect for traditional customs, including *the monarchy* and *civilized* manners. The suburban home bore the promise of the middle-class good life. "Privet Drive looked exactly as a respectable suburban street would be expected to look in the early hours of Saturday morning. All the curtains were closed" (*Harry Potter and the Goblet of Fire*).

Like class, ethnicity, and race, gender played a strong role in defining an identity appropriate to the new century. This is where we see a clash with a more *traditional* Britain. A letter by a person in Manchester laments the loss of old certainties thus: "When I was young, a woman's hair was her crowning glory. These days I can hardly distinguish whether someone on TV is male or female. They all have the same short haircuts" (*Daily Mirror*, 15 March 2000). In fiction, older generations resented the rejection of their wisdom in general but especially in conversations with modern figures desperate to project an image of confidence.

Reader letters showed ambivalence over changes in heterosexual, nuclear family structures that take *patriarchal* assumptions about British social and familial organization as a point of departure. In a letter to the editor about the case of a woman who publicly shamed her ex-husband's failure to pay child support (specifically speaking to the issue of whether her actions were just) published in the *Sun* on 15 May 2000, a reader writes: "It is becoming more common for women to show less natural affection and responsibility for their children. It is becoming more common for men to be left with the kids." (The editor is sympathetic to her frustrations but objects to the assumption that only single mothers are the victims of irresponsible fathers and, furthermore, expresses ambivalence over the changing role and expectations of mothers, decrying the loss of "natural" gender behaviour.) A letter in the same issue from a reader in Essex responds to a proposed public program to provide teenagers with personal mentors by declaring that "the same advice used to be given free – by parents."

The same newspaper worried about the young partygoers in the editorial column as well: "Sadly, they could fall victim to unscrupulous drug pushers. The vermin who prey on our children would have no qualms if they ended up dead. One girl, who was not sold drugs but whose drink was spiked, nearly did." The solution was in stronger state action: "Now the Government is being pressed to close clubs where pushers are found to be operating. Some might find that a harsh measure. Others will see the need for it. Young lives come first" (*Sun*, 15 January 2000). Young lives also come first in the Harry Potter novels, where the wizarding characters eschew and view with incredulity (and sometimes suspicion) the trappings of modern existence that the Muggles (non-wizards) consider necessities.

As in all other years, *declining* was a broad-tent identity. One dimension of Britain's decline is morality, which emerges in aforementioned debates about social organization, including gender roles, traditional family structure, and the state of working-class families and youth. Another dimension of decline was the nation's decreasing geopolitical influence in the world (more on this below). Yet some voices found all such talk either historical or misleading or irrelevant – or all three at once. Blair expressed this sentiment in his Brighton Speech thus: "Britain is no longer in decline."

The masses did not question that the UK still has an influence that extends far beyond what economic and demographic logic might suggest. Yet they were more sceptical than the elites about Britain capably adapting its institutions to the modern age. We indeed see considerable concern about the decline of the economic bases of the working class, for example, the offshoring of manufacturing, as captured in this letter to the *Sun* (15 May 2000):

> Yet another car plant to be scrapped. When is it ever going to end? Now it's Ford at Dagenham and Tony Blair has the cheek to tell us we've never had it so good. What is going to happen to all these poor car workers and their families – not that Tony Blair gives a hoot as long as he is alright.

Related to this was a claim that the working class was betrayed by New Labour, which had continued and deepened neoliberal economic policies implemented by Blair's Tory predecessors. In the same edition of the same newspaper: "So Tony Blair is now determined to sell off Air Traffic Control. That man won't be happy until he has sold off everything belonging to this country. Are the Crown Jewels next?" (*Sun*, 15 May 2000).

The nation that emerged from the mass archive was *rural* and pastoral, not urban. In the Harry Potter novels, Muggle life in London is presented as boring and spiritually impoverished. In *Chicken Run* the plotline centres on the protagonists' attempt to break out of a chicken farm into the countryside beyond. While attempting to mobilize her fellow hens to escape, Ginger responds to expressions of uncertainty about the hens' ability to break through the fence unnoticed: "The problem is the fences aren't just round the farm, they're up here in your heads. There is a better place out there somewhere beyond that hill. It has wide-open spaces and lots of trees. And grass. Can you imagine that? Cool, green grass." At the end of the movie, when the chickens make their successful escape, they are depicted as living harmoniously on a small island in the middle of a lake, itself in the middle of a hilly countryside, where eggs are not commodities but are hatched as chicks.

Insular was in fact an important category on its own, a constant reminder of Britain's identity as an island off the northwest coast of continental Europe. The Walsh (1996, 3) textbook states: "In the 19th century Britain had tried not to get involved in European politics. Its attitude became known as 'splendid isolation' as it concentrated on its huge overseas empire." Isolation and empire were also prompts for thinking about a glorious, simpler past. In *Chicken Run*, the character Fowler, an elderly rooster, first waxes nostalgic about his "RAF [Royal Air Force] days," which by his age implies service in the Second World War, and then laments the loss of *patriotic* respect for values like "discipline."

With respect to significant Others, the archive featured many familiar figures, but also some new ones. *The US* was once again the main creature of British imagination, animated by an exaggeration of powers held in Washington and occasional concern about the way they were wielded. The new category is *The Nationalists*, referring summarily to Scots, Welsh, and Northern Irish seeking greater national sovereignty for their respective regions, if not full secession from the UK. Going with *Chicken Run* again, consider a scene wherein the captive chickens assess the unexpected arrival of Rocky, an American who wants to fly:

FOWLER: I don't like the look of him [Rocky]. His eyes are too close together.
GINGER: Fowler!
FOWLER: And he's a Yank!
ROCKY: Easy, Pops. Cockfighting's illegal where I'm from.
GINGER: Where is that, exactly?
ROCKY: A place I call the land of the free and home of the brave.
MAC: Scotland!
ROCKY: No! America.
CHICKENS: Oooh, America!
FOWLER: Poppycock! Pushy Americans. Always showing up late for every war. Overpaid, oversexed and over here!

Here, America and Scotland are both significant Others against which British identity is distanced, with America standing in for the memory of American GIs sent to, and stationed in, the UK during the wars of the twentieth century. The same text positions the US as a land of freedom, as when Rocky says that "the open road" is his "style" and that back home he is called "The Lone Free Ranger." This is seen as positive (Chickens: "Oooh"). But while Rocky is much stronger and more confident than all the other chickens, he is also less substantial than them:

ROCKY: You see, over in America, we have this rule. If you want to
motivate someone, don't – mention – death!
GINGER: Funny; the rule here is: always tell the truth.

In comparison, the Scottish character in the movie, Mac, is more
closely aligned to the English, though not always – Mac's English is occasionally incomprehensible to both Ginger and Rocky. In the end,
Rocky is an in-group member. We see the same in the Culpin and Turner
(1997, 253) textbook: "The USA and the USSR had emerged from the war
as the two superpowers. In the 1930s other countries such as Britain and
France had been as important in international affairs. However, the war
had finally demoted Britain and France to a second division." Having
made this clarification, the textbook hands off the role of protagonist
to the US. And while some elites expressed worries about the American
stock market, no one foresaw the American superpower declining any
time soon.

The high presence of non-English identities in the archive for the year
2000 relative to the previous years reflects and reinforces a renewed
search for a uniquely British identity. Since Scotland and Wales voted on
devolution in 1998 and their regional parliaments were (re)established
in 1999, there was now a real question as to what Britain and British
means in a multinational state in which the constituent national identities
are institutionalized in devolved, regional parliaments. For example, in a
January 2000 *Daily Mirror* column, Paul Starling observes the increasing
leverage of Plaid Cymru, the Welsh nationalist party, in the Welsh assembly: "Plaid is set on bringing down Labour in the Assembly. They
will fail and in the process further discredit the Assembly." While high-
lighting Labour's historical attempts at promoting solidarity, he laments
its inability to sustain its role as a brokerage party: "For years the Labour
Party tried to hold together an impossible range of political views,
opinions and support. By the Eighties all that unraveled." Finally, Starling
worries that increasing nationalist sentiment in the regional assemblies
could also stoke English nationalism: "Why, their constituents are asking,
should Welsh and Scottish MPs vote on English matters, when English
MPs progressively will be unable to vote on Welsh and Scottish affairs."

On the issue of the stationing of the country's nuclear arsenal – the last US nukes were repatriated in 1996 – the *Sun* (15 March 2000) expressed unhappiness about Scottish politicians: "So where do they want the Nukes sited? Not in Scotland. So obviously somewhere in England, Ireland or Wales. That's us acting like the people who find a dog poop in the garden, scoop it up with a shovel and toss it over the fence on to the neighbour's lawn. Nice eh?"

In the struggle to repeal Clause 28, a.k.a. Section 28, legislation that banned local governments from engaging in "homosexuality promotion," Scotland was made foreign from, and even threatening to, the British Self. The *Daily Mirror* commented in March that the Scottish first minister "hit out at coverage of the recent Clause 28 campaign in some tabloid newspapers, saying: 'There has been a huge debate conducted on the basis of dishonest claims.' The Premier and his spokesman are furious that Clause 28 has been allowed to dominate the headlines for months."

Northern Ireland received less attention. One reason for this is that devolution there had already taken place in 1920, if only (mainly) for Protestant Unionists. Another reason is that Northern Ireland was still being subjected to excision, as in the talk of "the island nation," which rendered the region either completely invisible or folded into the Irish Other. At the same time, the Irish Other was now evaluated more positively than before. The "Irish Comment" section in the London edition of the *Daily Mirror* published op-eds from the *Irish Mirror*, suggesting that both Irelands were part of the larger British family of nationalities. An example from the 15 March 2000 edition:

Well, our national holiday is almost upon us. St Patrick's Day is when the streets are festooned with green, people wear green and drink green beer. And they'll be green in the face next morning. Mind you, the most interesting phenomenon about St Patrick's Day is the influx of tourists. By and large, they join in the spirit of things. But two points bug me when they invade our pubs. The first is Americans pronouncing our national drink as Gwinness. And the other is Brits who say "Bloody good Guinness here."

The *Sun* (15 February 2000), for its part, still worried about Ireland and the ability of Labour's Peter Mandelson, the secretary of state for Northern Ireland, to outwit the enemies of Britain in the period after the Good Friday Agreement:

> This is a real test of Mandelson's nerve – he knows he must deliver lasting peace, but equally knows he must not give any more concessions to the terrorists. Nor must he bow to pressure from the Irish government, which wants him to restore the assembly and power-sharing executive as quickly as possible.

Next on the list of the most significant Others was *Europe*, this time appearing ambiguously as either the EU ("Brussels") or as the two big nations of the western part of the European continent, *France* and *Germany*. In the elite discourse, British identity was not only trying to find a way of being cosmopolitan enough to appreciate the benefits of European integration but also seeking to retain the distinctions necessary for retaining Britishness and to support the British understanding of democracy – two key underpinnings of a *sovereign* Britain. The more popular of the two newspapers resented the EU and worried that the British elite would never grant a chance to the voters to express how they felt about the sovereignty issue:

> VAT [Value Added Tax] will be slapped on the price of baby clothes, newspapers, books and some foods under plans unveiled by Brussels last night. EU chiefs want all member states to have the same tax levels for everything – from business rates to VAT. And they plan to scrap Britain's right to veto it. (*Sun*, 15 March 2000)

> So the London Stock Exchange is planning to merge with the exchange in Frankfurt. We are being linked closer with Europe all the time so that when Tony Blair sees fit to grant us a referendum it will be too late to say no. (*Sun*, 15 May 2000)

In the mass discourse, references to the Second World War were still common, presumably because the British liked to remind themselves that they were "plucky" and possibly invincible — a nation that that kept itself safe from European invasion or occupation not just in 1940 but for centuries. Note also that *Chicken Run* dialogues hint that Europe can further be divided into Germany, *Russia*, and Eastern Europe, the latter two being a source of refugees and asylum seekers. *Chicken Run* is likewise the only source in which *communism* receives positive evaluation, whereby Ginger and her team scheme not only to escape their imprisonment but also to seize the means of production in order to make a better future.

Back to East of Suez

The story of the evolution of British identity narrated in this book thus far can be seen as broadly consistent with established historiographic theses on postwar Britain, from those on the transformation of "liberal political economy" to those on the slow-moving, partial shifts in "traditional" institutional and social structures of authority in postwar Britain. The analysis of British identity in this chapter follows this trend: all top organizing identity categories recovered in this analysis relate to ambiguities of Britain's liberal modernity. While classism is once again viewed as undesirable, working- and middle-class identities are generally presented in a favourable light. An important new issue is national unity, as Britain under Blair had decided to renew centuries-old relationships with its constituent nations. And beyond the Isles, it is Europe – still an "over there" – and America that reverberated through the archive as Others, with only the faintest echoes of Russia.

On this basis, Britain in 2000 was under the impress of two to three rival discourses. One, which we can call Adaptable Britain, was the product not only of the elites of London but also of a large mass segment. This discourse emphasized national unity and solidarity, modernity, urbanity, multinationality, multiculturalism, trade and travel, and the nation's globalized, cosmopolitan future. It accepted democracy and individual freedom as givens, rejected divisions and hierarchies at home and abroad, including various gendered oppressions, and believed in the success of political and social reforms and national purpose. In the same vein, Adaptable Britain foregrounded efficiency, thus at least implicitly acknowledging the Thatcherite reforms of the 1980s as crucial to improving the performance of the British economy. In short, everyone and everything in Britain was "adaptable" – even refugees.

The main challenger discourse, labelled Nostalgic Britain, approved change but in small, controlled doses. Emphasizing order, the rural over the urban, and English leadership of the Union, this discourse was distinctly middle-brow and attentive to what it argued was the growing gulf between the elite and ordinary Britain. It likewise argued that insularity was the main source of the kingdom's greatness, both geographically and temporally. Globalization and "Federal Europe" were not to be trusted, much like mindless consumerism and hedonistic individualism. A strong sense of patriotism revolved around memories of the Second World War, the message being that if Britain "stood alone" against the continent in 1940, it could do so again, if need be.

The second, more peripheral challenger was the discourse of Scottish identity. This discourse sought escape from the confining shackles of the past represented by Nostalgic Britain, while pointing out that "adaptability" is not the same as actual constitutional evolution. Yet the Scottish discourse, too, was nostalgic and not just for Scotland's own mythical past; rather, it looked to the 1950s and 1960s, when both Labour and Conservative governments built social institutions, public transport, education policies, and health services for everyone. Accordingly, today's bipartisan shift away from wealth redistribution and towards promoting global competitiveness was evaluated as wrong-headed.

Whereas the Scottish discourse was inward-oriented, Adaptable Britain and Nostalgic Britain each had strong opinions on the defining foreign policy events of the early 2000s: the EU's institutional progress, symbolized in the euro, and the US-led military interventions in Afghanistan and Iraq. The UK government stayed clear of the first but joined the other two, both times framing the country as a "bridge" between Europe and America. Of these three events, two proved to be deeply divisive issues, including within the ruling (New) Labour Party.

The idea of replacing the pound with the EU's new single currency had a number of champions in the Labour government: leader of the House of Commons and former foreign secretary Robin Cook, Trade

Secretary Patricia Hewitt, Home Secretary Charles Clarke, and, last but not least, the prime minister himself, for whom the euro was Britain's "destiny," as he said at the Labour Party conference in 2002.[2] Chancellor of the Exchequer Gordon Brown, Blair's friend turned rival, was philosophically interested in the euro but was, in practice, against it, as were, in fact, most Labour and Conservative politicians and most public opinion polls at the time. (To wit, Labour's manifesto had promised a referendum on the issue.) In addition to being in charge of economic policies – part of a deal he had made with Blair – Brown was also politically savvy: in 2001 he asked the Treasury to conduct a comprehensive economic test assessment on whether the UK stood to benefit from euro membership, the so-called Stage Three of Economic and Monetary Union. Released by the department in June, the assessment predictably supplied a negative answer to four of the five tests, thus shutting down much of the debate (the cabinet never came close to debating the subject). This was followed up by several more studies, all of which concluded that the economic argument for the euro was weak.[3]

While no discourse of British identity supported EU supranationalism per se, the analysis presented here suggests that UK entry into the single currency was in principle defensible because Adaptable Britain implied openness towards experiments in capitalism. From this point of view, the EU was becoming a new Britain – the most powerful global shaper of social and economic developments. Indeed, rather than a "mere" zone of peace, tolerance, and enlightened self-interest, the EU was now taking on opportunities to spread its stability, wealth, and liberal values to Eastern Europe, and possibly much further. That being said, the preceding analysis also suggests that Europe had not become less of an Other. The xenophobia that had once characterized mass discourse was now almost gone, but many still viewed the EU as a Franco-German scheme for a federal state. We could thus say that the euro entry decision was shaped less by categories such as, in Nostalgic Britain, tradition and patriotism or, in Adaptable Britain, dynamism or prosperity-seeking, and more by a negative evaluation of Brussels in *both* discourses.

This leaves us with at least two counterfactuals. First, recall that it was the counterhegemonic discourse, Nostalgic Britain, rather than the hegemonic Adaptable Britain, that emphatically rejected the notion of yielding sovereignty to the European Central Bank in Frankfurt, So, had Blair stopped Brown from his five-test schema, the transition from the pound to the euro might have been possible. Second, while it is true that the pound and the right of the UK government to conduct its own monetary policy had quasi-sacrality in British society, a spin-doctored manipulation of public opinion might have still been possible, much as it had been in 1975. With a successful framing of the bloc as an opportunity, Britain's participation in the Eurozone or, for that matter, the EU's constitutional process would have been more likely. We could also add a third counterfactual: had the pound been weaker than the euro, the newborn currency might have had a better chance. In reality, the political wriggle room was limited. The Blair government duly maintained the crucial euro opt-out, ending only the opt-out from the social chapter, one for which John Major had fought hard in the context of the Maastricht Treaty, as discussed in the previous chapter.

Oliver Daddow's (2011) comprehensive analysis of Blair's attempts to persuade the British to accept a European future confirms that elite agency was severely limited by a predominantly Eurosceptical media, including the *Sun*, and a mostly disinterested public. The prime minister's pro-Europe frames failed not only because they resisted clarity and coherence – recall differences with Brown – but also because the British public maintained a view of their country as an extra-European actor. A particular barrier was the pervasive and persistent "logic of history" that underpinned the dominant articulation of sovereignty as that which survives and thrives only in separation from a conflict-prone continent (Daddow 2011, chaps. 7–8). Here we have a basic similarity with Wallace's analysis of the European versus Anglo-Saxon "debate" circa 1990. The former, represented and led by a reformist elite, could not possibly rebrand Britain so long as civil society stuck to the traditional conceptions of the British state and claims of exceptionalism (Wallace 1991, 69).

Hadfield-Amkhan (2010) agrees. According to her study, the euro debate exhibited elements of both continuity and change from the perspective of national identity. The continuity had to do with specifically English attitudes towards Europe: "a collective belief in a destiny apart from Europe" (166) was as powerful in 2003 as it was in 1973 or earlier.

The change, she argues, was a function of the evolution of Britishness towards "a collective identity based on a strategic-symbolic mix of separateness defined in relation *with*, rather than in stark opposition *to*, the EU" (ibid., emphasis in original). However, British reticence towards the euro was always nested within the latter. Indeed, the "English self-referential core" of the British state was what hobbled not only the euro entry in 2003 but also, arguably, every other supranational policy that governments in London ever contemplated (187). As we see in the next chapter, this self-referential Englishness was precisely what drove the Brexit vote in 2016.

Hadfield-Amkhan (2010, 173; cf. Daddow 2011) observes that the euro debate did not carry into Labour's second term because of "significant internal and external distractions surrounding the Iraq War." Iraq would come to captivate British politics not only in 2003 but for many years afterwards as more and more evidence came to light to prove that the Blair government inflated the strength of the intelligence about alleged Iraqi weapons of mass destruction. In announcing to the House of Commons on 18 March 2003 that Britain was going to war, Blair indeed spoke of Saddam Hussein's Iraq as a rogue state in possession of weapons of mass destruction and with ties to international terrorism – twin claims first concocted in Washington. A large segment of British society did not buy it, but in the event Britain went all out, sending forty-six thousand troops to Iraq – so, again East of Suez, the third-largest deployment of British forces since the Second World War. With this, Britain joined the forty-five-member "coalition of the willing" led by the US in a war that the governments of France, Germany, Canada, and most other UK allies argued was premature, unnecessary, illegal, and illegitimate.

Britain's road to Iraq is often explained with reference to the special relationship and "the vice-like grip of Atlanticism on Britain's identity" – and on Blair in particular (Dunne 2004, 895; cf. Kampfner 2003; Parmar 2005; Hill 2005; Haseler 2007; Dyson 2009; Porter 2018). This is confirmed by the analysis presented here: America was a significantly closer and friendlier Other than either "Europe," France, or Germany. Blair's aforementioned bridge metaphor conveyed this geographically, given that it located the UK in the mid-Atlantic, closer to Bermuda than to

Calais, absent an obvious hierarchy or even a dichotomy between Europe and America. Though this metaphorization goes back to Macmillan and ultimately to Churchill's three circles trope, it was Blair who decisively reframed it in 1997: "There is no choice between the two. Stronger with one means stronger with the other ... We are the bridge between the US and Europe."[4] What this meant in 2002–03 was that Blair felt responsible for bridging the French and German "no" to the Iraq War with a British "yes." This put the entire British foreign policy at stake. If London let Washington attack Iraq alone – or rather only with Australia, Poland, and two dozen or so smaller but "willing" members of the US-led coalition – then this would jeopardize the future US commitment to the defence of Europe and the West.

Discursively speaking, Adaptable Britain did not necessarily have a problem with the illegality of the intervention, and neither did Nostalgic Britain, though the latter also opened up space for questioning British foreign policy subservience to American military leadership in general and to the trigger-happy administration of US president Bush in particular. In reality, however, Iraq was vigorously debated throughout (cf. Edgerton 2018b, 587). In August 2002, the British press reported on a "cabinet rift" on Iraq between the majority hawks and the minority doves. Blair led the former, while the latter camp included Cook (leader of the House of Commons), Clare Short (international development), Margaret Beckett (environment), Alastair Darling (transport), Andrew Smith (work and pensions), Jack Straw (Foreign Affairs), and Gordon Brown.

In October, the annual party conference endorsed a resolution calling for a strict following of the UN route, and more than a few Labour parliamentarians consistently joined forces with Liberal Democrats, Scottish and Welsh nationalists, and even some Tories to argue against the military option. (In contrast, the press and the Conservative opposition, now led by Iain Duncan Smith, were both hawkish.) On 17 March 2003, the day before the crucial Commons vote on the invasion, Cook famously resigned, while the next day more than a third of Labour MPs defied Blair by voting in favour of an anti-war amendment. (Short resigned later.) The defiance was only symbolic, however: for the subsequent pro-war motion, the majority of rebellious backbenchers actually abstained, giving it a pass. One imagines that parliamentary opposition would have been stronger still had the government not engaged in a series of (self-) deceptions about the casus belli or had the prime minister not threatened to resign. Even so, the vote was close, and had Blair lost it, he would have resigned. That this was a possibility is a testament to the fact that the idea of the Middle East had lost discursive salience in 2000 in comparison to earlier years – a point I make in the previous chapter.

Looking at the Iraq War debates in the House of Commons, we see ample elements of both Adaptable Britain and Nostalgic Britain: the nation's democratic spirit, individual freedom of opinion, and a commitment to justice but also to unity. Compared to this event, the interventions in Sierra Leone (2000) and Afghanistan (2001) count as the "easy cases" for foreign policy legitimation since the government could frame them as a matter of saving the world, using Atlanticist, moralist, and pragmatic arguments at once. The war against Taliban-dominated Afghanistan was particularly popular since British society could identify with the Americans and the brutal terrorist attacks they had experienced on 11 September 2001.[5] UK support for the war indeed held even when America's "War on Terror" began to take turns – the use of torture, for one – that contradicted British understandings of human rights and justice. Here, too, the closeness of the American Other relative to Europe offered ample discursive resources for decision makers in London to legitimate divergence from America's other allies.

Multiple constructivist analyses of Britain's road to Iraq have all emphasized "the Blair factor" – the fact that he was Labour's most successful leader ever going into this policy situation and also that some of this success can be attributed to his political communication skills. Jack Holland's (2013) account of Blair's War on Terror policy rhetoric finds that "rationality" and "British leadership" frames greatly resonated in British, and specifically English, society. On the first, Blair portrayed the attack on Hussein's Iraq as common sense, especially in light of what the prime minister said was the ability of Iraqi rockets to hit London within forty-five minutes of their launch – now known as the dodgy "45-minute" claim. On the second, Blair positioned the UK as having no choice but to continue with its activist foreign policy of co-leadership with America

– for reasons of identity, history and morality. Both frames appealed to ordinary British citizens, especially those in Middle England (Holland 2013, 59–60).

Jarrod Hayes (2016) similarly makes a convincing case that Blair legitimized the Iraq War by a series of savvy frames. Aware of brittle public opinion, he and his team focused attention on Hussein's authoritarian state rather than "simply" on presumed weapons of mass destruction. This, Hayes contends, activated Britain's democratic entity, thus making it easier for the government to frame Iraq as a national security threat to both Parliament and the public at large. James Strong (2017), in what is by far the most detailed constructivist study of the Iraq debate to date, also pegs Blair as an effective communicator. The prime minister knew much of the press had his back – the pro-war camp was led by the *Sun* – and he also reasoned, correctly as it turned out, that public support would "rally around the flag" at the onset of the invasion (37). But in order to legitimate an invasion that lacked clear party and public support, he and his ministers had to engage in dodgy claims that in the end generated "the legitimacy deficit" (59). Even the government's style – "ministers often only had to say something, anything, reportable" (33) – added to this outcome.

Little in these three analyses contradicts predictions made on the basis of the topography of Britishness in 2000. Rationality and British leadership frames resonated with both hegemonic and subaltern discourses, as did Blair's activation of democratic and militaristic identities. One aspect of the debate that identity under-predicts is the failure of the claim that Britain was right on political, legal, and moral grounds to join the US in waging war. Although it seems defensible in principle, the claim spectacularly backfired in the actual debate, rendering the war a difficult sell before the invasion and a nearly impossible sell afterwards (Strong 2017, chap. 9).

Every one of five "Blair's wars" (Kampfner 2003) drew on New Labour's expressed desire to add an "ethical dimension" to foreign policy, even if the government never actually promised an ethical foreign policy as such (Self 2010, 252; see also Holland 2013; Hill 2005).[6] Associated with Cook's tenure as foreign secretary (1997–2001), Britain's ethical foreign policy was controversial: former foreign policy-makers and much of the media rejected the talk of "good international citizenship" as either astonishingly naïve or deeply hypocritical (see Chandler 2003; Williams 2005; Wickham-Jones 2000; Mumford and Selck 2010; Vickers 2011, chaps. 6–7; McCormack 2011; Ralph 2011; Humphreys 2015). Yet, a realist policy à la Bosnia was unacceptable as well, and therefore part of the reason Blair "picked up the torch of Thatcher's more ambitious foreign policy" (Hill 2019, 100).

Arguably, "the ethical turn" built on elements of both Adaptable Britain and Nostalgic Britain in the sense that Cook's vision combined cosmopolitanism with claims to moral superiority. Yes, Britain was well-armed, but, more important, it was a country that retained a top position in the hierarchy of states by virtue of being well-governed for centuries.

The same finding would suggest that the New Labour insistence on appearing strong on defence – in contrast to the old Labour, especially the old Labour of Michael Foot – went against the evolution of Britishness. In 1998, Secretary of State for Defence George Robertson released the Strategic Defence Review, which his successor Geoff Hoon updated in 2002 with "A New Chapter." Meanwhile, the level of defence spending had fallen to 2.6 per cent of GDP, which many regarded as exceptionally low given a host of new roles that Western military forces were playing at the time. Indeed, the Hoon paper mentioned Afghanistan nineteen times – compare this to zero times in the review – and reiterated Britain's commitment to different global operations, including counterterrorism and expeditionary warfare. Both documents outlined the need for new forces ("two Joint Rapid Reaction Forces" in 1998 and the reserves-based "Civil Contingency Reaction Forces" in 2002), new conceptualizations, new technological adaptations, and ever-greater versatility and efficiency. In 2003, Hoon proceeded to produce a white paper, *Delivering Security in a Changing World*, which revisited all of the themes from 1998 and 2002 but with a recognition that the Armed Forces would now face a broader range of tasks both at home and abroad.

What these documents articulate is an acknowledgment of the limits of British power in the age of "new security challenges" (from the 1998 review) and "asymmetric attacks" (from the 2002 "New Chapter"). Yet they also ask the Armed Forces to maintain capability for concurrent operations in different parts of the planet. The Armed Forces are also expected to work with allies and an Atlanticist frame of mind. So, though the 2003 white paper highlighted the possibility of leading European-only interventions, the primary focus was on the need to develop sufficient "interoperability" with US forces so that Britain could continue to contribute even to "large-scale" operations, such as the one in Iraq. The magnetic attraction of Atlanticism was evident in all three documents. The US receives 34 mentions in 1998, compared to 30 for NATO and 15 for Germany; 6 in 2002, compared to 8 for NATO and 0 for individual allies; and 7 in 2003, compared to 17 for NATO and 1 for France. This, too, suggests that British defence officials still thought about the world more from an Atlanticist than from a European perspective. Looking at these documents and the surrounding debates, Rees (2001, 44) remarks:

> At the end of the century Britain still regarded itself as a major actor on the world stage – not on the scale of the 1940s and 1950s with its forces in numerous overseas bases – but in the sense that Britain should have a voice in all major international issues, a seat on the UN Security Council and military forces capable of global intervention alongside allies.

In this context we can understand why the Blair government committed to the building of two *Queen Elizabeth*-class aircraft carriers, the largest ships in the history of the Royal Navy – hence their nickname "super-carriers." Their relative closeness in size to the enormous *Nimitz*-class carriers fielded by the US Navy was not "merely" symbolic: "The aim was to provide a complete but small air, sea and land force, to assist US operations" (Edgerton 2018b, 584; see also Rogers 2006; MccGwire 2006; McCourt 2014b).

In sum, British foreign policy choices in the 2000s mostly followed the topography of British identity presented in this chapter. Iraq, the most fateful choice of all, stands as a partial exception. It was Blair, his inner circle, and much of the rest of the ruling elite who, through a combination of savvy politics and resolute Atlanticism, transcended a number of existing or aspirational British identities. Like the one in Suez forty years ago, this intervention backfired (Porter 2018, ix; cf. Edgerton 2018b, 588). In committing almost all of the kingdom's military might to an unnecessary and unwinnable war – a war that we now know was conducted on the pretexts that Iraq was producing chemical and biological weapons, and was harbouring terrorists – Blair ruined his reputation in the country and severely damaged Britain's reputation internationally. Absent this fiasco, and perhaps with exceptionally clever leadership, it is possible that the country could have pursued a more European turn in this period. Possible, but, I argue next, unlikely.

Conclusion

This book begins with the view that Britain's engagement with the post-Second-World War world is a puzzle. Since at least 1948, a large segment of Britain's political class had quietly accepted the fact that Britain could not sustain a truly independent foreign policy, not in the age of brooding American and Soviet power. Yet, even when the management of imperial decline became its full-time job, the same political class continued to strive for global leadership. Why?

My main contention is that this behaviour was not "merely" a function of elite interests, elite-level political culture, or of bipartisan consensus. Rather, it was rooted and promulgated through discourses of national identity, hegemonic or otherwise, that positioned Britain as politically and morally suited to lead the world. The preceding chapters demonstrate two dependable intersubjective realities. First, "greatness" was the product of a deep-seated, doxic agreement across civil society as a whole. Second, this agreement held for sixty years, impervious not only to the displacement of one prime minister by another but also to larger and far more dramatic social and institutional transformations in British society. Speaking as the shadow foreign secretary in the run-up to the 2010 general election, William Hague was therefore probably not wrong to remark: "British engagement in and influence on world affairs is, simply put, ... an indispensable part of the British character" (quoted in Morris 2011, 342).

In what follows, I start with a review of the main findings, in which I reflect on the overarching puzzle animating this study. From there I make suggestions for further avenues of research. First I compare my analysis to the literature on British public opinion and British foreign policy, which could be seen as the main alternative to the constructivist approach I have put forward. I then discuss complementarities with the growing IR literature on ontological security, which opens up new opportunities for theorizing the making and shaping of Britain's foreign policy from a constructivist perspective. I reserve the book's last pages for a reflection on some foreign policy implications of the nation's referendum-mandated decision to leave the EU, the obvious caveat being that only political anthropologists and survey specialists are well positioned to make reliable reflections on Britishness *in statu nascendi*.

Out of Tune?

The very term "national identity" risks implying uniformity where none exists. But here I approach it in a nonessentialist fashion, treating British national identity as fluid and constantly evolving rather than as something fundamental or unitary. For the purposes of this conclusion, however, I am compelled to offer a simplified visual reconstruction of the content, contestation, and evolution of Britishness based on the previous chapters. With a nod to Churchill's three majestic circles, I call this figure the five circles of Britishness, 1950–2000 (see figure C.1).

At the centre we see what I believe is the most dependable signifier of modernity, moral prestige, and national greatness more generally: Britain's *progressive* identity. The idea that the nation was more progressive than its geographical and historical peers was shared across different versions and iterations of dominant discourses: Recovery in 1950; Modern Britain in 1960, 1970, and 1990; Muddling Through in 1980; and Adaptable Britain in 2000. All of these discourses emphasized the necessity and attractiveness of broadly liberal – as well as broadly social democratic – responses to a world altered by advanced industrial capitalism and by new technologies. Symbols of progress varied, but the NHS usually dominated, especially once the welfare state came under attack or was turned into an object of nostalgia.

Discourses of reform, Socialism and Thatcherism, positioned the Self as inherently progressive as well, the former in relation to capitalism and communism and the latter in relation to Butskellism. In some regards,

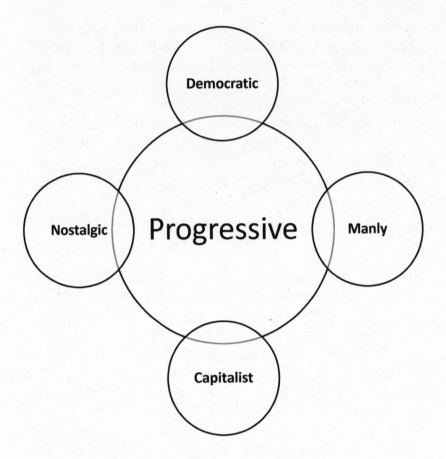

Figure C.1 Five circles of Britishness, 1950–2000

even Traditionalism in 1950 and Nostalgic Britain in 2000 agreed with
the idea of progress. Although resisting institutional efforts to modernize
public life and individual routines in favour of slower (i.e., more organic)
change, these discourses readily agreed that the UK was far more civilized
(i.e., more progressive) than the rest of the world. The denial of responsibility for imperial wrongdoings followed this logic directly: we let our
Empire go freely and without fuss.

Related, most racist tropes about the "lack of civilization" of Others
were interchangeable across different years and different referents, whatever the overall balance between overt and covert racism. So, whatever

the year, there was a "they" in some parts of national identity discourse, elite and/or mass: Irish, blacks, Asians, Muslims – "they" were fundamentally different, held illiberal beliefs, and were keen on procreation, crime, and violence, usually all three at once. In the surveyed popular fiction, the rest of the world was more often than not a stage for projecting racist imaginations.

The British sense of progress was centred specifically on England. This changed only in the last year of the study, following Blair's constitutional reforms. But change was partial. On the one hand, millennial Britain took pride in its adaptability, giving ample space to voices arguing that "the Isles" have always been a multicultural and multiethnic archipelago. On the other hand, however, we also see a certain longing for temporally marked Selves: a politically more united UK and also its aesthetic representation to southern counties of England. Either way, we see that English self-importance "at home" consistently informed and shaped Britain's self-importance "abroad."

All discourses likewise configured the UK as free and *democratic*, the word at the top of the figure. As with progressive, democratic was a prompt for thinking about the underlying hierarchy of capacities and potentialities across nations (and/or races, according to the textual archives for 1950 and 1960). Even those voices least likely to respect the official and officious codes of British state- and nationhood – voices close to Traditionalism in 1950 or Anti-Thatcherism in 1990 – failed to break with this part of the British common sense. A possible exception is the Scottish discourse in 2000, where we see a foreshadowing of sorts of the coming nationalist reactions to the lack of legitimate democratic power in London: first the (first?) Scottish independence referendum in 2014, then "England's Brexit" two years later. Overall, however, democratic identity informed the British sense of exceptionalism and exemplarity throughout, thus inflating the nation's sense of superiority and superciliousness in the world.

Moving clockwise from democratic we see *manly*, an adjective that conveys the fact that "Britain" was not gender-neutral but masculine. In the vast majority of texts, even in more recent years, men were constructed as physically and mentally strong, while women were weak and, therefore, the target of both protection and violence. Although explicitly feminist voices increased after 1970, there remained a constant awareness of the costs of expressing feminism – a lesson learned by women leaders everywhere. We also see that normal sexual activity was nearly consistently confined to heterosexual marriage – even as Modern Britain or Adaptable Britain revelled in the idea of British society becoming less heteropatriarchal and less dependent on narrowly defined gender roles. And, of the twenty-four works of popular fiction surveyed – and five of the twelve novels are authored by women – only four are mostly or equally female-driven, whereas twice as many can be safely described as misogynist (as opposed to merely strongly masculinist).

Building on the previous point, virtually every discourse justified the use of violent, hard-power means as a way of "maintaining order" and "reasserting control," whether in North Borneo or in Northern Ireland. In this sense, loss of empire was not emasculating. In 1970, for example, most Britons "knew" that their government would still keep more than a few military and intelligence assets throughout Asia – in Brunei, Hong Kong, Singapore, Diego Garcia, and across the Arabian Peninsula. They similarly "knew" in 1990 and 2000 that another Falklands War-style campaign could be successfully launched if needed, including as a humanitarian project completed on behalf of global freedom, democracy, and security. The same logic informed the rank-ordering of friends and allies: the Europeans were soft on terrorism and free riders on defence. Finally, contradictions between gender inequality on the one hand and Britain's progressive and democratic identities on the other were either put aside or relativized, usually as a way of affirming British success via then-now and there-here comparisons.

At the bottom of the figure is *capitalist*. Viewed as a set of regulatory and redistributive institutions within a market economy, the welfare state was already an established feature of British identity discourses in 1950. Established but contested, that is: the British vigorously debated the balance and integration of the capitalist and socialist elements in their society in *all* years under study. The position of Socialism, and also of Nostalgic Britain in 2000, was that welfare spending was much-needed insurance against various twentieth-century brutalities, *including* the upheavals of neoliberal market capitalism. The position of Recovery, Modern Britain, and Adaptable Britain was different: they agreed with the premise but then emphasized that the welfare state needs good capitalism. Traditionalism and Thatcherism (i.e., New Britain in 1980) despised the welfare state altogether, each for different reasons. Also, although debates on the meanings, history, and functions of the welfare state were often wide-ranging, no text in any year expressed a desire to abolish private property.

The fifth element of Britishness in figure C.1 is *nostalgic*. Bookended by Traditionalism in 1950 and Nostalgic Britain in 2000, two challenger discourses, this identity category was actually a more general desire to return to a better past, either to a time when the nation was an imperial, worldwide power or to the "good" postwar years. Save for Traditionalism, all discourses agreed that a more scientific, wealthy, technological, trading, innovative, efficient, and competitive Britain was a precondition for a just and fair Britain. Leadership speeches and most textbooks surveyed generally made this point consistently, either in the abstract or in the context of a Macmillan-style claim that collective British life was now better than ever before. When Britain was recovering or modernizing, the masses tended to agree – they did not think of themselves as particularly immiserated, certainly not in comparison to the masses elsewhere.

By 1980 and 1990, however, the Britains of the elite discourse were often at odds with the Britains of the mass discourse. The capitalism of tax cuts and selective rule-enforcement that developed under and after Thatcher certainly had fans across the elite-mass divide, but *most* texts classified as mass in this study rejected these reforms. For all the upbeat elite-level talk of post-Cold War change and progress later on, "ordinary people" remained suspicious of the establishment. This longing for a simpler past received full-blown discursive expression in 2000, with Nostalgic Britain bemoaning cynicism, materialism, and over-consumption, among many other modern ills. Per the same discourse, the British were supposed to know that their children would not be better off going forward.[1]

Together, these findings confirm my suspicions of theoretical frameworks that consider nation building as a manipulative process going from top to bottom; rather, they suggest the validity of viewing British common sense as a joint elite-mass project. If the discursive enactment of progress, democracy, or capitalism faltered among the masses, Britain could still constitute itself as masculine or nostalgic, thus still confirming the sense of British exceptionalism. Thus, if we accept that these five circles capture the basic temporal, spatial, and ethical coordinates of Britishness between 1950 and 2000, then we might indeed see why successive governments in London insisted on a global approach in foreign and defence policy. The overall picture that emerges is one of a weakened, yet self-confident nation consistently interested in all four corners of the globe. All discourses position the UK as superior to the rest of the world in at least some domains. This exceptionalism in turn bled into claims of exemplarity: the notion that the rest of the world stands to learn from the kingdom. Conversely, in no discourse was the UK fading into irrelevance. Whether in 1960, when it was becoming increasingly clear that British imperial power was no more, or in 1980, when more and more voices insisted that the UK was no longer the model for the rest of the world, *most* members of British society routinely believed that *change* did not, and should not, thwart efforts of the British state to *continue* to maintain order on a global scale. In other words, the sense of exceptionalism never dissipated, even though some of its elements did, at least proportionally speaking. We see this in the period after the Cold War, decades after (formal) empire: old feelings of moral and cultural superiority were still sufficiently strong in British society to allow Major's and Blair's governments to justify military interventions not only in relation to a desire for a more liberal world order but also in terms of civilizational, East-West differences.

Of the twenty-four "events" discussed in the previous chapters, some decidedly do not fit the notion that policy-makers follow the discursive playing field. Among these, most can be classified as "small misfits": policies at odds with dominant discourse that were either quickly reversed and/or were seen as pet projects of specific governments (and therefore easily reversible). The Major government's Bosnia policy as well as the defence reviews of 1957 (Sandys), 1966 (Healey), and 1981 (Nott) are all good approximations of this category. But Britain's "turn to Europe" is by no means a small misfit. In 1960, a year before Macmillan applied for EEC membership, the Commonwealth was much closer to the British hearts and minds than the Continent. In 1970, all three discourses, including the dominant Modern Britain, leaned towards the Churchillian-

Bevinite *with* but not *of* Europe policy, which was the actual policy of the governments in London that decade.

This discursive constellation did not significantly change: Britons remained convinced that their interests were different from those of their continental neighbours. In 1980, one can say, the EEC was still new, and European standards of security, prosperity, or beauty could not resonate with a civil society that saw Britain's future either as one of Britain alone or as connected to American modernity. Yet, neither in 1990, when the Soviet Union officially collapsed and the Maastricht Treaty became a household name, nor in 2000, when Britain was led by a fairly pro-EU government, was there much actual demand, at either elite or mass levels, for a more European life. Instead we observe the prevalence of the same old ideas: Britain as a transatlantic bridge, Britain as the global hub ("the very point of junction"), Britain as a plucky little nation and so on.

Going back to Wallace's terminology discussed in the introduction, we can therefore conclude that the nation continued to dance to the "Anglo-Saxon" tune right into the twenty-first century. While the motivations of individual and institutional actors who maintained this particular construction of Britain no doubt varied, the discourses of separation and difference with Europe continued to dominate in regular intervals from 1950 to 2000. In other words, although postwar British constructions of Europe drew upon many elements of positive identification, the basic Us and Them distinction remained constant throughout – sometimes as an explicit superiority claim, sometimes as a subtle one.[2]

These boundary-producing performances, as Wallace notes, had profound consequences for the "awkward" nature of British participation in the European integration project, with the ultimate consequence, we might add, being the 2016 referendum. As Daddow (2015b, 85) wrote in the year before the faithful vote: "withdrawal from the EU would be more in line with expressed British identity constructions than would continued EU membership."[3] And with Wallace's Anglo-Saxons and Europeans locked in a post-referendum struggle over power rather than in a struggle over the discursive terms expressive of that power, it was perhaps inevitable that Leave would prevail, paving the way for the country's exit from the European bloc.

Missed Opportunities?

Taking a longer view, some would suggest that the Anglo-Saxon tune is but a variation on the centuries-old "pragmatist" theme in British foreign policy, the manifestations of which are the policy of "limited liability" to Europe and Britain's "maritime strategy" more generally (Gamble 2003; Colley 2009 [1992]; Darwin 2009; Daddow 2015b; Simms 2016). Some would thus say that the basic Anglo-Saxon policy agenda was already set at the end of the Napoleonic Wars in 1815; others would link it back to the Glorious Revolution of 1688 and the Industrial Revolution; and still others would tie it to that crucible of colonialism, imperialism, racism, and patriarchy known as the long sixteenth century. Whatever the chosen point of origin, we see no shortage of historical axes of hierarchy and oppression that structured the logics of modern world politics in ways that privileged and protected some political communities over others. Consequently, we see why no account of postwar Britain is ever one of decline alone (Holland 1991, 2–4; Self 2010; 13–14, 31–4; Clarke 2004 [1996], 5).

Whether international or transnational in orientation, such scaled-up, interactive historical perspectives are also helpful in foregrounding the pitfalls of methodological nationalism. Indeed, if we accept that nations do not live in isolation – least of all England/Britain, whose military, cultural, economic, and other lives have always had a global constitution and circulation – then we must also acknowledge that discourses of Britishness emerged in and through the evolution of the global system as a whole, with its many core-periphery dynamics and coexisting social entities.[4]

To consider a possible means of integrating these different perspectives, let us look at the constitution of the special relationship one more time. Just as Western hegemony allowed Britain to prosper during the age of formal imperial expansion, so, too, did the post-Second World War and post-Cold War iterations of American hegemony. US power influenced postwar British foreign policy both directly, as with its massive loans or during the Suez crisis, and indirectly, as through processes such as "the imperialism of decolonization" or the so-called Englishization of the world.[5] Most fundamentally, American hegemony shaped British realities by deterring and, eventually, destroying the Soviet Empire. Had, for example, Western Europe *not* become safe for capitalism and democracy in the aftermath of the war, Britain's decline would have been much more precipitous, no matter how the British elites and masses might have thought of themselves during this time and since.

The present analysis suggests that most discourses of Britishness accepted this counterfactual. The moment the Cold War became nuclear, and especially after the Suez Crisis, the British – elites and masses alike, but with some exceptions in each case – came to a firm agreement that American pressure mattered and that London had to support Washington in defence of the West. Acknowledging this arrangement at once confirmed the reality of Britain's decline and fed the illusion that London could execute what Reynolds (2004, 178) has termed "the policy of power by proxy." What made this double vision possible was the fact that the British *also* recognized, again with some exceptions, the US as an extension of the Self – that is, as a modern, liberal, and "Anglo-Saxon" hegemon on a global mission. Tacit UK-US division of anti-Soviet labour helped legitimate such a construction, while also conveniently, if somewhat illogically, providing Britain's superiority vis-à-vis France.

Crucially, the "persistent inclination to pursue empire vicariously by clambering like a mouse on the American eagle's head," to use Linda Colley's phrase (quoted in O'Toole 2019, 10), had wide societal support. Neither elite nor mass discourses saw the UK as a prisoner of decisions taken in an allied country suffering from its own delusions of grandeur. On the contrary, they tended to represent their state as modernity's vanguard, a junior partner in a reconstructed but essentially continuous "liberal" hegemony. Yes, some voices always dissented from the pro-American view, pointing out that the US had always been an ally and a rival at once, not least in the way it consistently attacked the sterling area. For the vast majority, however, the operative term was "friend and ally," or, for the authors and readers of best-selling spy novels, "cousins." So, with our powerful cousins in charge, we could continue to sit, if not at the top of the table, as in all surveyed pieces of the James Bond franchise, then at least next to the very top, as in Forsyth's *The Devil's Alternative*.

Historians of the special relationship, like George Orwell before them, tend to view the idea of UK-US friendship as "almost entirely British in inspiration and authorship" (Danchev 1998, 155). One could certainly point out that this friendship was a by-product of the larger structure of the Cold War. In comparison to the Soviet analogue in Eastern Europe, American hegemony in the "free world" was always constructed as essentially non-coercive, and the UK voluntarily ceded sovereignty to Washington in exchange for US protection and assorted privileges. But France, Canada, South Korea, and many other countries experienced the same.

Britain did have one specifically British claim to specialness in Washington: the ability and willingness to stand and fight "shoulder to shoulder" with the Americans. The previous chapters show this clearly. British identity persistently avowed resistance to centralization and coercive power only within a narrowly defined "home." This did not apply to the locales constructed as "abroad," which is where liberalism and/or civilization were nearly always under threat. Indeed, most discourses accepted that "government" – meaning either the UK government or the UK and US governments working together – had to use overt and covert means to suppress agents of disorder and support their opponents, including some right-wing dictators, military juntas, and paramilitaries. The fact that this construction persisted throughout the period under study might help us appreciate why Britain's "warfare state," as Edgerton (2005) labels it, outlived the end of the Second World War, the end of empire, and the end of the Cold War.

The persistent, socially pervasive, and vertically shared character of Britain's liberal militarism, to use another one of Edgerton's famous terms, further illuminates the nature of the special relationship. Sir Oliver Franks made this connection already in the 1950s, as did, arguably, the entire role-theoretic scholarship on British foreign policy: the UK defines itself as an ally ready to "deliver" – that is, to make meaningful military contributions to the freedom of the free world (Danchev 1998, 6; see also Self 2010, 108–9; Vucetic 2011b; Gaskarth 2014; Holland 2020). Or in Danchev's (1998, 1601) words: "Being willing and able to intervene, globally, on the appropriate scale, and to agree on (or acquiesce in) what and where and when: this was the bedrock of the relationship for a hot and cold half-century, 1941 to 1991, from the Tyrant of Berchtesgaden to the Thief of Baghdad."

Shortly after these lines were written, the Anglo-American military coalition found other tyrants to slay – first in Serbia, then in Afghanistan, then again in Iraq. Each time, London expressed confidence that being able to "deliver" gave it influence over US policy. But these wars laid this self-delusion bare. "Afghanistan and Iraq," writes Robert Self, "brutally revealed the utter futility of the underlying assumption that participation in American adventures automatically enhanced Britain's influence over US policy."[6] Yet, even after Iraq, the special relationship continues. Virtually every defence policy document published in and after the Blair years admits that the UK is constrained by the need to work with its US ally effectively (Gaskarth 2014, 62; Edgerton 2018b, 584; cf. Morris 2011, 341–2). Conversely, very few UK government documents discuss the fact that ten thousand US military personnel remain stationed in "'little Americas' on British soil" (Harrison 2009, 96) three decades after the Cold War.

Combining the insights of scholarship that encompasses broader spatial geographies with the present approach brings us back to a point I make in the introduction about the mutual constitution of national identity and international order. With this in mind, we could ask if a less stable American hegemony would have permitted more opportunities for rethinking foreign policy nostrums everywhere in the West, not just in the UK. This is certainly plausible, but based on the analysis presented here, I see no counterfactual of a postwar period in which the UK would have abandoned the alliance with the US altogether and, in turn, a foreign policy that was to various degrees both global and muscular.

Let us start with the baseline year for this study, 1950, when, despite the weak pound, depleted gold and dollar reserves, rationing, and dozens of other problems, Britain's bid to great power status was still strong on most reasonable measures – the basic premise of Modern Britain. Had either Socialism or Traditionalism been dominant, a different foreign policy would have been possible in the sense that a more left-wing Attlee might have said no to the war in Korea and perhaps yes to a West European union, just as a less pragmatic Macmillan might have caused yet another Suez. That said, no government would have managed to get away with a fully pacifist foreign policy, let alone a policy aimed at taking Britain out of the US orbit.

Chapter 2 begins with a look at Britain's foreign policy under the conditions of accelerating decolonization and the nerve-wracking Cold War, and there I argue that the hegemonic grip of Modern Britain helps illuminate debates not only on the post-imperial adjustments, especially in so-called British Africa, but also on ways of shoring up British influence abroad. Socialism, a counterhegemonic discourse institutionally expressed on the left of the Labour Party, exerted some influence on Wilson's foreign policy – namely, on the Vietnam War. Had the Socialist alternative been more powerful, retrenchment would have been more defensible, but it is hard to see any meaningful rejection of a global role for Britain, especially given Socialism's interest in the promotion of peace, order, and good governance after decolonization. (Also keep in mind that a US-led free world that assigned less weight to anti-colonialism than anti-communism exerted significantly less pressure on London to change its foreign policy orientations than an actual free world would have done in a counterfactual scenario.)

Discursive affirmation of the primacy of a global role for the UK is in fact observable even in the years of hard decline. In 1980, covered in chapter 4, the UK was a nation that no longer counted on postwar miracles – near-full employment and the expansion of public services, for one. However, although New Britain, a discourse embodied in the new Thatcher government, attacked the old Modern Britain on most policy dimensions, it did not attack it on foreign policy. Even in the absence of the Falklands War, the British state would have proceeded with the Trident purchase while dragging its feet on implementing the recommendations of *The Way Forward*, the short-lived budget-cutting document put out by Thatcher's defence secretary John Nott. (We see similar continuities in the two defence policy documents discussed in chapter 5.)

Only three moments in my account constitute potential missed opportunities for recasting British foreign policy. Chapter 3 reconstructs British identity in 1970 as a three-cornered contest: Modern Britain versus Traditionalism versus Socialism. All three accepted some version of a global approach in foreign policy, but not all three agreed with the special relationship. This is evident in the discursively available range of reactions to the Nixon shock as well as in the debate over the Labour government's Mason review of defence. In light of the fact that the then leaders actually made two important U-turns in foreign policy – namely, East of Suez and entry into the Common Market – it is *possible* that a more daring Heath, acting under far more fortuitous political and economic circumstances, could have legitimated a turn to the more modest role of a trading nation à la West Germany and Japan, which, arguably, was the main policy recommendation of the Berrill Report of 1977.[7] It is similarly *possible* that a more powerful mid-1970s Labour Party comprising Wilson, Callaghan, Benn, and Foot might have led the UK towards a "Belgium-with-nuclear-weapons" scenario. I italicize the word "possible" twice because chapter 3 shows a different reality: Socialism, and to some extent Modern Britain, actually rejected Europe, while Traditionalism rejected both Europe and East of Suez. So, while at one level the Self was aware of its fundamental structural weakness, its habits continued to make it hard to translate that awareness into an acceptance of diminished status and reduced policy commitments.

The identity topography for 1990 likewise suggests *possibilities* for a more isolationist and more pacifist foreign policy, this one rooted in what in chapter 5 I call Anti-Thatcherism. Given that it shaped expressions of scepticism about the ethics and effectiveness of military interventions among some Labour MPS, the presence of this discourse does invite us to imagine a counterfactual timeline in which a government led by a Labour left leader says no wars, to nuclear weapons, and to the EC/EU all at once. (It is far more likely that this government would have stayed close to the actual historical course in most foreign policy situations while pursuing social democratic experiments at home.)

The last potential missed opportunity can be found in chapter 6, which deals with the heyday of Blair's New Labour. In 2000, Britishness was a contest between Adaptable Britain, which was dominant, and Nostalgic Britain, which was its alternative, with a more subaltern Scottish discourse that was opposed to both. I argue that only the first discourse supported Blair's wars – namely, the one in Iraq and the one on terror. The foreign policy orientation of Nostalgic Britain was akin to Anti-Thatcherism in the sense that it paused over military interventions, including those conducted in alliance with the US. Had Nostalgic Britain been dominant and Adaptable Britain subaltern, the debate over foreign and defence policy might have been different in both process and outcome, such that Blair would not have been able to authorize his East of Suez expeditions, least of all Operation Telic, which spectacularly strained UK Armed Forces at the time. With some luck, the prime minister might have even managed to consolidate the nation's role in the EU, too (the caveat being that in no counterfactual would British society actually accept the normality of being "just another" EU member state).

That all these conjectures refer to *potential* missed opportunities speaks volumes about a fundamental continuum in post-1945 British foreign policy. This, I think, has to do with discourses of British identity – they were all dynamic and supple but not infinitely so. For one, identification with America was strong throughout. This not only facilitated legitimation of the special relationship in particular foreign policy debates but also worked to amplify discourses and voices advocating for continuity over those advocating for shifts. Furthermore, at any given time, even in 1980, a larger part of British society strongly believed that Britain should be in charge, if not economically, then certainly morally, much as it was during the world wars, especially the second one, when it – all alone – faced a much stronger opponent. This might have been an illusion or a delusion, but it was one that was widely shared.

If this conclusion is even partially correct, then *none* of the aforementioned alternatives had much chance of breaking the frames of intelligibility available to decision makers in London and their fellow citizens in the rest of British society. What is more, even if one or more maverick pro-EC/EU, anti-American politicians, whether Conservative, Labour, or (Liberal) Democrat, had somehow had large majorities in the House of Commons at any point in the period under study, British foreign policy choices would have probably been as constrained as they were under actual prime ministers. On this basis, we could conclude that British foreign policy reflects the type of evolution associated with the concept of path dependency, which refers to situations in which opportunities for new directions are constrained by the development pathways that have long been institutionalized or habitualized (Vucetic 2011b, 153–4; Uttley, Wilkinson, and van Rij 2019). In these circumstances actors either choose inaction or are prevented from doing so by their environment – a configuration that can only be changed by an external, cataclysmic shock or crisis. More on this in a moment.

Public Opinion

Data on the British mass public's views of British foreign policy is large. Ben Clements (2019) has combed through a variety of sources to provide a comprehensive picture from 1945 to 2017. His sources include long-running recurrent national surveys: the British Election Survey (running since 1963) and the British Social Attitudes Survey (since 1983); cross-national surveys, namely the Eurobarometer (since 1973), Pew Global Attitudes Project (since 2001), and Transatlantic Trends (since 2002); and commercial surveys, such as Gallup and National Opinion Polls, which go back to the early postwar decades, to the more contemporary YouGov and Ipsos MORI. His synthesis of the main areas of change and continuity in the public's views makes for an excellent point of comparison with the findings presented in the preceding chapters.

Clements's overview is generally in line with the arguments made here. To begin with, the aggregate data point to a continuity in civil society support for a "big" foreign policy.[8] They also capture the transition from an imperial to a post-imperial order. In one of the National Opinion Polls, conducted in 1965, 40 per cent of the respondents saw Britain's economic future to be Churchill's first circle, while 21 per cent and 17 per cent saw that future to be in Europe and America, respectively. In 1969, the respective figures changed to 30 per cent, 24 per cent, and 11 per cent, and then changed further in Europe's favour in the following decade. Gallup polls from the same period differ somewhat because they show a clear and consistent preference for Europe over America, albeit in the context of an overwhelming desire for close relations with all three circles at once.[9]

America and Americans are positively evaluated throughout, while the reception of US governments and their foreign policy actions has been mixed.[10] The British public was both savvy and critical about the special relationship: in addition to recognizing the asymmetric interdependence involved, the respondents often regarded their government as too eager to cheerlead for the US in international affairs.[11] A partial exception to these trends is NATO, which has received strong and enduring commitment irrespective of the context.

As for Europe and European integration, opinions have varied over time. Clements shows that from the 1980s until 2017, the last year covered in his study, the British public perceived the relationship with "Europe" – the Common Market, EU, Brussels, and so on – as either important or very important. (In December 2015, famously, only 1 per cent of respondents thought that Britain's membership in the EU was the most significant issue facing the country [Rasmi 2009; cf. Copeland and Copsey 2017].) The mood, however, was decidedly ambivalent. The bloc was both loved and loathed, depending on the context. Polls taken in the run-up to the 1975 referendum show the public divided on membership, the exact split sensitive to the timing and sequencing of questions. Following the 1978–79 Winter of Discontent, the popularity of membership declined.[12] Clements (2018, chap. 4) also reports that the political and ideological basis of anti-EU feelings shifted over time, while, demographically speaking, older people and the less educated tended to be mostly Eurosceptic throughout. An approximate fifty-fifty split in public opinion on Europe following the 2016 Brexit vote roughly follows these trends. (The British public has also come to evaluate the relationship with the EU as the most crucial issue facing the country [Rasmi 2019].)

Clements's overview, and survey research in general, is useful for my purposes because it provides additional context for some of the more limited observations about Britishness I make earlier. In chapters 1 through 4, I trace the discursive transition from the uppercase "Empire" and "the British world" to the multi-racial Commonwealth family of nations. Yet ordinary British citizens always "knew" that their actual family was white. Of course, by 1970 it was increasingly impolitic to call the "old" Commonwealth "white," so this community came to be articulated differently – namely, with references to the rule of (common) law, British-style education, the English language, Westminster institutions, good governance, or, simply, collective sacrifice. (In chapter 3, for example,

Force 10 from Navarone and *Battle of Britain* each feature an Old Commonwealth protagonist, a New Zealander and a Canadian, respectively.)

Surveys confirm that feelings of intimacy with white-majority Commonwealth countries carried on well beyond 1970. Indeed, they have carried into the twenty-first century: a 2010 Chatham House-YouGov study of British foreign policy views – the first in what has since become an annual survey – showed respondents favouring the fellow Westminster democracies of New Zealand, Canada, and Australia the most (in that order), followed by Switzerland, the Netherlands, and the Scandinavian countries.[13] This additional context is important because it supports the aforementioned claim that we cannot evaluate the opportunities postwar Britain missed as if an alternative foreign policy, oriented towards Europe, was readily available and waiting for political champions such as Heath or Blair.

Survey research might help situate some of the seemingly paradoxical observations I make, such as the one that the British saw their country as peaceful and well armed at once. This likely has to do with enduring partisan differences on hard and soft power projection – namely, defence spending and the provision of foreign aid to developing countries, respectively. Clements notes that Conservative supporters have been more in favour of defence and less in favour of foreign aid than their Labour and Liberal (Democrat) counterparts. Nuclear weapons, including Trident, likewise tended to be close to Conservative supporters' hearts, while unilateral disarmament was more likely to be championed by those on the left.[14] Also relevant is evidence that the British public has preferred "just wars" and "wars of necessity" over "wars of choice," especially if the former are thought to be winnable or confined to air strikes and special forces operations only (Reifler et al. 2014). That being said, the British public's aggregate views have tended towards policies that privilege more spending on health and education rather than on foreign and defence policy goals – a fact consistent with my own analysis (Clements 2018, chaps 5–7). Next, the British public grows more sceptical over time about the reasons given to it for the necessity of using force – a fact consistent with other social-scientific research on changing orientations towards politics, parties, and elections in Britain over time (Clarke et al. 2018).

Looking at the post-Cold War period, Gaskarth (2013, 78), too, questions "the durability of the public's commitment to Britain's identity as a global leader – at least in the military field."

Most constructivists – and not just Bourdieusians and Foucauldians – harbour healthy scepticism towards the public opinion literature. Asking respondents to answer a battery of questions about foreign policy or about what makes their country special, or to rank-order other countries in terms of their importance for trade or security, allows researchers to assemble said answers into large datasets. One problem is that said data are often contradictory and heavily context-dependent (Strong 2017, 16–17; Colley 2019, 11–12). Another problem is that the survey questions are designed by scholars, not subjects themselves, and so they cannot gauge how the latter understand and practise their identities. For example, we know from recent YouGov polls that between two-thirds and three-quarters of Britons in 2018 thought their country and/or their communities were caught in the triple helix of social, economic, and cultural decline (Gaston and Hilhorst 2018). We also know that fewer and fewer Britons are expressing pride in the British Empire, from 59 per cent in 2014 to 32 per cent in 2019 (Smith 2020). Yet we also know that cues such as "decline," "pride," and "shame" cannot tell us much about the range of intersubjective understandings of the contemporary economy or of the history of colonial empires, let alone about the ways in which people deal with imperial legacies every day.

But the public opinion literature and constructivist analyses of British foreign policy also stand to learn from each other. One example is James Strong's study of the UK's road to the Iraq War, which we encountered in the last chapter. There, the analytical focus is on how elite actors contest and construct public opinion as a social fact and on what ramifications this process has for actual foreign policy decision making. Democratic governments can make an issue more or less publicly salient but they cannot make it more or less legitimate. Blair's successors appear to have learned this lesson, which is also why we have seen fewer military actions abroad (Strong 2017, 2; see also Holland 2020).

In light of Strong's contention that ultimately only elite publics matter, we should pause over an ongoing debate in the public opinion literature on the relative merits of the so-called top-down versus bottom-up models. The former holds that public opinion on foreign policy follows cues from elites – primarily state officials and party leaders but also military generals and celebrities – as well as from international institutions and foreign leaders. The latter suggests that members of the public base their opinions on principles, not information, which is what generates stable foreign policy predispositions and attitudes independent of the cues they receive from elites. So, if, as Joshua Kertzer and Thomas Zeitzoff (2017, 546) write, scholars of public opinion accept the actual publicity of public opinion, then they should have an abiding interest in "the social context and network in which citizens are embedded." Constructivist IR, the authors continue, might offer a source of knowledge on precisely such things, especially if one follows the Gramscian argument that *senso comune* renders public opinion "uncueable" (546).[15] Two directions for future research might be aligned with their argument. One, topographies of postwar Britishness could inform knowledge of cues and cue-ability and, therefore, the designs of studies standing at the nexus of public opinion and British foreign policy. Two, bringing together analyses of public opinion and discourse could lead to a better understanding of the range and texture of British common sense and, therefore, of the drivers of British foreign policy.

Turning to methodology, we can also see potential complementarities between this book's discourse analytic approach and quantitative content analysis.[16] Rather than manually extracting content from the written word, some researchers might prefer to rely on machines. In the study of British foreign policy, Blair's foreign speeches have received considerable attention from scholars looking for ethically loaded opinions and sentiments (Mumford and Selck 2010) or evidence of certain leadership characteristics (Dyson 2009). Similar analyses can of course be done with many other types of texts. In general, quantitative content analysis approaches use preconstructed dictionaries of positive and negative words, and then use measures such as word counts to score all the opinions in the corpus. The latter part is similar to the approach undertaken here, but the former requires a degree of exogenous pretheorization, a result of which is a reduction in the validity of measures and findings (Grimmer and Stewart 2013; Allan 2016). In discourse analytic approaches, the primary goal is not so much to trace what was said or written and how often as it is to identify linguistic commonplaces and interpret them in context, such as Britishness.

One way to ameliorate the problem of low validity in quantitative content analysis is through so-called machine learning. Here, researchers use computers to classify a subset of texts from a larger corpus according to their content and then deploy this classifier to compute semantically similar terms from the remainder of the corpus. Many currently available machine-learning research designs still rely on human coders to produce basic content benchmarks and otherwise "train data" before allowing machines to assign any content scores. However, methods for large-scale analysis of political content in texts are becoming ever more sophisticated. A study of British identities based on, for example, a Google Ngram assembling the content of books published in the UK over several decades could conceivably inform analyses of British foreign policy in ways that might complement interpretative analyses.[17] One can likewise imagine quantitative researchers subjecting the same or similar data to systematic analysis as a way of evaluating qualitatively made claims about continuity and change in Britishness in the UK as a whole or within its constituent parts.[18]

Ontological Security

Many, if not most, constructivists would caution against "exploring" such complementarities because of their potential to marginalize non-positivist, anti-positivist, and post-positivist scholarship. Ontological security theory, or OST, is a case in point. The engine behind this scholarship in IR is the idea that states care as much about their ontological security, or the security of a consistent self, as about their materially defined well-being. One way to understand the UK's behaviour, as Steele (2008), Hadfield-Amkhan (2010), and Whittaker (2017) have shown, is to comb through (ruling elite) texts with an eye on state identity narratives – narratives about Britain's past and destiny, as well as its imaginary centres and future destinations.[19]

But what if, as Stuart Croft (2012) asks, we acknowledge that the social institutions of the state are in fact inseparable from other social institutions? The modern state, he reminds us, is paradoxical because it claims universality while simultaneously drawing legitimacy from the geographical and historical specificity of its society. The same point can be made from a Gramscian perspective, which says that the modern capitalist state as well as political and civil society – or, to use the jargon, the juridical-administrative apparatus of government and the apparatus of cultural and ideological reproduction – are parts of a single integrated whole.[20] This broader perspective on what OST calls state identity implies that ontological (in)security researchers should in fact treat mass publics as co-authors of autobiographical narratives rather as nebulous entities (ruling) elites can ignore, patronize, or hail, depending on the political moment. Croft (2012, 103) does just that when he looks at the telling and retelling of jokes about Muslims on the internet and many other negotiated practices of everyday Britishness in order to show how Muslims and Islam became "securitized" in the wake of the terrorist attacks on New York and Washington in 2001 (9/11) and on the London transport network in 2005 (7/7). Colley's (2019) analysis of British public narratives of war makes a similar wager: to understand how identity and ontological (in)security are constructed, we must take into account the everyday stories of ordinary people.

This book showcases one methodology for furnishing such accounts historically.[21] What is more, reconstruction of national identity topographies in regular time intervals could help ontological security researchers probe the consistency and coherence of Self over time, thus tracing the disruption of routines that could produce anxiety. Due to the dialogical character of identity, such disruptions are frequent, which leads to ontological discontinuity. States are no exception. Recognition, validation, and confidence that the world will continue as before are all uncertain even within states' own societies, to say nothing of uncertainties generated within international society as a whole.[22] This is why, OST scholars argue, states become attached even to destructive and dangerous routines: because they provide a sense of continuity and certainty in a world characterized by constant change and uncertainty. This is also why crises are so anxiety-inducing for *all* states, from semi-peripheral Serbia (Ejdus 2020), with its loss of Kosovo, to the world-leading US, with its loss of international hegemonic status (Suboti and Steele 2018).

To identify crises as such, OST scholars look for evidence of discursive representations of stress and anxiety and, most important, for disruptions in dominant storylines about the Self. This is clearly easier said than done.[23] In objectivist terms, post-1945 Britain should have been deeply insecure throughout, from the day it "lost India" onwards. Not so intersubjectively. While *some* evidence of ontological insecurity can be found in *most* discourses of Britishness, I found no fundamental uncertainty over "who we are" in the six years under study. Even Suez, which, as we see in chapter 2, put the limits of Britain's claim to great powerhood out in the open, does not constitute what OST scholars call a "true crisis" – a crisis that succeeds in disrupting the dominant biography of the state. So, even as "the British world system" came crushing down, and even as the metropole suffered years of economic stagnation, British society, at both elite and mass levels, was able to structure, stabilize, and adapt its mainstream identity scripts in ways that kept ontological insecurity at bay.

In speculating why this might be, two hypotheses immediately come to mind. First, one's place in international society matters. Some states are more likely to be anxiety-ridden because they already feel provincialized and marginalized in, or even excluded from, international life (Zarakol 2011). In light of Britain's history as a hegemon of hegemons, as well as its special privileges in the US-run free world, we might thus appreciate why none of its post-1945 crises were catastrophic, let alone apocalyptic, or why its autobiographies *always* managed to anchor themselves to *some* certitudes about greatness. The outstanding case in point is the myth of well-managed decolonization, which the ruling elites already propagated in 1960: the notion that "we" lowered the Union Jack down hundreds of overseas flagpole "out of our own volition."

The second hypothesis is related to the first and refers to what could be called creative agency. A UK-Japan comparison might be instructive here. According to Shogo Suzuki (2018), Japan's decline in relation to China, South Korea, and Japan's own history – the measures include everything from military power to a combination of a growing national debt and shrinking population – has brought about major ontological insecurities for the Japanese, both elites and masses. But rather than denying or correcting this position, Japanese society has moved to coping strategies aimed at "partial acceptance of decline followed by a search for alternative markers of 'greatness,'" such as the promotion of "civilian power" identity and of Japanese popular culture (13).

We could see similar coping mechanisms at work in the UK. Whenever their economy or military power suffered, the British reached for various "soft power" markers of their high status in the world: social policy, higher education, television, or music. As time went on, some of these markers of course became less defensible, but the general approach never lacked discursive resonance at either elite or mass levels. And if exceptionalism no longer provided sufficient ontological security, exemplarism still did. Greatness and material power are not necessarily connected, observed the sociologist (and later politician) Michael Young in 1960 (Harrison 2009, 544). "Let us now have enough sense to accept the position of a small country and try to show the world how to preserve some elements of civilisation and decency that the large ones are rapidly stamping out," wrote the Cambridge University economics professor Joan Robinson in 1972 (quoted in O'Toole 2019, 8). One could even argue that a similar tendency towards self-flattery amidst resignation to smallness can be found in self-deprecating "British humour," especially in the commonplace urge to inject irony and its derivative, sarcasm, in everyday conversations.[24] Of course, all such coping mechanisms are always embedded in the intersection of the domestic and the international, which is why some of them have a global reach and a global influence while others do not. The aforementioned Englishization of the world, for example, empowered and still empowers Britain's creative agency with alternative markers of greatness in ways that are simply not replicable in the case of Japan.

The preceding discussion raises the question of the relationship between discourses of national identity and state identity narratives. In the abstract, they are very similar because they both refer to (partially unselfconscious) practices of communication shared between elites and non-elite members of a state via consumption of the same media and same deployments of first- and third-person pronouns. However, if, as Colley (2019, 6, 10) argues, narratives are "units of discourse" that revolve around "plot," then OST scholars might have another reason to consider a more societal perspective.[25] Consider Colley's own study. Having interviewed sixty-seven ordinary Britons – meaning, "British citizens resident in England from non-military families" (13) – in late 2014 and early 2015, he identifies two basic "narratives of war" in the UK, a narrative of "Continuous War" and a narrative of "Material Decline," together with five more competing narratives that citizens use to morally evaluate said continuous war, from the familiar "Punching above Its Weight" to the Marxist "Selfish Imperialist" (85).

Situating Colley's findings against mine, I would suggest that discourses of national identity subsume or at least structure mainline (autobiographical) narratives.[26] For one thing, the twin notion that Britain is at war non-stop and that it is also progressively losing the material capacity to fight is in fact the basic story of greatness amidst decline told and retold by successive generations of British citizens, both elites and masses (cf. Reynolds 2017). For another thing, the existence of competing narratives by which the British morally evaluate their wars is similarly consistent with the reconstruction of Britishness I present in this book. Indeed, Modern Britain and Adaptable Britain, much like their Socialist and Thatcherist challengers, narrated British self-identity with references to progress and change, both of which were sources of anxiety for the Self constructed in successive iterations of the Traditionalist discourse.

This brings us to the scholarship on emotions in IR, which I believe intersects with, and potentially complements, my theoretical approach. For many constructivists, emotions are linked to, circulating within, and ultimately co-constituted with the discourses that undergird world politics.[27] Many constructivists also think that, in contexts in which their national identity is at stake, people are likely to have stronger emotional reactions to political processes and outcomes. While nationality is not the only identity a person has, it often aligns with other identities in ways that are emotionally charged, and not just for that one person. So viewed, discourses of British identity are not simply conduits for the circulation of emotions but, in fact, constitute whole patterns of emotional experience: recovery- and progress-induced joy, anxiety, shame, and fear revolving around decline, love, desire for greatness, and so on. If this is correct, then we might say that national identity topographies should be important to scholars interested in analyzing the dynamics between emotions and foreign policy.

Nora Femenia's (1996) analysis of (both British and Argentine) national identity and the Falklands Crisis is an important step forward in this direction. In her account, Argentina's surprise invasion ("recovery") of the islands by military means stunned the entire world and shamed and enraged the British, whose ire was also directed at their own defence planners for failing to anticipate and counter this threat to British territory. These emotions were mixed with humiliation and fear, both of which were compounded by the memories of the Suez episode in 1956, when Britain was forced to accept defeat at the hands of a supposedly backward nation, Egypt, whose military junta succeeded in stealing what the British believed was their land and property.

As Femenia details, the British leadership deliberately constructed the entire Falklands affair as an emotionally charged drama. Thatcher, members of her cabinet, and countless MPs referred to Argentine military aggression as, in the words of MP John Peyton, "a humiliating experience, and a grave affront to the people of the Falkland Islands above all, and to the people of the United Kingdom" and, according to MP Richard Luce, as an "indignity and humiliation ... Of course we are angry and shocked that the country should have been taken completely by surprise when we might have been warned and prepared."[28] Statements such as these were not delivered with an eye to political mass mobilization and support in favour of reinvasion. By the time of the British victory on 14 June 1982, the pervasive sense of shame and humiliation had been thoroughly replaced by its polar opposite – pride.[29] As Thatcher put it that day: "The Falklands factor is a symbol of a nation that built an empire. Too long submerged, too often denigrated, too easily forgotten, the springs of pride in Britain flow again" (Femenia 1996, 199). She then seized the opportunity to capitalize on the emergence of pride and trust to win the next election and so continue to work on restoring this version of British greatness (17, 23).

To theorize processes through which these and similar emotional registers became a social and political force in this context, we could invoke discursive fit. According to the analysis presented in chapter 4, Britain was then both a nation that was mostly muddling through and a nation that was led by a government intent on building a new Britain, one that would be able to regain self-control and, in turn, greatness. Such context is helpful for understanding not only why some emotional representations performed by political figures become salient within a community while others do not but also why some emotional representations emerge in the first place. Consider two ideas Thatcher enunciated at the beginning of the Falklands Crisis: one, that Britain's objectives were simultaneously the objectives of international law (Femenia 1996, 122, 170) and two, that the purpose of British foreign policy was to slay dictators rather than to appease them (39, 182). Based on my analysis, these claims were not only intelligible at the level of the British public circa 1980 but also compatible with their emotional responses – namely, love for moral leadership and pride for being on the right side of history.

Although but one aspect of emotions research in IR, discourse analyses of emotional representations are nevertheless a useful point of departure for developing and evaluating new theories of foreign policy. National identity topographies can assist in this effort because they provide insight into a broader discursive context within which scholars can examine how some emotional representations might or might not fit. Indeed, national identity topographies might provide insights into the prevailing emotional moods in multiple national contexts, thus helping scholars analyze the nature of emotional interactions between state actors, whether in conflictual forms, as in Femenia's analysis, or in cooperative ones.

Global Britain, Little Britain

Based on the previous discussion, we can conclude that post-Second World War American hegemony provided Britain with many more benefits – whether in physical or in ontological security – than the country might otherwise have had. Fast forward to the twenty-first century, when the coronavirus pandemic is spreading havoc and the climate crisis threatens humanity's future, and we see the structure of the international system shifting almost beyond recognition. Some observers are describing this period as an interregnum – a prolonged, in-between period of uncertainty, disruption, indeterminacy, and what Gramscian scholars call morbidity, meaning a deep crisis of authority. Others, looking at Donald Trump, America's radical far-right president, are lamenting the passing of the liberal, a.k.a. rules-based, order, fearful about what comes next.

An act of direct democracy concocted by the right wing of the Conservative Party, the 2016 referendum plunged Britain into a crisis that can also be seen as a symptom of a larger malady within the capitalist world order.[30] Following the decisive Leave victory in the 2019 election, the Conservative government of Boris Johnson embarked on a mission to quickly negotiate a comprehensive EU trade agreement, what he called a "super Canada-plus" deal.[31] Just four months later, Johnson was admitted to the intensive-care unit of a London hospital after days of fighting a serious COVID-19 infection. With the number of virus-related deaths in the UK approaching the levels seen in the worst-hit European nations, the so-called transition period will last much longer than anticipated, with the UK bound to the EU, albeit without any ability to influence its rules.

Looking at the state of British foreign policy on 8 September 2019, the *Guardian* pointed to a bitter irony: "To say that Britain's hard power has long been in decline is merely an expression of the obvious, not of doomsaying. Now the Brexiters who dreamed of restoring glory are daily eroding the soft power it amassed as its empire shrank" ("The World and Brexit: Rue Britannia"). This irony could well turn tragic for the British state, too. First, under the most likely EU withdrawal scenario, Northern Ireland will gain a special economic and legal status, thus altering the UK's constitutional fabric. Then, having consistently voted against Brexit, Scotland could decide to hold another independence referendum, whereby a Scottish "yes" would render Britain smaller than at any time since the 1707 union. In fact, whatever the future holds – the pandemic's economic, geostrategic, political, and social consequences will take years and decades to play themselves out – ontological insecurity beckons for the UK.

The same *Guardian* editorial suggests that the break with the bloc was fuelled by "a wholly unrealistic assessment of Britain's international status and heft, rooted in a vague, nostalgic vision of its imperial past."

This thesis is hackneyed but not without merit.[32] In her 2017 Lancaster House Speech, then prime minister Theresa May famously called for a "Global Britain," with two members of her cabinet following up with pro-Commonwealth trade speeches shortly thereafter.[33] Johnson took this rhetoric to yet another level, promising to liberate the economy from as many taxes and regulations as possible so that the country could take on the world through trade. "The people who bet against Britain are going to lose their shirts," he declared in his first speech as prime minister on 24 July 2019.

To better appreciate the symbiosis between Brexit-era fantasies and a highly selective reading of the nation's imperial past, consider the curious parallels between Global Britain and "Greater Britain," a Victorian-era imperialist fantasy that Duncan Bell (2019, 89) describes as "one of the most grandiose identity politics projects of the last two centuries" (see also Kenny and Pearce 2018; Bell and Vucetic 2019; Daddow 2019; Ward and Rasch 2019; Wellings and Mycock 2020). Introduced in an eponymous 1868 bestseller penned by the politician and author Charles Dilke, "Greater Britain" became a rubric for a programmatic effort to consolidate the British Empire economically, militarily, and politically and so establish a discrete global space in which Britannia would continue to rule the waves, either alone or in tandem with the US. This idea has now been reborn as "the Anglosphere." As several leading right-wing Brexiters have argued, since English-speaking countries already have so much in common – in history, politics, economics, law, media, culture, and even in familial ties – and since technology is making physical distance smaller, new Anglosphere arrangements are eminently viable. While most of them are interested in securing bilateral trade deals, starting with a giant one with the US, some have their eyes on a multilateral Anglosphere of free movement of goods, services, and labour. Some go so far as to imagine new defence pact and transcontinental (con)federal arrangements. As the Brexiter historian Andrew Roberts explained in 2016, with a combined population of 130 million mostly rich people, CANZUK – a recently relaunched label for a future ever-closer union of Canada, Australia, New Zealand, and the UK – would be the world's third most powerful polity as well as a third pillar of Western civilization, alongside the US and the EU.[34]

However, historians caution us against linking Brexit to imperial nostalgia (Edgerton 2018b; Ward and Rasch 2019; Thackeray and Toye 2019; Saunders 2019). Two of their criticisms will suffice here. First, while it is true that the UK's foreign policy ambitions derive from its former imperial role, the associated delusions of grandeur are by no means exclusive to the UK, much less are they the exclusive province of Leavers keen on triumphalist "Rule Britannia" panegyrics. Robert Saunders (2019) writes: "The idea that Britain should *lead* the EU – widely deployed in 2016 – has as strong an imperial heritage as the aspiration to *leave* it."[35] Surveys might qualify this statement somewhat, as does the fact that few Remainers framed the EU as a means of making Britain great as the Yes campaign did in 1975.[36] But the author's main point stands: British society is yet to come to terms with the British Empire, its legacies, and its sense of exceptionalism. And even if Remain had won, the UK would have still stayed out of the eurozone and so been unable to lead the European project forward.

Second, the connection between Brexit and empire is conceptually much closer to (selective) amnesia, aphasia, "forgetfulness," or myopia than to nostalgia. Saunders (2019) again:

> In Eurosceptic readings of history, the dominant memory is not of empire but of "our island story": of plucky "little Britain," standing alone against overpowering odds. It's the story of Dunkirk, of Sir Francis Drake, and of Britain fighting "alone" in 1940 – a story that reduces empire to an *expression* of British power, rather than its *source*. The myth it fuels is not that empire can return, but that it hardly mattered in the first place: that Britain can flex its muscles on the world stage without the sinews of imperial power.[37]

My analysis bears both of these observations out. First, the history that was taught at schools, in leadership speeches, newspapers, films, and novels seemed more interested in the wars of the twentieth century than in empire. We have also seen from chapter 1 onwards that dominant discourses of British identity routinely linked Britain's industrial rise to good luck and clever institutions rather than to other factors, violent colonial theft from other lands and other peoples being the principal one. Indeed, a basic premise of progressive identity mentioned earlier is that Britain was exceptionally endowed with peace, order, and good governance.

We have also seen that all discourses accepted that greatness is sometimes a function of smallness. This is particularly evident in Second World War novels and movies – part and parcel of Britain's history in which empire plays only a secondary role. There, British warriors win their battles by being brave, resilient, and resourceful, not by having superior resources; what we lack in hard power, we must make up for with wits and willpower. Debates over Skybolt and Trident, East of Suez and Iraq, and, above all, the Falklands send the same message, as do, of course, various Brexit(e)er refrains: never underestimate "the British underdog."[38] So, whether attributed to luck or to pluck, Britain's historic role was always great.

The urge to lead was equally deeply rooted in everyday identity discourses, thus configuring the kingdom as being naturally in charge, whether going solo, as in 1950, or co-jointly with the US. The one major adjustment governments in London made in the face of these two identities was therefore a maladjustment: the transfer of habits of leadership from the Commonwealth to the EC/EU, an effect of which was a persistently awkward participation in the latter. Indeed, what this analysis could not find is an identity discourse that would authorize a view of Britain as just another European power. Even France was consistently constructed as inferior – a fellow state-empire that, once its colonies won independence, reinvented itself as a major power with, among other things, a seat on the UN Security Council, an actual independent nuclear deterrent, and sufficient military might to engage in overseas interventions on its own.

The apparent longevity of these repertoires proves that "certain habits of mind and structures of feeling" (Ward and Rasch 2019, 7) are as impervious to changing material circumstances today as they were in the 1950s, when Franks first puzzled over the same fact. If we accept that Global Britain and "little Britain" are two sides of the same coin, then we have reasons to speculate that a segment of British, and specifically English, society will press on for a global foreign policy – if not necessarily a muscular one (Hill and Beadle 2014; MacDonald 2019) – even if the country's material capacity and international status precipitously dissipate. In fact, we might well conceive something similar happening in an actual little Britain scenario in which the Union disintegrates (McCourt 2014a, 176–9; cf. Strong 2017; Uttley, Wilkinson, and van Rij 2019).

Temptation to revert to old habits will be tested like never before. "Today," Edgerton (2018a) wrote in 2018, "the UK is 'just' another European power – a big Canada rather than a small United States, on a par with France and Germany, and on many measures behind them." This relative weakness, coupled with the geography that renders the kingdom "European despite itself" (Hill 2019, 16, 73, 174), means that London will be forced to search for a new partnership with Paris and Berlin as well as, via NATO and the EU, with Brussels.[39]

That said, we can also fully expect the Johnson government to try to mould a different "another Canada" strategy, one that positions the UK as a state that is close to the EU but closer to the US (Johnson 2019). This scenario, however, hinges on geostrategic developments. In case of a major rift within NATO, the UK might side with the US over the European powers, thus almost certainly weakening its overall position. A worse scenario is an isolated UK spinning in the vortex of global governance contestations between Washington, Beijing, and Brussels (and possibly some regional ones, depending on the future of the EU.)

Here we come back to the co-constitution of geopolitics and everyday political life. Since at least the Global Recession, British – and particularly English – politics has been reconfigured by the rising radical right, a phenomenon that has found expression in some of the Brexit-at-all-cost rhetoric of Johnson and Nigel Farage, the former leader of the United Kingdom Independence Party and the Brexit Party. Rooted in a critique of globalization and economic liberalization, this politics has many commonalities with mid-twentieth-century racism à la Enoch Powell. In it, the national "we" and "white race" are tightly linked together, as in the oft-made contemporary claim that the defence of the latter – the code words are "the people" and "ordinary working class" – is as legitimate as is the defence of other groups and identities, especially those related to immigration and multiculturalism.[40]

These radicals are part of a transnational movement. As Farage declared in 2016: "Voters across the Western world want nation state democracy, proper border controls and to be in charge of their own lives."[41] This is nothing less than a call for an alternative international order in which free market capitalism thrives but is firmly anchored in myths of inherited communities and their traditional sources of authority. This Britain is small and global at once: a member of CANZUK as well as "Singapore-on-Thames," a fantasy land in a fantasy world where money and goods can move freely but not people and viruses, and where human rights give way to citizenship rights and legal contractual obligations are codified through private mechanisms of arbitration. In addition to rehashing old Thatcherist ideas, this vision also advanced the political agenda of the Atlas Network, a large and mostly "Anglobal" coalition of right-wing think tanks and campaign groups that links into Johnson's cabinet.[42] Imperial amnesia is part of the same mix: "The UK rose to greatness because of our championing of global free trade," stated the prime minister in a BBC interview on 14 January 2020.[43]

Meanwhile, four decades after Thatcherism and three decades after the end of the Cold War, socialism came back to UK politics on the wings of a Labour Party led by Jeremy Corbyn. And although the party's 2019 election fiasco killed this momentum, a series of quasi-Keynesian responses to the coronavirus pandemic by Western governments – the Johnson government's own "disaster socialism" was no exception – could revive it. Younger generations, energized over the need to deal with the climate emergency and at ease with Britain's postcoloniality, could also turn to left-wing ideas and policy possibilities that were previously made unthinkable, or at least wholly marginalized. Either transformation in principle has potential to break at least some habitualized foreign policy formulations.

Alternative, progressive British foreign policies have long been put forward. Tarak Barkawi and Shane Bright's concept of "Brown Britain" is a "generational project" to move UK strategy away from wishful thinking and towards a future in which Britain is not only global but also postcolonial: "a follower and a leader of networks and peoples across the global North and South" (Barkawi and Brighton 2013, 1,121 and 1,111). Much like Wallace in 1991, the authors pin their hopes on a reformed national curriculum. By foregrounding area studies, languages, and the global histories of empire, they argue, the kingdom would reverse the cultural exclusion of minorities from British identity and therefore gradually lay a foundation for a more imaginative global foreign policy (1,123). A postcolonial cultural revolution that would cross borders and language barriers would similarly help make "Brown Britain" a reality.

A future foreign policy for Britain's left could also begin with talk of "another Canada," which in this case would be used as a progressive middle power trope.[44] Some might use it to legitimate a reduction in huge gaps between the Ministry of Defence and the Foreign and Commonwealth Office's pre-COVID-19 commitments and their post-COVID-19 budgets. Others might wish to "Canadianize" the most explicitly militarized aspects of the kingdom's global power role – if not the Trident nuclear deterrent, then certainly the Royal Navy's super-carriers and "forward-deployed" task forces.[45] Still others might reach for "Canada" to advance pro-gender equality, a.k.a. feminist, foreign policy. Like Brown Britain, this last scenario would throw the differences between left-liberal and postcolonial positions into sharp relief but within the "just-another-country" imaginary.

Whoever wins the political future, global uncertainties will continue and so deepen an abiding sense of insecurity for Britain and the British. This is where Gramsci's much-quoted reference to the morbidity of the 1930s once again appears apt: "The crisis consists precisely in the fact that the old is dying and the new cannot be born; in this interregnum a great variety of morbid symptoms appear." This applies well beyond British foreign policy: the old approach is dying, but the alternative is missing. What we are left with in the meantime – and I really mean "we," for we are all affected – is a long string of delusions, some old, some new: morbid symptoms of the wicked and super-wicked upheavals going on in our world.

Appendix A

Archive

Given that ethnography is limited to the present and the immediate past, the most valuable interpretivist methodology for reconstructing postwar Britishness is an inductively oriented discourse analysis. Assembling an archive or corpus for such analysis can be a challenging task in that there seems to be both a huge number of possible texts from which national identity categories can be recovered and an abundance of different, often conflicting, texts about what counts as elite versus mass discourse in a given historical period. This selection strategy follows the theoretical and methodological rationale set out in the Making Identity Count project: https://www.makingidentitycount.org/.

Leadership Speeches

Our aim was to select two speeches that were at once high circulating, regular ("annual"), and on "anything but national identity" (nothing on devolution or "The Future of Britishness," for example). The prime minister's statements in the "State Opening of Parliament," a new session of Parliament, and the "annual party conference speech" met these criteria. With respect to the first, the UK government's legislative program (a.k.a. the ministerial agenda) for the forthcoming parliamentary session is traditionally laid out in the Queen's Speech (in 1950, it was the King's Speech), a.k.a. the "Most Gracious Speech from the Throne."

Set in 1852, the ceremony is part of the UK's "unwritten" constitution, which relies heavily on understandings and assumptions more than on hard rules. The Queen's Speech is prepared by the Prime Minister's Office, and the monarch reads it as a matter of her constitutional duty. In the period under study, the combination of the royal pomp and disclosure of the upcoming policies and pieces of legislation by the government naturally attracted significant media attention, including a live television audience.

Party conferences in the UK serve to rally their constituencies, gain a few days of newspaper headlines, and raise money. They also normally take place in early fall and away from the capital city – in Birmingham or Brighton, for example. They have also evolved over time, with latter years witnessing the emergence of workshops, book fairs, movie screenings, and other events within them. In the immediate postwar decades, the party conference was a site of policy-making; from about 1980 onwards, it became an opportunity for image-making. The prime minister's speech was always the central event, however.

We departed from this rule thrice. In 1970, the UK had a change of government and we decided to have one leadership speech from each the two prime ministers that year: the outgoing Wilson (Labour) and the incoming Heath (Conservative). We selected the speeches the two leaders gave in the post-election State Opening on 2 July. Both speeches were given during the "Debate on the Address," a.k.a. "Loyal Address," which is occurs when members of both houses debate the content of the speech (an "Address in Reply to Her Majesty's Gracious Speech") – another longstanding parliamentary ritual.

In the year 1990 the UK again had two prime ministers: Margaret Thatcher resigned on 22 November. The subsequent leadership contest within the Conservative Party was carried by John Major, chancellor of the exchequer, who then became the nation's leader on 28 November 1990. His speech at the Queen Elizabeth II Conference Centre on 4 December 1990 was his first as prime minister.

In 2000, we selected Tony Blair's "Britain Speech" on 28 March, rather than the Queen's Speech or his statement in the Debate on the Address on 6 December. This was done to reflect the changing nature of mass mediation of leadership speeches in the internet age and because of the fact that this speech had been widely received as "the" statement of "Blairism" and Blair's attempt to "rebrand" the UK.

Newspapers

We followed the rankings based on the Press Council and Audit Bureau of Circulations circulation figures or the closest equivalent. Accordingly, we selected the *Daily Express* and the *Daily Mirror* from 1950 through 1980, the *Sun* and the *Daily Mirror* for 1990, and the *Sun* and the *Daily Mail* for 2000. Although in national circulation numbers the *Sun* had already overtaken the *Daily Express* in 1980, we continued to use the latter due to some difficulties in gaining access to the former's archive. With this selection, we achieved some variance in the ownership structures and ideological orientations of newspapers known as "popular" or "mass-market" (a.k.a. "red-tops" or "tabloids"). We sampled the editions published on the fifteenth day of each month, including, when appropriate, Sunday equivalents of the selected newspaper (the *Sunday Mirror*, the *Sunday Express*, the *Mail on Sunday* but not the *News of the World*).[1]

History textbooks

For each year under study we selected the two high school-level publications on modern English or British history that were most likely to have been used at the time in private and state schools in the UK, primarily in England. To that end, we reviewed the histories and institutional contexts of the educational program in history in England and then combed contemporary and historical reviews and discussions in the journals *Teaching History* and *History of Education Review*. While it is true that UK history teachers began to use textbooks in their classrooms only following the introduction of the history General Certificate of Education Exam (GCSE) and the National Curriculum initiative in the late 1980s, it is still the case that numerous textbooks – and "topic-books" – existed and circulated throughout the period under study. Whenever appropriate, we used publications catering to students between the ages of fourteen and nineteen, particularly those studying for history GCSE and history A Level exams (the more advanced qualifications generally required for university entrance) or their closest historical equivalents (CSE/O-Level). Next, for ample reflection we looked at "the last hundred years," whatever the type of history (economic, social, cultural, political etc.), as well as at "recent editions" – that is, editions published in the beginning of the year or in the preceding year or two – 1958 or 1959 for 1960, for example. If one of the two textbooks we selected covered only a short period of history and/or was exceptionally short, we added a third textbook to our sample.[2]

Novels

Identifying "bestselling novels" was challenging. To select two top-selling items on the consumer market of books, bought by private individuals for their own use or as gifts, in each year, we first consulted scholarly histories of the book and of the UK fiction industry. For 1950 and 1960, we consulted annual round-ups of the bestseller market produced by W.H. Smith's *Trade News*, the *Observer*, the *Bookseller*, the *Evening Standard*, the *Evening News*, *Time and Tide*, the *Sunday Telegraph*, and the *Daily Express* and picked the two British-authored novels closest to the top of each list.[3] For 1970 and 1980, the reliability of bestseller lists improved thanks to the introduction of surveys, automated data collection (after 1980), and other ranking instruments. Especially helpful were secondary assessments of said lists published in specialist magazines such as the *Listener*, a weekly BBC magazine published until 1991, and by journalist Alex Hamilton in the *Guardian* (from 1970 onwards). For 1990 and 2000, we followed the rankings generated by computerized data capture via Electronic Point-of-Sale equipment and disseminated by companies such as Nielsen BookScan. As Table I.1 in the introduction shows, several authors appear in multiple years: Fleming, Christie, Smith, Forsyth, and Rowling.[4]

The paperback revolution changed our selection criteria as well since it rendered paperback the dominant format for bestsellers. First, the paperback revolution changed the meaning of high-circulating: in the late 1940s, a top hardback novel would achieve sales of 100,000 over several years, whereas in the 1990s a bestselling paperback would have 500,000 copies sold in weeks. Second, this means that some our "bestselling novels of the year" after 1960 were in fact paperback editions of a hardback released a year, or two or three, before the year of the study. In 1960, we thus selected Ian Fleming's *Dr No*, released in March 1958 over Fleming's *For Your Eyes Only*, released in April 1960. In principle, either one would have been acceptable as UK readers en masse were enjoying multiple of Fleming's Bond novels. However, *Dr No*, the sixth book in the espionage adventure series, topped that year's bestseller with more than 150,000 copies sold thanks to the paperback release in February as well as, to a lesser extent, to both text and comic-strip serializations occurring that year in the *Daily Express*. *For Your Eyes Only*, in contrast, was released in hardback and sold fewer than 22,000 copies.[5] The same rationale applied to *4.50 from Paddington*, a novel by Agatha Christie first published in November 1957 but appearing in paperback three years later with Fontana Books.[6]

Movies

To select top watched movies by UK directors we followed two strategies. For the 1950 to 1980 period, we referred to the end-of-the-year movie reports published in the *Times*. Based on the annual surveys of box-office returns (including both "general release" and "reserved tickets") collected and analyzed by the industry publication *Motion Picture Herald*, these reports do not provide details such as the numbers of viewers, but they helpfully identify and sometimes rank-order most watched movies in the UK.

For 1990 and 2000, we used the box-office data reported in the histories of British film – the British Film Institute's BFI *Film and Television Handbook* above all. In the case of a tie, we went for the more British of the two. For 1980, for example, we selected *McVicar* over *Yanks* because the former was a UK production and the latter a UK-US production. In 2000, however, we selected the greater box-office popularity of *Gladiator*, a sword-and-sandal drama directed by a British filmmaker and delivered in British accents, over *Billy Elliot*, an identity-rich story of a coal miner's son in Northern England who takes up ballet.[7] Film histories likewise helped determine release dates, which, too, occasionally helped us break a reasonable rankings tie. Here, we usually opted for the more recent release: *McVicar*, released in August 1980, over *Yanks*, released in September 1979, for example. For the earlier years, however, we acknowledged that movies released in the previous year *often* topped most watched estimates in the following year. In the 1950s, for instance, showings of popular movies in some cases went on for eighteen consecutive months.

Appendix B

Events

The rationale for finding events is set out in the introduction.

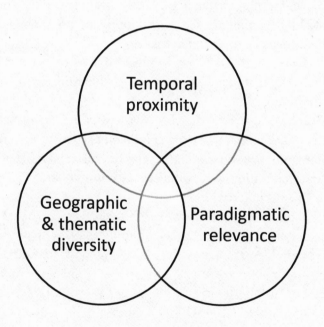

Figure App.B.1 Selecting events

UK Defence Reviews, 1957–2003

Sandys, D. 1957. *Statement on Defence, 1957*. London: Ministry of
Defence. http://filestore.nationalarchives.gov.uk/pdfs/small/cab-129-
86-c-57-69-19.pdf.

Healey, D. 1966. *Defence Review: The Statement on the Defence Estimates*.
London: Ministry of Defence. http://filestore.nationalarchives.gov.
uk/pdfs/small/cab-129-124-c-33.pdf.

Mason, R. 1975. *Statement on the Defence Estimates* London: Ministry
of Defence. http://filestore.nationalarchives.gov.uk/pdfs/small/
cab-129-181-c-21.pdf.

Nott, J. 1981. *The United Kingdom Defence Programme: The Way Forward*. London: Ministry of Defence. http://fc95d419f4478b3b6e5f-
3f71d0fe2b653c4f00f32175760e96e7.r87.cf1.rackcdn.com/991284B4011
C44C9AEB423DA04A7D54B.pdf.

King, T. 1990. *Defence (Options for Change)*. London: Ministry of
Defence. https://api.parliament.uk/historic-hansard/commons/
1990/jul/25/defence-options-for-change.

Rifkind, M. 1994. *Front Line First*. London: Ministry of Defence. https:/
/publications.parliament.uk/pa/cm199394/cmhansrd/1994-07-14/
Debate-1.html.

Hoon, G. 2002. *The Strategic Defence Review: A New Chapter*. London:
Ministry of Defence. http://webarchive.nationalarchives.gov.uk/2009
0805012836/http://www.mod.uk/DefenceInternet/AboutDefence/
CorporatePublications/PolicyStrategyandPlanning/StrategicDefence
ReviewANewChaptercm5566.htm.

Hoon, G. 2003. *Delivering Security in a Changing World: Defence White
Paper*. London: Ministry of Defence. http://webarchive.national-
archives.gov.uk/20121018172935/http://www.mod.uk/NR/rdonlyres/
051AF365-0A97-4550-99C0-4D87D7C95DED/0/cm6041I_white
paper2003.pdf.

Notes

Introduction

1 The first aphorism, which likely belongs to late Belgian prime minister Paul-Henri Spaak, came from Danish finance minister Kristian Jensen (Boffey 2017) and then also from Spanish foreign minister Joseph Borrell (Sharma 2019). The second comment came from the president of the EU's European Council Donald Tusk (Reuters 2019).

2 The phrases are from Prime Minister Theresa May (Blagden 2019; Daddow 2019; Ward and Rasch 2019).

3 This is a vast literature that begins with Gallagher and Robinson (1953).

4 Craig and Radchenko (2008, 79–80). See also Harrison (2009, 9); Hopf (2012, 79–80); and Shifrinson (2018, 1). On status recognition as a function of assorted competitive performances in international society, see Røren and Beaumont (2019); Ward (2019); and Murray (2019).

5 The definition is from Shifrinson (2018, 13–15). In his estimation, the UK's European capabilities declined from 11 to 14 per cent to 8 per cent and from 22 to 33 per cent to 20 per cent vis-à-vis the US (16, chap. 2). For a range of alternative characterizations of Britain's great powerhood, see Blagden (2019, 4–7).

6 Gamble (2000, 5; 2003, 27–8). See also Holland (1991); Clarke (2004 [1996]); English and Kenny (2000); Hall (2000); Croft (2001a); Hall (2012, 4); Simms (2016, chap. 9); Tomlinson (2017, chap. 2); and Green (2020, chap. 1).

7 On the consensus and its subsequent iterations, see McCourt (2014a, 4; 2014b, 165); Self (2010, 6, 36–7); Heinlein (2002, 137); and Harrison (2009, 5, 115–16). Note also that the descriptor "postwar" works to elide the

history and politics of imperial decline (Bailkin 2012; Schofield 2013; Burkett 2013).

8 Bevin pitched the notion to the French and continued to champion it well into 1949. He was not alone. Some Third Forcers in London argued for territorial expansion (Bevin had an eye on the Italian colonies in particular), others for a rapid industrial development of empire, and still others for bringing select European countries into the Commonwealth (Bevin's "Western Union" speech of 1948 can be read this way). France had its Third Forcers at the time too. See Barker (1983); Vickers (2003); Daddow (2004); Darwin (1991); Heinlein (2002); Deighton (2013); and Grob-Fitzgibbon (2016).

9 The sequel, *The Friends of Harry Perkins*, was published in March 2019. In Mullin's vision of the future, set in 2025, Brexit negotiations are still inconclusive, the Labour Party is in continued opposition, and the US is at war with China. Note that Haseler (2012) counts Attlee, Wilson, and Blair among potential change agents.

10 Larsen (1997, chap. 1); Bell (1997, chaps. 5–8); McCourt (2014a, 5, 182n24); Hill (2016, 395; 2019, 137–9); and Thomas and Toye (2017, 230–7). On comparative post-imperial pathways more generally, see Thomas (2014); and Buettner (2016).

11 "Reverential" is from Gaskarth (2013, 68). "Unsinkable aircraft carrier" is Churchill's phrase (Campbell 1986, 1); Orwell actually preferred "Airstrip One" (Vucetic 2011b, 1).

12 Powell's was in fact a double critique of British foreign policy: against the idea of global leadership – whether via the Commonwealth or the Common Market – and against the nineteenth-century idea of a free-trading little Englandism (Schofield 2013; see also Shilliam 2018, 96–106; Kenny and Pearce 2018, chap. 4).

13 On Labour's attraction to the Swedish model, see Harrison (2009, 119). Exemplarity can be defined as "the social process through which standards of conduct are formulated, sustained, and re-worked" (Noyes and Wille 2020). On the UK case, see Harrison (2009, 544–5; Harrison 2010, 547–8); and Gaskarth (2014, 47). For the anti-nuclear movement in particular, see Heuser (1998); and Croft (2001b).

14 Speech in Manchester on 4 July 1948, quoted in Edgerton (2018b, 82).

15 See, inter alia, Holland (1991); Mangold (2002); Darwin (2009); Self

(2010); Morris (2011); and Simms (2016). The argument is sometimes extended to defence policy as well (Baylis 1989; cf. Rees 2001).

16 For examples, see Cain and Hopkins (2016); Wearing (2014, 2018).

17 Introduced by Robinson and Gallagher, writing with Alice Denny, in 1961, the term "official mind" originally referred to the body of bureaucrats tasked with governing colonial affairs from London, but it has since been stretched to refer to the foreign and defence policy apparatus more broadly or even to a larger group of professionals sharing a common set of beliefs about said policy (Robinson, Gallagher, and Denny 1961; see also Heinlein 2002; Haseler 2007; Self 2010; Haseler 2012; Bevir and Daddow 2015). In general, the bureaucrats were *less* willing to cling to grandeur than were the politicians (Blackwell 1993, 25–7; Self 2010, 300).

18 Sanders and Houghton (2017, x). See also Mabon, Garnett, and Smith (2017, chap. 1). Some of these concepts now appear even in parliamentary documents on foreign policy (Gaskarth 2014, 42–3; Vucetic 2020b, 79–80).

19 Quotes from Wallace (1991, 79, 66, 75, 69). See also Wallace (2000, 2005a, 2005b). On exceptionalism, see also Larsen (1997); Young (1998); Rees (2001); Baker (2002); Gamble (2003); Marcussen et al. (1999); Grob-Fitzgibbon (2016); Sanders and Houghton (2017); Daddow (2011, 2015b, 2018); and Wellings (2019, esp. chap. 4).

20 Note the semantics here: some argue the third "e" in Brexiteer was inserted strategically to invoke pride in the buccaneers and privateers of the sixteenth century, and their legendary "swashbuckling" endeavours (Ward and Rasch 2019, 3; see also Barnett 2018, chap. 13). On the historical constitution of Anglo-Saxons and Anglo-Saxonism, see, for example, Vucetic (2011b, chap. 2) and Shilliam (2018, chap. 3), and compare to Atlanticists and Atlanticism (Gamble 2003, 80–2; Dunne 2004).

21 There are now hundreds of discrete studies of foreign policy that conceptualize nations as intersubjective social-cognitive structures that constitute the space where ideas, emotions, institutions, and practices intersect to affect collectively binding actions at the level of states, regions, and the international system as a whole (Vucetic 2017a, 2018). Constructivist IR, however, is similar but not identical to interpretivist British foreign policy scholarship (Bevir, Daddow, and Hall 2013; Bevir, Daddow, and Schnapper 2015; Daddow and Gaskarth 2011; Schnapper 2011; Gaskarth 2013; Edmunds, Gaskarth, and Porter 2014; Bevir and Daddow 2015).

22 His context is Norman Tebbit's infamous "cricket test" (Ward 2004, 82–3, 115). Compare with Doty (1996b, 126). On the conflation of state and national identity in IR, see Berenskoetter (2014, 263).

23 These are simplified definitions only: *senso comune*, or common sense, refers to the content of popular, everyday knowledge. Structures of feeling and *habitus* both refer to the broader intersubjective dispositions that produce common sense, whereby the former concept stresses the affective dispositions and the latter stresses the cognitive ones. *Doxa* refers to the unarticulated, taken for granted elements of common sense.

24 For recent examples of Hallsian analyses of British life in history and sociology, see, respectively, Vernon (2017); and Valluvan (2019).

25 Students of popular culture in IR and political geography see it the same way: masses routinely elaborate, negotiate, rework, or challenge elite positions. See, for example, Saunders and Strukov (2018), and compare with studies of British foreign policy that focus on liberal propaganda, capitalism, and/or the class system (e.g., Curtis 1995; Haseler 2012; Cain and Hopkins 2016; Wearing 2018).

26 For a more sustained engagement with this large literature, including the work by Jon Fox and Cynthia Miller Idriss (2008), Michael Skey (2009), and others from a loosely Gramscian perspective, see Vucetic and Hopf (2020).

27 Since the mid-2000s (e.g., Mitzen 2006), ontological security has become a workhorse for constructivist IR theorizing of the social-cognitive and emotional underpinnings of agents' motivation for action (Gaskarth 2013, 61–4; cf. Skey 2010).

28 Neoclassical realism posits that all states seek survival because the international system is fundamentally anarchic, but it explains foreign policies by focusing on the interaction of (independent) systemic and (intervening) domestic-level variables such as, in this case, national identity.

29 See Henderson, Wincott, and Jones (2017); Oliver (2018); Wellings (2019); and O'Toole (2018). For further context, See Kumar (2003); and Kenny (2014).

30 This goes double for attempts to pursue clashing role orientations: "One cannot be an influential/rule of law state and at the same time seek to transgress international law in an opportunist-interventionist fashion" (Gaskarth 2014, 64).

31 McCourt (2014a, 15). Elsewhere he has intimated that roles are at once si-
tuation-specific and sensitive to societal transformations (McCourt
2014b, 175). We could thus say that role theory sees foreign policy as a
practice performed in and through joint actions involving Self-Other
relations in multiple locales and at different scales, and not "just" at the
intersection of the international and domestic environments. Space prevents me from engaging with this rich literature further, but see, inter
alia, Hill (1979); Breuning (1995); Macleod (1997); MccGwire (2006);
Gaskarth (2014, 2016); McCourt (2011); Morris (2011); Aggestam (2012);
Daddow (2015a; 2019); Blagden (2019); Strong (2018); and Oppermann,
Beasley, and Kaarbo (2019).

32 Only Lecture 3, "The Atlantic Bridge," is available for listening: https://
www.bbc.co.uk/programmes/p00hg2c7. On the significance of Franks,
see Danchev (1993).

33 Franks (1954). He likewise correctly dismissed isolationism as impossible
(Gaskarth 2014, 48–51; Hill 2019, 8).

34 Two additional points. First, like Doty, most interpretivists shy away
from making causal claims (e.g., Hansen 2006, 22–5). Whether *how* questions are causal also depends on one's underlying theory of causation
(compare, inter alia, Wendt 1999, 55–6, 87; Klotz 2008, 50–1; Navari 2008,
40–1; Kurki 2008, 184; Vucetic 2011a, 1307–11; McCourt 2014a, 46–53). Second, the "ideal type" interpretivist research design encompasses *detailed*
accounts of how situated agents exert their agency (Bevir and Daddow
2015, 281–3). This is beyond the scope of my study, which in any case
aims to supplement, not supersede, other approaches (Humphreys
2015, 580).

35 On elite-mass verticality, see Colley (2019, 4–5); Clarke et al. (2018, 6);
and, more broadly, Hall (1996a); and Whitmeyer (2002).

36 The project website is https://www.makingidentitycount.org. See also
Hopf and Allan (2016).

37 All supplementary files are available at https://www.makingidentity-
count.org/united-kingdom (see, in particular, Vucetic, "A How-to Guide
for Project Contributors," December 2015; and Vucetic, "The United
Kingdom, 1950–2000: Primary Texts," 23 June 2016). On research design
and methodological details, see Allan (2016); cf. Hansen (2006, chap. 5).

38 Polities centred on Istanbul, Madrid, and Moscow come to mind. On

British political development and Britishness, see, inter alia, Colley (2009 [1992]); Burton (1997); Paul (1997); Robbins (1998); Kumar (2003); Gamble (2003); Ward (2004); Darwin (2009); Barkawi and Brighton (2013); Kenny (2014); Bhambra (2016); Vernon (2017); Shilliam (2018); and Wellings (2019).

39 For an argument that a unifying, national, and mass democratic culture in the UK had already emerged in the 1930s – thanks to the deep penetration of popular daily newspapers, the cinema, and other media infrastructures into daily life – see LeMahieu (1998). On the role of scholars, such as Richard Hoggart and Raymond Williams, and scholarly methods, such as Mass-Observation, see Savage (2010).

40 Britishness is not the same as British citizenship (Croft 2012, 4; Doty 1996b, 130). While in 1948 the latter encompassed all subjects of the empire, in 1962, as we see in chapter 2, it came down to the territory of the UK and British Overseas Territories, plus the diaspora – British-born people living abroad. As for the national UK, Edgerton locates its decline in the 1970s, which witnessed the beginning of the internationalization of finance and production and the rise of subnational nationalism. To this we could also add the decline in political participation since the late 1980s.

41 On mass media and Britishness, see LeMahieu (1988) and McClintock (1995). While weekly cinema audiences went down from around 26 million circa 1950 to around 14 million circa 1960, this was still about the same as the total circulation of all daily national newspapers and more than the total television program consumption figure. Note also that, in 1960, the BBC and ITV were each restricted to a seven-hour broadcasting day. For further details, see Appendix A; Webster (2005, 6); and Harrison (2009, 54–8).

42 Consider any number of James Bond films: in addition to looking at how camera angles and light illuminate, say, the portrait of the Queen, the coder must also pay attention to music, sound, and bodies, including the manner in which the protagonist touches objects and people (Funnell and Dodds 2017).

43 British print media consumption likewise reflected and reproduced one's class and political identification. In Agatha Christie's *Murder Is Announced*, which is one of my sources in chapter 1, most characters seem

to read more than one newspaper daily, in addition to the village newspaper and newsmagazines. Colonel Easterbrook reads the *Times*, the
main establishment newspaper. The rich Miss Blacklock likes the conservative *Daily Mail*. The eccentric Miss Hinchcliffe and Miss Murgatroyd
prefer the Liberal Party-leaning *New Chronicle*. Only the cranky (and
wealthy) writer Edmund Swettenham reads the pro-communist *Daily
Worker*.

44 The analysts – none of whom resided in the UK at the time of research –
were asked to tune out UK news (especially Brexit) and UK history
(especially social and cultural [e.g., Spiering 2014]) until all coding and
analysis was complete. My own researcher subjectivity reflections are
in Vucetic (2017b).

45 Together, Steps 3 and 4 could be dubbed "interpretive quantification"
(Barkin and Sjoberg 2017). Compare Doty (1996a) and Hansen (2006).

46 For summary tables as well as for lists of all counted identity categories
with coding examples, see full-length UK identity reports at the project
website: https://www.makingidentitycount.org/united-kingdom.

47 Scholars often lament the fact that no word but "British" exists to describe UK citizens as a group (e.g., Harrison 2010, xv). The term "British
and Northern Irish" is merely a regional census category, whereas Tom
Nairn's 1980s-vintage "Ukanians" has adherents only among the New
Left.

48 On eventfulness as a methodological technique, see Hansen (2006, 27–9);
Skey (2009, 8, 117–19); and Guzzini (2012, 52–4). Compare to the concept
of a dilemma (Bevir and Daddow 2015, 275, 280–1).

49 Nearly fifty years after Churchill introduced this trope, Blair insisted that
Britain was a "power that is at the crux of the alliances and international
politics which shaped the world and its future" (quoted in Self 2002, 5).
See also Kenny and Pearce (2018, 55–6); Sanders and Houghton (2017,
1-4); Simms (2016, 672); Gaskarth (2013, 66-68); Daddow and Gaskarth
(2011, 13); Gamble (2003, 220); Reynolds (2000, chap. 8); Young (1998,
32–5); and Larsen (1997, 52).

50 On paradigmatic cases, see Flybjerg (2006, 15–16). On case selection in
constructivist IR, see Klotz (2008).

51 A sample: Deighton (1990); Taylor (2016) [1991], chap. 4); Dell (1995);
Clarke (2004 [1996]); Bell (1997); Young (1998); Peden (2012); Bevir,

Daddow, and Schnapper (2015); Daddow (2015b); Grob-Fitzgibbon
(2016); Smith (2017); and Hill (2019, chap. 2).

52 Even if we accept that audience effects are potentially present even in the
most secretive policy arenas (e.g., Cormac and Aldrich 2018; Gun 2020),
the fact remains that overt and covert foreign policy actions are qualitatively different (e.g., Heuser 1992; Cormac 2018), as are ("American,"
"Blairite") "sofa circle" discussions in comparison to parliamentary
debates or white papers in comparison to cabinet-level memos (e.g.,
Wallace 1975; Gaskarth 2013).

Chapter One

1 Terminological alternatives for the US ("America") and the Union of Soviet Socialist Republics ("Soviet Russia") are subject to the usual caveats.
Although the Commonwealth (of Nations) was established in 1949, both
"British Commonwealth" and "empire" reminded widely in usage, alone
or together (Harrison 2009, 6; Edgerton 2018b, 256). See also under the
"third" British Empire in historiography (Vernon 2017).

2 Word counts were generated in NVivo and are here used for presentational, not analytical, purposes. For the full raw counts table, biblio-
graphic details, and other materials, see the UK 1950 report (Vucetic
2019a) and other supplementary materials on the project website. Leading identity categories are identified in *italics*. When appropriate, I extend the discussion to include the less frequent identity categories.

3 An alternative label would be "collectivism" or even "social democracy,"
with a caveat that the latter was far more technocratic than democratic
(Vernon 2017, 378). The "welfare state" does not appear in the 1950
archive.

4 Though viewed as "half-educated," the masses were (supposed to be)
well informed. In the works of fiction dealing with war, education is
always a lifesaver. In Shute's *A Town Like Alice*, the heroine's basic famil-
iarity with the Malay language and the Koran helps her survive her wartime ordeals.

5 The First, Second, Third, and Free Worlds did not yet exist as terms in
the British popular imagination as sampled in this study. And those
who actually used the term "Third World" later in the decade – French

demographer, anthropologist, and historian Alfred Sauvy coined it only in 1952 – were anti-colonial advocates who described their politics as that of the "Third Estate," the sans culottes, of the world.

6 Attlee did not just have British people in mind here; rather, he basically described his party ("our Movement") as the vanguard of the *international* socialist democratic revolution. Note also that the House of Commons had no more communist MPs after 1950.

7 While also keeping quiet on the first anti-apartheid riots in South Africa (Hyam 2007, chap. 2; Heinlein 2002, chap. 2).

8 Darwin (2009, 128–9). Officials routinely lied, denying reports of British atrocities, but when news of the Hola massacre reached London, even the far-right imperialist Enoch Powell reacted with indignation. See also Curtis (1995, chap. 4); Hyam (2006, chaps 2–3); Walton (2013, chap. 5); and Buettner (2016, chap. 1).

9 Webster calls this "a wider globalized identity, bringing together the special relationship and the 'people's Empire' of a racial community of Britons in Australia, Canada, and New Zealand" (Webster 2005, 16–17).

10 Considering that this helped Britain retain the sterling area (Campbell 1986, chap. 1), it is doubtful that a counterfactual Churchill government would have said no to the Americans (Barker 1983, 243).

11 Not least because the US bases in the UK made the latter the main first-strike target (Verrier 1983, 94–6; Self 2010, 109). For context, see Self (2010, 160–1); Dorman (2001, 11–12); and Baylis and Macmillan (1993).

12 See Pierre (1972). See see Croft (2001b, 82–3); and Baylis and Stoddart (2015, 213–17). Pierre's is arguably the first book-length discussion of the British identity-foreign policy nexus.

13 As the first non-superpower to go nuclear, the UK actually spurred proliferation (Baylis and Stoddart 2015, 214).

14 They were partially right: operations were different from procurement. See the discussion of the so-called Mark 1 and Mark 2 independence, and of the "Moscow criterion" in Baylis and Stoddart (2015, 215–16).

15 Intelligence was indeed "the last penumbra of empire" (Walton 2013, 329). And while the US and the UK simultaneously cooperated and competed in postwar covert operations, the former remained the dominant form of interaction. See also Aldrich (2001); Cormac and Aldrich (2018); and Heuser (1992).

16 The history of the Schuman Plan and the ESCS is well known: the Pleven
   Plan is not – it refers to a poorly designed, poorly executed scheme for an
   army made of troop contributions from the ESCS countries (Milward
   2003, chaps. 3–4).

17 Quoted in Grob-Fitzgibbon (2016, 116). Fearing a French-led "Continental bloc," Bevin called the Pleven Plan "a sort of cancer in the Atlantic
   body" (Milward 2003, 85).

18 Lord Plowden, referring to an anonymous "forthright colleague" in his
   memoirs (quoted in Mangold 2001, 60). For further context, see Young
   (1989); and Schaad (1998).

19 This draws on Richardson (1992); Shaw (1996, 74–6); Onslow (1997); and
   Thomas and Toye (2017, 200–12).

20 House of Commons, 27 July 1956, cited in Richardson (1992, 380).

21 The special relationship has many beginnings, one of them being early
   1947, when London "passed the buck" by withdrawing its troops from
   Greece and Turkey. For a sample of interpretations, see Kolko and Kolko
   (1972); Barnett (1972); Charmley (1995); Dobson (1995); Ingram (1997);
   Danchev (1998); Curtis (2003); Haseler (2007); Vucetic (2011b, 2011c);
   Tate (2012); Murphy (2012); Dobson and Marsh (2017); Haugevik (2018);
   Haglund (2019); Marsh (2019); and Green (2020).

22 Also note that covert cooperation with the Americans rarely suffered
   because of high-office disagreements.

23 See Harrison (2009, 5, 87–8). Measured in terms of per centages, the peak
   year was 1953, but the GDP share is not the only relevant measure in this
   regard. For discussions, see Edgerton (2018b, chap. 13, 459); Harrison
   (2009, 90, 93); and Chalmers (1985, 44, 45). For cabinet-level discussion
   of British defence at the time, see Baylis and Macmillan (1993); and
   Peden (2012).

24 On the gradual reorientation to the defence of Europe, see Dockrill
   (2002, 22–6).

25 As was the case during the Battle of France, in the 1950s some French
   officials were actually open to the idea of economic and political integration with the UK (Bell 1997, 155–8; Crouzet 2004, 312–15).

26 Bevan had previously supported a British atomic bomb and the rearmament program. See Edgerton (2018b, 345); Vickers (2003, 185).

27 The text of the full speech is online: https://api.parliament.uk/historic-hansard/commons/1951/apr/23/mr-aneurin-bevan-statement.

28 Compare Dorman (2001); Rees (2001); Darwin (2009);and Harrison (2009). Suez certainly disrupted Britain's claim to great powerhood in the sense that it became obvious to decision makers in London that future interventions would require US fiat (Grob-Fitzgibbon 2016, 249–50).

29 Similarly, if we extend McCourt's framework backward in time, we might see that Washington repeatedly attempted to altercast London into leadership in Western Europe via the Marshall Plan. One hypothesis would be that this altercasting failed because Britain had not yet configured itself as a transatlantic bridge, certainly not one in which the traffic was supposed to go in the direction of a vanquished, impoverished Europe.

Chapter Two

1 Figure UK 1960 shows the top 25 per cent of categories. A more detailed analysis, including the supplementary materials containing full raw count tables and more are available in Vucetic (2019b) and on the project website. Some labels are simplifications: "Just & fair" and "Soviet/Communism" were created by combining two heretofore separately coded identity categories, while the "Third World" is an amalgam of various significant Others located outside of both the East and the West.

2 Notwithstanding the conceptual distinction, I coded this category as interchangeable with "sexist," which here means believing that women are inferior to men intellectually, morally, and otherwise. Masculinist identity is separate as it refers to explicit claims that Britain is "manly" – that is, that it has traits of male-identified persons.

3 Class hierarchy appeared fixed in the sense that lower classes generally accepted their subordinate status vis-à-vis the upper class. The movie *Doctor in Love* depicts these relations well. At the bottom of the socioeconomic hierarchy are chauffeurs and strip club dancers, then nurses and secretaries, then junior doctors, all of whom are middle class, then senior doctors. Sir Lancelot Spratt is the most dominant figure. His very presence renders everyone insecure (everyone except Lady Spratt, that is), as does his reckless driving and insistence on using an unapproved drug

(which suggests that he sets himself above the law). Spratt comes off as benevolent and caring in the end.

4 The Queen's Speech: "My Government will seek to maintain a sound economy ... My Government will follow out their policy of advancing the social welfare of My People ... A high rate of house-building will be maintained." And these policies were working, according to Macmillan, with Britain rising again: "One family in every six in this island [has] a new home. And for many of them not just a home, but a home of their own" (Scarborough Speech).

5 In the story, Bond is sent out to Jamaica to investigate a loss of espionage assets. He ends up on a guano-rich island between Jamaica and Cuba, where he comes face to face with an international mega-villain bent on stealing American missile technology in order to sell it to the Soviets (or Communist Chinese, if they pay more). Bond defeats the villain, saving the missiles and defusing a potential Cold War crisis.

6 Winston Churchill also materializes in the movie as a telephone voice – a reminder of his famous morale-boosting radio speeches at the time – that makes the fateful command: "Sink the Bismarck at any cost!"

7 This discussion owes a great deal to Heinlein (2002); Milward (2003); Louis (2004; 2006); Hyam (2007); Parr (2006); Stockwell (2008); Smith (2008); Darwin (1991); Darwin (2009); Harrison (2009); Beck (2009); Self (2010); Peden (2012); and Grob-Fitzgibbon (2016).

8 This applied throughout the twentieth century. "Most people in Britain," Lord Tebbit opined in 1989, "did not want to live in a multicultural, multiracial society, but it has been foisted on them" (Harrison 2010, 205).

9 On Macmillan's emotional blackmail at Nassau, see Self (2010, 204).

10 See Heuser (1998, 3). A product of Macmillan's wit and charm, however, Nassau was never since been replicated (Danchev 1998, 156). On British defence policy under Macmillan in general, see Ball (1996).

11 Churchill's son Randolph read out the letter in a televised ceremony at the White House. See NBC News (1963).

12 Which, as McCourt (2014a, 91) notes, would entail only "a temporary lapse in the quality of the deterrent."

13 See Sanders and Houghton (2017, 122–3). EFTA, Britain's counter-project, was likewise bringing little clout.

14 See Grob-Fitzgibbon (2016, 222). The same nowhere-to-go logic equally drove Wilson's 1967 application (365).

15 "Big units" is from Macmillan's speech on the Schuman "no customs" Plan in 1956, https://www.britishpathe.com/video/macmillan-speaks-on-european-no-customs-plan. At the 1962 Tory party conference, Macmillan spoke of the EEC's "doubling" Britain's influence (Grob-Fitzgibbon 2016, 295).

16 And while France had developed the atom bomb, it still had but a handful of them, together with the most rudimentary delivery system. The politics and policies of the Fifth Republic under de Gaulle appeared directionless as well, especially in foreign policy, where the Fouchet Plan failed to bear fruit (Thomas and Toye 2017).

17 "La voie qui un jour peut-être le conduira à s'amarrer au continent." The video and full transcript of the press conference is available online: https://fresques.ina.fr/de-gaulle/fiche-media/Gaulle00085/conference-de-presse-du-14-janvier-1963-sur-l-entree-de-la-grande-bretagne-dans-la-cee.html. De Gaulle and Macmillan previously held three summits to discuss a range of topics, including the possibility of Anglo-French nuclear cooperation.

18 Wilson's tiny majority in the House of Commons was another factor. Wilson was convinced that, under Gaitskell, the British troops would have duly gone to Vietnam (Pythian 2007, 74). For further discussion, see Parr (2006) and Hyam (2006, chap. 5).

19 The review came in the midst of an economic crisis and after a controversial decision to scrap the TSR-2 project in April 1965, a high-performing tactical strike and reconnaissance aircraft that marked the end of world-leading aerospace research, development, and procurement in the UK (Dorman 2001, 14; Self 2010, 166).

20 See Vickers (2011, 75). None of the texts in the 1960 archive argued for abandoning Britain's "residual imperial role" and turning to Europe as Britain's first and last line of defence.

21 The popularity of the phrase "East of Suez" originates in Rudyard Kipling's 1890 poem "Mandalay." In the mid-1960s, approximately 25 per cent of all *military* expenses fell on units deployed east of Suez, and this includes those engaged in violent conflicts in both Southeast and West

Asia. For discussions, see Rees (2001, 37–40); Ashton (2007); Stockwell (2018); and Cormac (2018).

22 The secrecy of the 1965 deal was a function of internal Labour politics (Vickers 2011, 72).

Chapter Three

1 For further details, see (Vucetic 2019c) and supplementary materials on the project website.

2 Titley's (1969) textbook, *Machines, Money and Men*, thematically covers the growth of England/Britain from its agricultural beginnings through the Industrial Revolution to the rise of organized labour and the welfare state. The narrative is that of progress through state action in a number of areas (education, women's and children's rights, industrial relations, and anti-slavery). The Georgian, Victorian, and Edwardian periods stand as significant Others.

3 Titley explained this well. "Farmers lost heavily" in the late nineteenth century due to the depression and foreign competition (Titley 1969, 59), while "the years from 1900 to 1914 were prosperous for the country as a whole but as prices rose faster than wages, the workers tended to be worse off" (196).

4 And in addition to being an impregnable fortress, Britain is able to mass-produce solid weaponry. Towards the end of the same movie, Göring asks German pilots what they need to win. "A squadron of Spitfires!," exclaims one.

5 See Self (2002, 4). A Gallup polls suggest that most Britons disagreed with him (Harrison 2009, 540).

6 And possibly as early as 1961 (Rees 2001, 38; Self 2002, 165).

7 Cited in Mangold (2001, 120). See also Darwin (2009, 638–9) and Deighton (2003). On Crossman more generally, see Honeyman (2007). On the erroneous beliefs in the sterling bloc's persistence, see Harrison (2009, 7–8, 40).

8 Quoted in Harrison (2009, 543). Macmillan's memoirs, published in 1972, repeat the same (Buettner 2016, 59n117).

9 Wilson's 1967 application was never actually withdrawn, and already in 1969 the UK was participating in the EEC via "European Political Co-

operation." For context, see Bell (1997, chaps. 10–11); and Vickers (2011, chaps 3–4).

10 Gibbins (2014, 25). This is a rich, focused study that covers the election manifestos of the Conservative, Labour, and Liberal parties in the February and October 1974 general elections, the House of Commons debate that occurred between 7 and 9 April 1975, memoirs and biographies, and declarations and press releases, including the referendum leaflets distributed by the Post Office in May.

11 By 1978, the spending would go down to 4.6 per cent of GDP (Harrison 2009, 107).

12 For context, see Smith (2017, chap. 2); and Saunders (2018).

13 Jenkins's campaign was harder than Heath's since the former contradicted the party's 1964 and, to a lesser extent, 1966 election manifestos, while also stoking extant tensions between the ex-Gaitskellites and ex-Bevanites.

14 And even though Nixon's withdrawal from Vietnam, the Watergate scandal, and Congressional threats to reduce US military presence in Europe in principle made it even harder to reinvest in the American alliance, UK leadership proceeded to do exactly that (Spelling 2009; Hughes and Robb 2013).

15 On the closeness and complexities of UK-Saudi relations, see Wearing (2018).

Chapter Four

1 On this analysis, see the project website and Vucetic and Orr (2019).

2 Also in the same newspaper: NHS, once the pride of British political ingenuity, was now characterized by "lengthy wait times and low quality service provision" (*Daily Mirror*, 15 October 1980, letter) and misallocation of scarce resources (*Daily Mirror*, 15 February 1980, letter).

3 In the UK, public schools are private, not run by the state.

4 Contrast this with "the heavy features" of Belgian and Dutch peasants, a "bloody wog," a "Chinese manservant," a "half-caste Indian woman," and a Spanish don with "that fierce Moorish rake to his thin features." Forsyth uses similar language to describe his characters (e.g., "the blond white Anglo-Saxon Protestant from the Midwest, and the dark, taciturn,

devout Roman Catholic who had come over from Krakow as a small boy").

5 The protagonist of the former, Stride, uncovers the existence of a power-ful network of unscrupulous men who rule the world behind the scenes, a group of "politicians and industrial leaders dedicated to restoring power to the hands of those fitted by training and upbringing to govern." Worse still, Caliph, the mastermind behind all of the international ter-rorism, is none other than Stride's boss, Dr Kingston Parker, the US counterterrorism tsar.

6 The article then proceeds to defend this argument by pointing out that the Thatcher premiership was no indication of female empowerment: "Women account for half of the country's population and 38 per cent of the workforce," but "only three per cent of our members of Parliament are female" and only "38 have served in Government and 12 have reached the Cabinet." In assigning blame, the article draws attention to the char-acter of the House of Commons – a "man's club – organized and run as such"– as well as to "women's attitudes to themselves"– namely, their failure to resist "the accepted tradition that a woman should tailor her ambitions to those of her husband."

7 The terrorist that Stride decides to kill at the beginning of the novel is a tall, blonde, bisexual, and US liberal college-educated German woman named Ingrid. Homosexuality is deviant in *McVicar* as well.

8 The wild popularity of this movie shows that the British were keen to lampoon religious illusions and double standards in 1980. The fact that the movie was banned by the Vatican and in some rural parts of the UK – Cornwall, for example – only added to its mainstream popularity.

9 The movie's palpable othering of the Third World did not contradict the satire against modernity, capitalism, colonial exploitation, and racism.

10 The phrase, long a familiar descriptor of postwar British politics and policy (e.g., Baylis 1989; Hennessy 1997), originates with Churchill, who used "Keep muddling through" interchangeably with "Keep buggering on" and "Keep plodding on," but was popularized by the American polit-ical scientist Charles Lindblom after the Second World War.

11 I was tempted to call this discourse "Thatcherism," given that this label had already appeared in British elite discourse in 1979, thanks to a pair of articles in *Marxism Today* – the famous one by Stuart Hall (1979), pub-

lished in January *before* Thatcher's electoral victory, and the one by Martin Jacques, which appeared in October. But because said journal catered almost exclusively to the well-educated members of the Communist Party of Great Britain, I opted for "New Britain" (even if this one smacks of Labour's 1964 election slogan, "A New Britain").

12 This discourse might have emerged three years later, when Labour, then under the leadership of Michael Foot, decided to run on a platform calling for a planned economy, the nationalization of industry, large-scale public spending, more power to unions, withdrawal from the EC, and unilateral disarmament.

13 The proposed cuts targeted the navy (Self 2010, 169).

14 The procurement woes with the V-Bomber force as well as the cancellations of the Blue Streak, TSR2, and Skybolt all led to the same conclusion: more cooperation with the US. France, in contrast, always insisted on developing indigenous systems, regardless of financial costs and technological disadvantages (Baylis and Stoddart 2015, 216–17; see also Pierre 1972; Heuser 1998; Ritchie 2012).

15 Thatcher (1982). Speaking to a rally in Bedfordshire in April, she even countered Acheson: "Britain has now found a role. It is in upholding international law and teaching the nations of the world how to live" (Harrison 2009, 547; Self 2010, 300).

16 This was a coup for a leader called the least popular prime minister since polling began in 1980, particularly since Labour was reduced to three seats in south England outside London.

17 See Falkland Islands debates in the House of Commons on 7 April and April 14 1982, respectively, *Hansard*. For a discussion of moral role claims, see Femenia (1996, 122). Note also that the Argentines were at first childlike and then, after April 2, dangerous (145).

18 The episode could be seen as part of a more continuous story of asking for exemptions going back to 1978 (Daddow 2015b; Smith 2017, chap. 3).

Chapter Five

1 For more detailed analysis, see Vucetic and Olver (2019).

2 The term is imperfect, but it usually refers to policies associated with anti-trade unionism, law and orderism, low taxation, privatization, and

more (Hall 1979). Though it does not appear in the archive for this year, the term "neoliberalism" could be used interchangeably with "Thatcherism" (Vernon 2017; Slobodian 2018).

3 The importance of this issue in British politics in 1980 cannot be emphasized enough. Shortly before the tax was due to come into force in England and Wales – it had already been introduced in Scotland – riots took place in London, contributing to the replacement of Thatcher by Major as well as the replacement of the poll tax by the more progressive but still controversial Council Tax.

4 Both the *Sun* and the *Daily Mirror* published op-eds addressing the rifts in industrial relations: autoworkers versus Ford (*Sun*, 15 January 1990); a local government worker union, NALGO, versus the government (*Sun*, 15 May 1990); and of course the miner strikes (*Daily Mirror*, 15 June 1990).

5 East of Suez had much to do with it: unlike in 1950 and 1960, when Britain's Middle East Land Forces still claimed control of a stretch of land from Libya to Aden to Bahrein, in 1990 the Middle East was no longer a top local in Churchill's first circle of British foreign policy.

6 This was made possible only by a creative reassemblage of units (Self 2010, 188). In contrast, Germany assisted the war effort only via "chequebook diplomacy," while France initially appeared uncertain (to the point at which its defence minister resigned). Note also that, while the 1991 British contingent constituted about 5 per cent of the total coalition forces, it was still larger than that sent to fight Hussein's troops in 2003.

7 For example, *Hansard*, 6 September 1990, vol. 177, col. 746, and 11 December 1990, vol. 182, col. 838. On Labour's tendency to follow the UN, see Pythian (2007).

8 Benn likewise took a number of opportunities to express concerns about the British troops serving under foreign command and to criticize the constitutional procedures that gave the government the power to decide whether to have any substantive debate on the issues of war. For example, *Hansard*, 15 January 1991, vol. 183, cols. 777–8.

9 The King review was not, in fact, a formal review (Self 2010, 171; see also Dorman 2001).

10 The policy difference was resolved only in the 1998 Strategic Defence Review (Dorman 2001, 23–4).

11 A number of observers have called this episode a (Conservative) foreign policy disaster on par with Suez (Simms 2001, 51–2, 132, 336).

12 Hansen (2006, chap. 7). Her analysis breaks the British debate on Bosnia into seven time periods over three and a half years, each corresponding to an exemplary debate in the House of Commons and a selection of articles published in the *Independent*, the *Guardian*, and the *Times*, for 120 articles in total (Hansen, 2006, 88–90).

13 The speech contained a number of positive evaluations of the EEC (Daddow 2015b, 79). For more context, see Daddow (2015b, 77–81); Smith (2017, chaps 3–4); Daddow, Gifford, and Wellings (2019).

14 For a summary, see O'Toole (2019, 17).

Chapter Six

1 This section draws on MIC's UK 2000 report (Grahame and Vucetic 2019) and its supplementary materials.

2 While Blair's pro-European stance had support from some tabloids in the late 1990s, many of his policy proposals – a call for "step-change" in UK-EU relations in September 1998, for example – typically hit the wall at the level of the media and public opinion. For more, see, inter alia, Self (2010, chap. 5); Daddow (2011); and Smith (2017, chap. 4).

3 The euro debate occurred in parallel with a more elite debate on the EU's "constitutional process." Launched at the European Council meeting in December 2001, this major reform reached an impasse by 2003, one of the causes being a shift in British policy towards ever greater reticence and obstructionism. Though a draft constitutional treaty came to reflect the anti-federalist position as entirely in line with the preferences of successive UK governments, the British negotiators publicly spoke against the EU's institutional progress. Again, for details, see Daddow (2011); and Smith (2017, chap. 4).

4 Quoted in Vucetic (2011b, 106). On the bridge metaphor, see Hill (2005, 397, 391) and compare to Daddow (2011, 226). More generally, see Gamble (2003) and Wallace (2005a).

5 For a more nuanced discussion, however, see Towle (2009, 142–55).

6 Kampfner (2003). The Blair government's first two military interven-

tions, against Hussein's Iraq in December 1998 and against Slobodan Milošević's Serbia in the spring of 1999, can also be seen as broadly consistent with the topography of British identity discussed above.

Conclusion

1 In a pilot study for this book, I looked at British identity in the year 2010 and found further evidence of this tendency. While the elites carried on as before, insisting on adaptability under the conditions of globalization, the masses were increasingly critical about a democracy in which politicians obsessed with how things were perceived, not with how they actually were, while all but ignoring those who suffered because of circumstances beyond their control (Vucetic 2016a).

2 This is not to say that factors such as the right-wing press or "issue capture" played a lesser role in shaping Britain's stance on European integration (Daddow 2011, 2015b; Copeland and Copsey 2017).

3 Daddow breaks post-1945 British European integration policy into several distinct outsider orientations: first as "supporter," then, after 1955, as "saboteur" and "rival," then, after 1960, as "supplicant," then, from 1973, as "insider."

4 In the sociological tradition of W.E.B. Du Bois and Immanuel Wallerstein, for example, see Taylor (2016 [1991]); McClintock (1995); Webster (2005); Go (2010); Tate (2012); Cain and Hopkins (2016); and Shilliam (2018).

5 Respectively, see Louis and Robinson (1994) and Grocott and Grady (2014), and Harrison (2009, 76–8) and Vucetic (2011d: 262–4). These and similar processes must be seen as a two-way street. UK support facilitated US foreign policy and defence (Self 2010: 110–11), much like British capitalism facilitated US financial power (Gamble 2003, 102-7; see also Strange 1971; Fichtner 2017; Green 2020).

6 Self (2010, 101). On previous disillusionments, see Rees (2001, 36).

7 Leaked to the *Economist* in June 1979, the report ignited much debate (Hill 2019, 189n20; Self 2010, 280).

8 A succession of Chatham House surveys in the 2010s confirms this as well (Colley 2019, 11; Gaskarth 2014; Edmunds 2014).

9 Clements (2018, chap. 3). Only one Gallup poll, conducted in 1969, seems

to show a clear preference towards the Commonwealth (34 per cent) over Europe (26 per cent) and the US (25 per cent). On British survey research in general, see Savage (2010).

10 Ordinary British people, as Clements (2018) shows in the third chapter of his book, were generally able to separate America and the Americans from developments such as American-led military actions and American-led globalization.

11 Yet, compared to other allies, such as France, Germany, and Japan, the US was always rated as significantly more valuable (Dumbrell 2006, 26).

12 In one poll taken in 1980, for example, 65 per cent of respondents said that in a referendum they would vote to leave, and only 26 per cent said they would vote to stay. Saunders (2018) provides ample polling history discussion.

13 See discussion in Gaskarth (2013, 68–9). More targeted surveys have yielded similar results, to the delight of Brexit-era advocates of new geo-political alliances (Bell and Vucetic 2019). More on this in a moment.

14 The expressed attitudes of young respondents were less militaristic than those of older respondents (Clements 2018, 176–7).

15 On the notion that the British public might be more "prudent" than the elites, see Towle (2009, 135–41) and Colley (2019, 12).

16 On quantitative content analysis as a subset of survey research, see Neuendorf (2004, 33). On the symbiotic and mutually dependent relationship between the press, public opinion, and national politics, see Todd (2016, 111); Strong (2017, 4-5, 15-6); and Copeland and Copsey (2017, 712).

17 Mitts's (2018) study of the role of mass media in cultivating and sustaining nationalist sentiment and right-wing politics in Israel relies on a content analysis of thousands of books published in that country between 1980 and 2008. Hills et al. (2019) mine online texts from millions of fiction and non-fiction books and newspapers published over the past two hundred years in the UK, US, Italy, and Germany to create a quantitative picture of historical subjective well-being, which they call the "National Valence Index."

18 See, for example, Bayram and Ta (2019), who use latent semantic analysis – better known by its abbreviation, LSA – to measure degrees of inter-subjectivity, with an eye of informing constructivist IR research.

19 This arguably both reflects and reinforces OST's preference for state identity over national identity. See also Mattern (2005); Hansen (2006); and Berenskoetter (2014). On other ontological security-providing entities, see Zarakol (2017).

20 Vucetic and Hopf (2020). Some liberal theories of (mass) democracy would readily agree with this perspective as well, as would some theories of nationalism. The other basic Gramscian view is that both civil and political society developments must be situated in the politics of *international* hegemony.

21 The everyday nationalism literature would also advise that researchers consider local news media, popular songs, ceremonies, cartoons, built environments and other materials, and spatial and performative dimensions of nationhood (Vucetic and Hopf 2020). On everyday jokes and ontological (in)security, see Vucetic (2004).

22 This is a simplification, for there are many different theoretical models for understanding the inherent instability of state/national identity: Giddensian (e.g., Ejdus 2020); Butlerian (e.g., Rossdale 2015); Lacanian (e.g., Vieira 2017); Honnethian (e.g., Murray 2019); and so on.

23 Doty (1996a, 13). On crisis theory and narrative theory in general, see Hay (1999). In OST, see Steele (2008); Subotić (2015); Kinnvall, Manners, and Mitzen (2018); and Ejdus (2020). For Gramscian discussions of the same, see Hozic and True (2016); and Babic (2020).

24 They are separate from the everyday irony and sarcasm of the postmodern age (*Economist* 1999).

25 Narratives and discourses are similar in the sense that they can both be defined as both conscious and unselfconscious practices of communication shared between elites and non-elite members of a state via consumption of the same media and same deployments of first- and third-person pronouns.

26 I underline the term "mainline." The narrative of "Led Astray" (by the US) in Colley's analysis does point to a major narrative gap between Britain's mass discourse in 2015, on the one hand, and postwar British society as reconstructed here, on the other (Colley 2019, 11–124).

27 In other words, emotions are intersubjective as opposed to purely subjective inner states (Koschut et al. 2017). Note also that IR sometimes treats emotions as synonymous with affect and feelings. Technically the former

are non-reflective, unselfconscious experiences of emotions – therefore akin to Williams's structures of feeling and Bourdieu's *doxa*, mentioned in the introduction – while the latter are available for reflection. Either way, emotional reactions have implications for world politics.

28 MPs Peyton and Luce, House of Commons 7 April 1982. Cited in Femenia (1996, 137). Some, like MP George Foulkes, spread the blame more broadly: "We are sending an aircraft carrier that has already been sold to meet cash limits from a port that is to be closed and with 500 sailors holding redundancy notices in their pockets. I find that humiliating, too" (House of Commons, 3 April 1982).

29 In fact, the very image of the Royal Navy departing to wage the war re-awakened the emotions of pride (Femenia 1996, 188). The image on the cover of McCourt's (2014a) book aptly captures this moment.

30 For different perspectives, see Hozic and True (2016); Henderson, Wincott, and Jones (2017); Jessop (2017); Oliver (2018); Browning (2018); O'Toole (2019); Oppermann, Beasley, and Kaarbo (2019); and Babic (2020). The idea of interregnum comes from Oswald Spengler's *Decline of the West*, published between 1918 and 1923.

31 The exact phrase is from a video he posted via his Twitter account on 10 November 2019: https://twitter.com/BorisJohnson/status/11935628894 84951552. The actual EU-Canada deal, which came into force provisionally in 2017, removes *most* tariffs on goods only. Johnson's goal is a "super-plus" deal that removes *all* tariffs and, crucially for the UK economy, covers the service sector. These negotiating aims will *not* be met.

32 The thesis is central to Wallace's argument (1991, 70), for example.

33 The slogan "Global Britain" was used before, not only by Gordon Brown but also by Frederick Forsyth, the author of the blockbusters we encountered in the 1980 and 1990 archives (Haseler 2007, 215). The de-linking of the EU from the globe was illogical but arguably effective in rhetorical terms. Below I address a postcolonial conceptualization of global Britain (Barkawi and Brighton 2013, 1,119).

34 On this initiative, see Bell and Vucetic (2019). Though dreams of settler colonial unity always remained just that, they nevertheless inspired countless discourses, policies, institutions, and practices that can be observed even today (Gamble 2003; Wallace 2005; Vucetic 2011b, 2020; Harris 2015; Fichtner 2017; Wellings 2019; Legrand 2020; Holland 2020).

35 Saunders (2019), emphasis in the original. The author adds that empire nostalgics were only a small minority in the Leave camp and that many Black and Asian voters were attracted to a Britain oriented more towards the Commonwealth than the EU.

36 A 2019 YouGov poll found that 50 per cent of Leave voters expressed pride in the Empire, and 51 per cent felt that Britain's former colonies were better off under British rule, whereas the equivalent figures for Remain voters were 20 per cent and 22 per cent, respectively. The same poll indicates that in Europe the Dutch are "most proud" of their former empire, at 50 per cent, and the Germans "least proud," at 9 per cent (Smith 2020). Once again, surveys are a rather rough tool for gauging how people understand the imperial past (cf. Runnymede Trust and the TIDE Project 2019).

37 On smallness, see also Whittaker (2017) and Colley (2019). On "the Dunkirk spirit," see Barnett (1982, 48); Gilroy (2004, 96); Daddow (2006, 320); Harrison (2009, 534; 2010, 548); Barkawi and Bright (2013, 1,115); and Wellings (2019, chap. 6). On nostalgia, see, inter alia, Gilroy (2004); Grob-Fitzgibbon (2016); Smith and Gray (2016); Namusoke (2016); Bhambra (2016); Beaumont (2017); Barnett (2017); Kenny (2017); Daddow (2019); and Wellings (2019).

38 This is the title of a 2012 Centre for Policy Studies pamphlet penned by Dominic Raab, who in 2019 became the foreign minister and deputy prime minister (Raab 2012).

39 On future UK-EU relations, see Oliver (2018); Martill and Sus (2018); and Whitman (2019).

40 On race and Brexit, see Bhambra (2016); Mondon and Winter (2018); Shilliam (2018, chaps. 7–8); and Valluvan (2019). On Powellism, see Gamble (2003, chap. 2); Schofield (2013; 2019); and Kenny and Pearce (2018, chap. 4).

41 Quoted in Allan, Vucetic, and Hopf (2018, 863). On the "utterly distinct" foreign policy views of Farage voters, see Gaston (2019). On the global imaginaries of the newest "New Right," see Abrahamson et al. (2020).

42 On the Singapore imaginaries, see Wellings (2019, 8). On the Atlas network and Johnson, see Lawrence et al. (2019), and compare Tooze (2017) and Eaton (2018). The network's website denies links to *Atlas Shrugged*, Ayn Rand's 1957 libertarian fantasy, but neither confirms nor denies links

to the Atlas Command, a shadowy force for good appearing in Smith's *Wild Justice*, as discussed in chapter 4. Smith's novel was published in 1979, two years before the first iteration of the Atlas Network.

43 The video of the interview is available here: https://twitter.com/BBC Politics/status/1217000741153464320. A day earlier in the House of Commons, his foreign minister, Raab, argued in favour of "expanding our global horizons to grasp the enormous opportunities of free trade" and "reinforc[ing] our national mission as a force for good in the world." See http://www.ukpol.co.uk/dominic-raab-2020-statement-on-britain-in-the-world/.

44 To be sure, "progressive Canadian foreign policy" is a matter of wish-fulfilment and illusion, too (Vucetic 2017c).

45 Unlike the 1980s Labour, Corbyn's Labour was unprepared for such a radical rethink. See its 2017 and 2019 manifestos. On defence policy alternatives, see Rogers (2006); Ritchie (2012); McCourt (2014b); and Wearing (2018).

Appendix A

1 For further details, see Srdjan Vucetic, "The United Kingdom, 1950-2000 —Primary Texts," 23 June 2016. Available at https://srdjanvucetic.word press.com/research/id/srdj-postwar-uk-sources-final/. We assumed letters to editors to be genuine.

2 Connolly and Phillips (1989), for example. For further details, see Vucetic (2020a).

3 British interest in translated fiction was, in any case, low throughout.

4 For advice, I am grateful to Professor Shafquat Towheed, director of the Book History Research Group and the UK Reading Experience Database, the Open University.

5 This is based on Bennett and Woollacott (1987, 26) and Benson (2015, 17). Analyses of Bond as a nationalist, anti-declinist fantasy are of course plentiful (e.g., Buettner 2016; Funnell and Dodds 2017). We relied on our own coding.

6 Neither is to be confused with "the steady longterm sellers" such as the Bible, Tolkien's three-volume fantasy *The Lord of the Rings* (1954–55), and, arguably, George Orwell's *Animal Farm* (1945). In all cases we selected

novels dealing with contemporary themes. To go with the year 1960 again, we were initially drawn to *Lady Chatterley's Lover* by D.H. Lawrence, a book that sold over 200,000 paperback copies within weeks following the infamous obscenity trial in November–October of that year. However, this was a Penguin paperback of a book published in 1928. Our runners-up included John Braine's *Room at the Top* (1957), which sold well thanks to a lucrative paperback-movie tie-in in 1959; David Storey's *This Sporting Life*, which won the 1960 Macmillan Fiction Award; and Nevil Shute's *On the Beach*, a novel first published in 1957 that sold well in the tens of thousands due to the author's death in 1960 and the story's cinamatization in 1959, but without quite reaching the numbers of the Fleming and Christie books.

7 On why *Gladiator* is a British and not merely "another Hollywood movie," see Dalby (2008, 443).

References

Speeches

British Political Speech, online archive, http://www.britishpolitical
speech.org/.
The Official Report (*Hansard*), https://hansard.parliament.uk/.

Newspapers

Daily Express
Daily Mail
Daily Mirror
Sun

Textbooks

Barker, William Alan, G.R.St Aubyn, and Richard Lawrence Ollard. 1960. *A General History of England, 1832–1960*. 2nd ed. London: A & C Black.
Carter, .H., and R.A.F. Mears. 1948. *A History of Britain, 1876-1953*. 2nd ed. Oxford: Clarendon Press,
Connolly, P., and Barry Phillips. 1989. *Britain, 1900–1939*. Southwick: Spartacus Educational Publishers.
Culpin, C., and Brian Turner. 1997. *Making Modern Britain: British Social and Economic History from the 18th century to the Present Day*. London: Collins Educational.
Hill, C.P. 1977. *British Economic and Social History, 1700–1975*. 4th ed. London: Edward Arnold.

Kavanagh, Dennis, and Peter Morris. 1989. *Consensus Politics from Attlee to Thatcher*. 1st ed. Oxford: Basil Blackwell.

Larkin, Patrick John. 1964. *English History for Certificate Classes, 1789–1939*. London: Hulton Educational Publications.

May, Trevor. 1987. *An Economic and Social History of Britain, 1760–1970*. 1st ed. Harlow: Longman.

Rayner, R. 1948. *A Short History of Britain*. Harlow: Longman.

Sked, Alex, and Chris Cook. 1979. *Post-War Britain: A Political History*, 1st ed. Sussex: The Harvester Press.

Strong, Charles Frederick. 1956. *History of Britain and the World, Book Five: The Twentieth Century and the Contemporary World*. 2nd ed. [S.I.], London: U.L.P.

Titley, D.P. 1969. *Machines, Money and Men. Economic and Social History of Great Britain, 1700–1960's*. London: Blonde Educational.

Walsh, Ben. 1996. GCSE *Modern World History*. 1st ed. London: John Murray Pubs Ltd.

Novels

Christie, Agatha. 1960. *4.50 from Paddington*. London: Fontana, paperback.

– 1967. *Endless Night*. London: Collins Crime Club, paperback.

– 2007. *A Murder Is Announced*. New York: Harper (originally: London: Collins Crime Club, 1950).

Fleming, Ian. 1960. *Dr No*. London: Pan Books, paperback.

Forsyth, Frederick. 1979. *The Devil's Alternate* London: Hutchinson.

– 1989. *The Negotiator*. London: Bantam Press.

MacLean, Alistair. 1968. *Force 10 from Navarone*. London: Collins Crime Club, paperback.

Rowling, J.K. 1997. *Harry Potter and the Philosopher's Stone*, London: Bloomsbury.

– 2000. *Harry Potter and the Goblet of Fire*. London: Bloomsbury.

Shute, Nevil. 1971. *A Town Like Alice*. London: Heinemann, (originally: London: Heinemann, 1950).

Smith, Wilbur. 1979. *Wild Justice*. London: Heinemann.

– 1989. *A Time to Die*. London: Heinemann.

Movies

Battle for Britain (dir. Guy Hamilton), 1970.
The Blue Lamp (dir. Basil Dearden), 1950.
Chicken Run (dir. Peter Lord and Nick Park), 2000.
Doctor in Love (dir. Ralph Thomas), 1960.
Gladiator (dir. Ridley Scott), 2000.
The Krays (dir. Peter Medak), 1990.
Life of Brian (dir. Terry Jones), 1980.
McVicar (dir. Tom Clegg), 1980.
On Her Majesty's Secret Service (dir. Peter R. Hunt), 1970.
Sink the Bismarck! (dir. Lewis Gilbert), 1960.
Shirley Valentine (dir. Lewis Gilbert), 1990.
What the Butler Saw (dir. Godfrey Grayson), 1950.

Articles and Books

Abrahamsen, Rita, Jean-François Drolet, Alexandra Gheciu, Karin Narita, Srdjan Vucetic, and Michael C. Williams. 2020. "Confronting the International Political Sociology of the New Right." Collective Discussion. *International Political Sociology* 14 (1): 94–107.

Adamthwaite, Anthony. 1985. "Britain and the World, 1945–9: The View from the Foreign Office." *International Affairs* 61 (2): 223–35.

Aggestam, Lisbeth. 2012. *European Foreign Policy and the Quest for a Global Role: Britain, France and Germany.* London: Routledge.

Aldrich, Richard J. 2001. *The Hidden Hand: Britain, America and Cold War Secret Intelligence.* London: John Murray Publishers.

Allan, Bentley. 2016. "A Method for Uncovering National Identity." In *Making Identity Count: Building a National Identity Database*, ed. Ted Hopf and Bentley Allan, 20–48. Oxford: Oxford University Press.

Allan, Bentley, Srdjan Vucetic, and Ted Hopf. 2018. "The Distribution of Identity and the Future of International Order: China's Hegemonic Prospects." *International Organization* 72 (4): 839–69.

Ashton, S.R. 2007. "British Government Perspectives on the Commonwealth, 1964–71: An Asset or a Liability?" *Journal of Imperial and Commonwealth History* 35 (1): 73–94.

Aulich, James, ed. 1992. *Framing the Falklands War: Nationhood, Culture and Identity*. Milton Keynes: Open University Press.

Babic, M. 2020. "Let's Talk about the Interregnum: Gramsci and the Crisis of the Liberal World Order." *International Affairs*. https://doi.org/10.1093/ia/iiz254.

Ball, Simon J. 1996. "Macmillan and British Defence Policy." In *Harold Macmillan and Britain's World Role*, ed. Richard Aldous and Sabine Lee, 67–96. London: Palgrave Macmillan.

Bell, Duncan. 2019. "Anglospheres: Empire Redivivus?" In *The Anglosphere: Continuity, Dissonance, Location*, ed. Ben Wellings and Andrew Mycock, 38–55. Oxford: Oxford University Press.

Bell, Duncan, and S. Vucetic. 2019. "Brexit, CANZUK, and the Legacy of Empire." *British Journal of Politics and International Relations* 21 (2): 367–82.

Bailkin, Jordanna. 2012. *The Afterlife of Empire*. Berkeley: University of California Press.

Barkawi, Tarak, and Shane Brighton. 2013. "Brown Britain: Post-Colonial Politics and Grand Strategy." *International Affairs* 89 (5): 1109–23.

Baker, David. 2002. "Elite Discourse and Popular Opinion on European Union: British Exceptionalism Revisited." *Politique Européenne* 2 (6): 18–35.

Barker, Elisabeth. 1983. *The British between the Superpowers, 1945–50*. London: Macmillan.

Barkin, J. Samuel, and Laura Sjoberg, eds. 2017. *Interpretive Quantification: Methodological Explorations for Critical and Constructivist IR*. Ann Arbor: University of Michigan Press.

Barnett, Anthony. 1982. *Iron Britannia*. London: Busby.

– 2017. *The Lure of Greatness*. London: Unbound.

Barnett, Correlli. 1972. *The Collapse of British Power*. London: Methune.

Basham, Victoria M. 2018. "Liberal Militarism as Insecurity, Desire and Ambivalence: Gender, Race and the Everyday Geopolitics of War." *Security Dialogue* 49 (1–2): 32–43.

Baylis, John. 1989. *British Defence Policy: Striking the Right Balance*. Basingstoke: Macmillan.

Baylis, John, and Alan Macmillan. 1993. "The British Global Strategy Paper of 1952." *Journal of Strategic Studies* 16 (2): 200–26.

Baylis, John, and Kristan Stoddart. 2015. *The British Nuclear Experience: The Roles of Beliefs, Culture, and Identity*. Oxford: Oxford University Press.

Bayram, Burcu, and Vivian Ta. 2019. "Measuring Common Knowledge: Latent Semantic Analysis, Linguistic Synchrony, and Common Knowledge in International Relations." *Sage Journals* (International Relations), 8 September 2019, 1–24.

Beaumont, Paul. 2014. "Performing Nuclear Peace: How Nuclear Weapons Have Kept Britain Great from Thatcher to Blair." Master's thesis, Norwegian University of Life Sciences.

– 2017. "Brexit, Retrotopia and the Perils of Post-Colonial Delusions." *Global Affairs* 3 (4–5): 379–90.

Beck, Peter J., 2009. "'The Less Said about Suez the Better': British Governments and the Politics of Suez's History, 1956–67." *English Historical Review* 124 (508): 605–40.

Bell, Duncan. 2007. *The Idea of Greater Britain: Empire and the Future of World Order, 1860-1900.* Princeton: Princeton University Press.

Bell, Duncan, and Srdjan Vucetic. 2019, "Brexit, CANZUK, and the Legacy of Empire." *British Journal of Politics and International Relations* 21 (2): 367–82.

Bell, P.M.H. 1997. *France and Britain, 1940–1994: The Long Separation.* London: Longman.

Bennett, Tony, and Janet Woollacott. 1987. *Bond and Beyond: The Political Career of a Popular Hero.* London: Macmillan Education.

Benson, Raymond. 2015. *The James Bond Bedside Companion.* London: Crossroad Press.

Berenskoetter, Felix. 2014. "Parameters of a National Biography." *European Journal of International Relations* 20 (1): 262–88.

Bevir, Mark, and Oliver Daddow. 2015. "Interpreting Foreign Policy: National, Comparative and Regional Studies." *International Relations* 29 (3): 273–87.

Bevir, Mark, Oliver Daddow, and Ian Hall. 2013. "Introduction: Interpreting British Foreign Policy." *British Journal of Politics and International Relations* 15, 2: 163–74.

Bevir, Mark, Oliver Daddow, and Pauline Schnapper. 2015. "Introduction: Interpreting British European Policy." *Journal of Common Market Studies* 53 (1): 1–17.

Bew, John. 2016. *Citizen Clem: A Biography of Attlee, Winner of the Orwell Prize.* London: Hachette UK.

Bhambra, Gurminder K. 2016. "Viewpoint: Brexit, Class and British 'National' Identity." *Discover Society.* https://discoversociety.org/2016/07/05/viewpoint-brexit-class-and-british-national-identity/.

Billig, Michael. 1995. *Banal Nationalism*. London: Sage.

Blackwell, Michael. 1993. *Clinging to Grandeur: British Attitudes and Foreign Policy in the Aftermath of the Second World War*. Westport, CT: Greenwood Press.

Blagden, David. 2019. "Two Visions of Greatness: Roleplay and Realpolitik in UK Strategic Posture." *Foreign Policy Analysis* 15 (4): 470–91.

Boffey, Daniel. 2017. "Brexit broadside: British Officials Bristle at Danish Scorn." *Guardian*, 14 June. https://www.theguardian.com/politics/2017/jun/14/road-to-brexit-is-paved-with-amusement-danish-and-brave-faces-british.

Breuning, Marijke. 1995. "Words and Deeds: Foreign Assistance Rhetoric and Policy Behavior in the Netherlands, Belgium, and the United Kingdom." *International Studies Quarterly* 39 (2): 235–54.

Brown, Gordon. 2004. Speech by the Rt Hon Gordon Brown MP, Chancellor of the Exchequer, at the British Council annual lecture, 7 July. On file with the author.

Browning, Christopher S. 2018. "Brexit, Existential Anxiety and Ontological (In)security." *European Security* 27 (3): 336–55.

Buettner, Elizabeth. 2016. *Europe after Empire: Decolonisation, Society, and Culture*. Cambridge: Cambridge University Press.

Burkett, Jodi. 2013. *Constructing Post-Imperial Britain: Britishness, "Race" and the Radical Left in the 1960s*. London: Palgrave.

Burton, Antoinette. 1997. "Who Needs the Nation? Interrogating 'British' History." *Journal of Historical Sociology* 10 (3): 227–48.

Cain, P.J., and A.G. Hopkins. 2016. *British Imperialism, 1688–2000*. 3rd ed. London: Routledge.

Campbell, Duncan. 1986. *The Unsinkable Aircraft Carrier: American Military Power in Britain*. London: Michael Joseph.

Chalmers, Malcolm. 1985. *Paying for Defence Military Spending and British Decline*. London: Pluto Press.

Chandler, David. 2003. "Rhetoric without Responsibility: The Attraction of 'Ethical' Foreign Policy." *British Journal of Politics and International Relations* 5 (3): 295–316.

Charmley, John. 1995. *Churchill's Grand Alliance: The Anglo-American Special Relationship, 1940–57*. New York: Harcourt Brace.

Clarke, Peter. 2004 [1996]. *Hope and Glory: Britain 1900–1990*. London: Penguin Press.

Clarke, Nick, Will Jennings, Jonathan Moss, and Gerry Stoker. 2018. *The Good Politician: Folk Theories, Political Interaction and the Rise of Anti-Politics*. Cambridge: Cambridge University Press.

Clements, Ben. 2018. *British Public Opinion on Foreign and Defence Policy: 1945–2017*. London: Routledge.

Colley, Linda. 2009. *Britons: Forging the Nation, 1707–1837*. New Haven, CT: Yale University Press.

Colley, Thomas. 2019. *Always at War: British Public Narratives of War*. Ann Arbor: University of Michigan Press.

Cormac, Rory. 2018. *Disrupt and Deny: Spies, Special Forces, and the Secret Pursuit of British Foreign Policy*. Oxford: Oxford University Press.

Cormac, Rory, and Richard Aldrich. 2018. "Covert Action Is Theatre – And the Curtain Isn't Coming Down Yet." *OUP Blog*. https://blog.oup.com/2018/05/covert-action-secrecy-security/.

Copeland, Paul, and Nathaniel Copsey. 2017. "Rethinking Britain and the European Union: Politicians, the Media and Public Opinion Reconsidered." *Journal of Common Market Studies* 55 (4): 709–26

Craig, Campbell, and Sergey Radchenko. 2008. *The Atomic Bomb and the Origins of the Cold War*. New Haven: Yale University Press.

Croft, Stuart. 2001a. "Introduction." In *Britain and Defence, 1945–2000: A Policy Re-Evaluation*, ed. Stuart Croft, Andrew Dorman, Wyn Rees, and Matthew Uttley, 1–8. London: Pearson Education Limited.

– 2001b. "Britain's Nuclear Weapons Discourse." In *Britain and Defence 1945–2000: A Policy Re-Evaluation*, ed. Stuart Croft, Andrew Dorman, Wyn Rees, and Matthew Uttley. 69–87. London: Pearson Education Limited.

– 2012. *Securitizing Islam: Identity and the Search for Security*. Cambridge: Cambridge University Press.

Crouzet, François. 2004. "L'Entente cordiale: Réalités et mythes d'un siècle de relations franco-britanniques." *Études Anglaises* 57 (3): 310–20.

Curtis, Mark. 1995. *The Ambiguities of Power: British Foreign Policy since 1945*. London: Zed Books.

– 2003. *Web of Deceit: Britain's Real Role in the World*. London: Random House.

Daddow, Oliver. 2004. *Britain and Europe since 1945: Historiographical Perspectives on Integration*. Manchester: Manchester University Press.

– 2006. "Euroscepticism and the Culture of the Discipline of History." *Review of International Studies* 32 (2): 309–28.

– 2011. *New Labour and the European Union: Blair and Brown's Logic of History*. Manchester: Manchester University.

– 2015a. "Constructing a 'Great' Role for Britain in an Age of Austerity: Interpreting Coalition Foreign Policy, 2010–2015." *International Relations* 29, (3): 303–18.

– 2015b. "Interpreting the Outsider Tradition in British European Policy Speeches from Thatcher to Cameron." *Journal of Common Market Studies* 53 (1): 71–88.

– 2018. "Brexit and British Exceptionalism: The Impossible Challenge for Remainers." *LSE Brexit*, 10 April. http://blogs.lse.ac.uk/brexit/2018/04/10/brexit-and-british-exceptionalism-the-impossible-challenge-for-remainers/.

– 2019. "GlobalBritain™: The Discursive Construction of Britain's Post-Brexit World Role." *Global Affairs* 5: 5–22.

Daddow, Oliver, and Jamie Gaskarth. 2011. "Introduction: Blair, Brown and New Labour's Foreign Policy, 1997–2010." In *British Foreign Policy: The New Labour Years*, ed. Oliver Daddow and Jamie Gaskarth, 1–21. London: Springer.

Daddow, Oliver, Christopher Gifford, and Ben Wellings. 2019. "The Battle of Bruges: Margaret Thatcher, the Foreign Office and the Unravelling of British European Policy." *Political Research Exchange* 1 (1): OnlineFirst, doi:10.1080/2474736X.2019.1643681.

Dalby, Simon. 2008. "Warrior Geopolitics: *Gladiator*, *Black Hawk Down* and *The Kingdom of Heaven*." *Political Geography* 27 (4): 439–55.

Danchev, Alex. 1993. *Oliver Franks: Founding Father*. New York: Clarendon Press.

– 1998. *On Specialness*. London: Macmillan.

Darwin, John. 1991. *The End of the British Empire: The Historical Debate*. Oxford: Basil Blackwell.

– 2009. *The Empire Project: The Rise and Fall of the British World-System, 1830–1970*. Cambridge: Cambridge University Press.

Gun, Katharine. 2020. "Britain's Secret State and the Need for Whistle-Blowing." *Declassified UK*, 5 March. http://declassifieduk.org.

Deighton, Anne. 1990. "Missing the Boat: Britain and Europe, 1945–61." *Contemporary British History* 3 (3): 15–17.

– 2003. "The Labour Party, Public Opinion and the 'Second Try' in 1967." In *Harold Wilson and European Integration: Britain's Second Application to Join the EEC*, ed. Oliver Daddow, 49–51. London: Frank Cass Publishers.

– 2013. "Ernest Bevin." In *Mental Maps in the Early Cold War Era, 1945–1968*, ed. Ralph Levering. London: Palgrave Macmillan.

Dell, Edmund. 1995. *The Schuman Plan and the British Abdication of Leadership in Europe*. Oxford: Clarendon Press.

Dillon, G.M. 1989. *The Falklands, Politics and War*. London: Macmillan.

Dobson, Alan. P 1995. *Anglo-American Relations in the Twentieth Century: Of Friendship, Conflict and the Rise and Decline of Superpowers*. London: Routledge.

Dobson, Alan, and Steve Marsh, eds. 2017. *Churchill and the Anglo-American Special Relationship*. London: Routledge.

Dockrill, Saki. 2002. *Britain's Retreat from East of Suez: The Choice between Europe and the World?* London: Palgrave Macmillan.

Dorman, Andrew. 2001. "Crises and Reviews in British Defence Policy." In *Britain and Defence, 1945–2000: A Policy Re-Evaluation*, ed. Stuart Croft, Andrew Dorman, Wyn Rees, and Matthew Uttley, 9–28. London: Routledge.

Doty, Roxanne Lynn. 1996a. *Imperial Encounters: The Politics of Representation in North-South Relations* Minneapolis: University of Minnesota Press.

– 1996b. "Sovereignty and the Nation: Constructing the Boundaries of National Identity." In *State Sovereignty as Social Construct*, ed. T.J. Biersteker and Cynthia Weber, 121–47. Cambridge: Cambridge University Press.

Dumbrell, John. 2006. *A Special Relationship: Anglo-American Relations from the Cold War to Iraq*. 2nd ed. London: Macmillan.

Dunne, Tim. 2004. "'When the Shooting Starts': Atlanticism in British Security Strategy." *International Affairs* 80 (5): 893–909.

Dyson, Stephen Benedict. 2009. *The Blair Identity: Leadership and Foreign Policy*. Manchester: Manchester University Press.

Eaton, George. 2018. "How the Right's Brexit Dream Died," *New Statesman*, 28 November. https://www.newstatesman.com/politics/uk/2018/11/how-right-s-brexit-dream-died.

Economist. 1999. "British Irony: A Quiet Joke at Your Expense." 16 December. https://www.economist.com/christmas-specials/1999/12/16/a-quiet-joke-at-your-expense.

Edgerton, David. 2005. *Warfare State: Britain 1920–1970.* Cambridge: Cambridge University Press.

– 2018a. "The Idea of Deep Continuity in British History Is Absurd: We've Always Been in Flux." *Guardian*, 18 November. Retrieved on 18 November from https://www.theguardian.com/commentisfree/2018/nov/18/brexit-delusional-conmen-britain-never-never-land-eu.

– 2018b. *The Rise and Fall of the British Nation: A Twentieth-Century History.* London: Allen Lane.

Edmunds, Timothy. 2014. "Complexity, Strategy and the National Interest." *International Affairs* 90 (3): 525–39.

Edmunds, Timothy, Jamie Gaskarth, and Robin Porter. 2014. *British Foreign Policy and the National Interest: Identity, Strategy and Security.* Basingstoke: Palgrave Macmillan

Ellison, James. 2007. "Britain and Europe." In *A Companion to Contemporary Britain 1939–2000*, ed. Paul Addison and Harriet Jones, 517–38. Oxford: Blackwell Publishing.

Ejdus, Filip. 2020. *Crisis and Ontological Insecurity Serbia's Anxiety over Kosovo's Secession.* London: Palgrave Macmillan.

English, Richard, and Michael Kenny. 2000. "Decline or Declinism?" In *Rethinking British Decline*, ed. Richard English and Michael Kenny, 279–300. Basingstoke: Macmillan.

Femenia, Nora. 1996. *National Identity in Times of Crises: the scripts of the Falklands-Malvinas War.* New York: Nova Science Publishers.

Fichtner, Jan. 2017. "Perpetual Decline or Persistent Dominance? Uncovering Anglo-America's True Structural Power in Global Finance." *Review of International Studies* 43 (1): 3–28.

Flyvbjerg, Bent. 2006. "Five Misunderstandings about Case Studies." *Qualitative Inquiry* 12 (2): 219–45.

Foster, Kevin. 1997. "To Serve and Protect: Textualizing the Falklands Conflict." *Cultural Studies* 11 (2): 235–52.

Fox, Jon, and Cynthia Miller-Idriss. 2008. "Everyday Nationhood." *Ethnicities* 8 (4): 536–63.

Fox, William T.R. 1980. "The Super-Powers Then and Now." *International Journal* 35 (3): 417–36.

Franks, Oliver. 1954. "Britain and the Tide of World Affairs, Reith Lecture No 1." http://downloads.bbc.co.uk/rmhttp/radio4/transcripts/1954_reith1.pdf.

Freedman, Lawrence. 1999. *The Politics of British Defence*. Hampshire: Macmillan Press.

Freedman, Lawrence, and Michael Clarke, eds. 1991. *Britain in the World*. Cambridge: Cambridge University Press.

Funnell, Lisa, and Klaus Dodds. 2017. *Geographies, Genders and Geopolitics of James Bond*. London: Palgrave Macmillan.

Gallagher, John, and Ronald Robinson. 1953. "The Imperialism of Free Trade." *Economic History Review* 6 (1): 1–15.

Gamble, Andrew. 2000. "Theories and Explanations of British Decline." In *Rethinking British Decline*, ed. Richard English and Michael Kenny. New York: St Martin's Press.

– 2003. *Between Europe and America: The Future of British Politics*, Basingstoke: Palgrave Macmillan.

Gaskarth, Jamie. 2011. "Identity and New Labour's Strategic Foreign Policy Thinking." In *British Foreign Policy: The New Labour Years*, ed. Oliver Daddow and Jaime Gaskarth, 84–9. Basingstoke: Palgrave Macmillan.

– 2013. *British Foreign Policy: Crises, Conflicts and Future Challenges*. Cambridge: Polity.

– 2014. "The National Interest and Britain's Role in the World." In *British Foreign Policy and the National Interest: Identity, Strategy and Security*, ed. Timothy Edmunds, Jamie Gaskarth, and Robin Porter, 42–65. Basingstoke: Palgrave Macmillan.

– 2016. "Intervention, Domestic Contestation, and Britain's National Role Conceptions," in *Domestic Role Contestation, Foreign Policy and International Relations*, ed. Christian Cantir and Juliet Kaarbo, 105–21. London: Routledge.

Gaston, Sophie. 2019. "The Impact of Returning UKIP Voters on Conservative Foreign Policy." *British Foreign Policy Group blog*. 5 November. https://bfpg.co.uk/2019/11/ukip-homecoming-foreign-policy/.

Gaston, Sophie, and Sacha Hilhorst. 2018. *At Home in One's Past: Nostalgia as a Cultural and Political Force in Britain, France and Germany*. London: Demos.

Gibbins, Justin. 2014. *Britain, Europe and National Identity: Self and Other in International Relations*. London: Palgrave Macmillan.

Gilroy, Paul. 2004. *After Empire: Melancholia or Convivial Culture?* London: Routledge.

Grahame, Alyssa M., and Srdjan Vucetic. 2019. "Making Identity Count: UK 2000." *SocArXiv*. https://osf.io/eyd4b/.

Green, Jeremy. 2020. *The Political Economy of the Special Relationship: Anglo-American Development from the Gold Standard to the Financial Crisis*. Princeton, NJ: Princeton University Press.

Grimmer, Justin, and Brandon Stewart. 2013. "Text as Data: The Promise and Pitfalls of Automatic Content Analysis Methods for Political Texts." *Political Analysis* 21 (3): 267–97.

Grocott, Chris, and Jo Grady. 2014. "'Naked Abroad': The Continuing Imperialism of Free Trade." *Capital and Class* 38 (3): 541–62.

Grob-Fitzgibbon, Benjamin. 2016. *Continental Drift: Britain and Europe from the End of Empire to the Rise of Euroscepticism*. Cambridge: Cambridge University Press.

Go, Julian. 2011. *Patterns of Empire: The British and American Empires, 1688–Present*. Cambridge: Cambridge University Press.

Guzzini, Stefano. 2012. "The Framework of Analysis: Geopolitics Meets Foreign Policy Identity Crises." In *The Return of Geopolitics in Europe? Social Mechanisms and Foreign Policy Identity Crises*, ed. S. Guzzini, 45–74. Cambridge: Cambridge University Press.

Hadfield-Amkhan, Amelia. 2010. *British Foreign Policy, National Identity and Neoclassical Realism*. London: Rowman and Littlefield.

Haglund, David G. 2019. *The US "Culture Wars" and the Anglo-American Special Relationship*. New York: Palgrave Macmillan.

Hall, Ian. 2012. *Dilemmas of Decline: British Intellectuals and World Politics, 1945–75*. Berkeley: University of California Press.

Hall, Stuart. January 1979. "The Great Moving Right Show." *Marxism Today*, 14–20.

– 1981. "Notes on Deconstructing 'the Popular.'" In *People's History and Socialist Theory*, ed. Raphael Samuel, 227–40. London: Routledge.

– 1996a. "Gramsci's Relevance for the Study of Race and Ethnicity." In *Stuart Hall: Critical Dialogues in Cultural Studies*, ed. David Morley and Kuan-Hsing Chen, 411–40. London: Routledge.

– 1996b. "The Question of Cultural Identity." in *Modernity: An Introduction to Modern Societies*, ed. Stuart Hall, David Held, Don Hubert, and Kenneth Thompson, 595–634. Oxford: Blackwell.

– 1996c "The West and the Rest: Discourse and Power." In *Modernity: An Introduction to Modern Societies*, ed. Stuart Hall, David Held, Don Hubert, and Kenneth Thompson, 184–227. Cambridge: Blackwell.

– 2000. "Reflections on British Decline: An Interview." In *Rethinking British Decline*, ed. Richard English and Michael Kenny. 104–16. Basingstoke: Macmillan.

Hansen, L. 2006. *Security as Practice: Discourse Analysis and the Bosnian War.* London: Routledge.

Harris, Peter. 2015. "America's other Guantánamo: British Foreign Policy and the US Base on Diego Garcia." *Political Quarterly* 86 (4): 507–14.

Harrison, Brian. 2009. *Seeking a Role: The United Kingdom 1951–1970.* Oxford: Oxford University Press.

– 2010. *Finding a Role? The United Kingdom, 1970–1990.* Oxford: Oxford University Press.

Haseler, Stephen. 2007. *Sidekick: Bulldog to Lapdog: British Global Strategy from Churchill to Blair.* London: ForumPress.

– 2012. *The Grand Delusion: Britain after Sixty Years of Elizabeth II.* London: IB Tauris.

Haugevik, Kristin. 2018. *Special Relationships in World Politics: Inter-State Friendship and Diplomacy after the Second World War.* London: Routledge.

Hay, Colin. 1999. "Crisis and the Structural Transformation of the State: Interrogating the Process of Change." *British Journal of Politics and International Relations* 1 (3): 317–44.

Hayes, Jarrod. 2016. "Identity, Authority, and the British War in Iraq." *Foreign Policy Analysis* 12 (3): 334–5.

Heinlein, Frank. 2002. *British Government Policy and Decolonisation, 1945–63: Scrutinising the Official Mind.* London: Frank Cass.

Henderson, Ailsa, Charlie Jeffery, Dan Wincott, and Richard Wyn Jones. 2017. "How Brexit Was Made in England." *British Journal of Politics and International Relations* 19 (4): 631–46.

Henderson, Jo. 1996. "The Falklands: National Identity and the Experience of War." In *Acts of War: The Representation of Military Conflict on the British Stage and Television since 1945*, ed. Tony Howard and John Stokes, 192–203. Aldershot: Ashgate.

Henderson, Sir Nicholas. 1979. "Britain's Decline: Its Causes and Consequences."

FCO WRF 020/1 Diplomatic Report No. 129/70. Available at the Margaret
Thatcher Foundation. https://www.margaretthatcher.org/archive/1979_
Henderson_despatch.asp.

Hennessy, P. 1996. Muddling Through: Power, Politics and the Quality of
Government in Postwar Britain. London: Weidenfeld and Nicolson.

Heuser, Beatrice. 1992. "Covert Action within British and American Concepts
of Containment, 1948–1951." In British Intelligence Strategy and the Cold
War, 1945–1951, ed. Richard Aldrich, 65–84. London: Routledge.

– 1998. Nuclear Mentalities? Strategies and Beliefs in Britain, France and the
FRG. Basingstoke and New York: Macmillan.

Hill, Christopher. 1979. "Britain's Elusive Role in World Politics." British
Journal of International Studies 5 (3): 248–59.

– 2005. "Putting the World to Rights: The Foreign Policy Mission of Tony
Blair." In The Blair Effect, 2001–5, ed. Anthony Seldon and Dennis Kavanagh,
384–409. Cambridge: Cambridge University Press.

– 2016. "Powers of a Kind: The Anomalous Position of France and the United
Kingdom in World Politics." International Affairs 92 (2): 393–414.

– 2019. The Future of British Foreign Policy: Security and Diplomacy in a World
after Brexit. London: Polity.

Hill, Christopher, and Sarah Beadle. 2014. The Art of Attraction. Soft Power
and the UK's Role in the World. London: The British Academy.

Hills, Thomas, Chanuki Illushka Seresinhe, Daniel Sgroi, and Eugenio Proto.
2019. "Historical Analysis of National Subjective Wellbeing." Nature Human
Behaviour, online first.

Hogan, Michael J. 1987. The Marshall Plan: America, Britain and the Reconstruction of Western Europe, 1947–1952. New York: Cambridge University
Press.

Holland, Robert. 1991. The Pursuit of Greatness: Britain and the World Role,
1900–1970. London: Fontana.

Holland, Jack. 2013. "Foreign Policy and Political Possibility." European
Journal of International Relations 19 (1): 49–68.

– 2020. Selling War and Peace: Syria and the Anglosphere. Cambridge: Cambridge University Press.

Honeyman, Victoria. 2007. Richard Crossman: A Reforming Radical of the
Labour Party. London: IB Tauris.

Hopf, Ted. 2002. *The Social Construction of International Politics*. Ithaca: Cornell University Press.

– 2010. "The Logic of Habit in International Relations." *European Journal of International Relations* 16 (4): 539–61.

– 2012. *Reconstructing the Cold War: The Early Years, 1945–1958*. Ithaca, NY: Cornell University Press.

– 2013. "Common-Sense Constructivism and Hegemony in World Politics." *International Organization* 67 (2): 317–54.

Hopf, Ted, and Bentley B. Allan, eds. 2016. *Making Identity Count: Building a National Identity Database*. Oxford: Oxford University Press.

Hozic, Aida, and and Jacqui True, eds. 2016. *Scandalous Economics: Gender and the Politics of Financial Crises*. Oxford: Oxford University Press.

Hughes, R. Gerald, and Thomas Robb. 2013. "Kissinger and the Diplomacy of Coercive Linkage in the 'Special Relationship' between the United States and Great Britain, 1969–77." *Diplomatic History* 37 (4): 861–905

Humphreys, Adam R. C. 2015. "From National Interest to Global Reform: Patterns of Reasoning in British Foreign Policy Discourse." *British Journal of Politics and International Relations* 17 (4): 568–84.

Hyam, Ronald. 2007. *Britain's Declining Empire: The Road to Decolonisation, 1918–1968*. Cambridge: Cambridge University Press.

Ingram, Edward. 1997. "The Wonderland of the Political Scientist." *International Security* 22 (1): 53–63.

Jackson, Ashley. 2007. "Empire and Beyond: The Pursuit of Overseas National Interests in the Late Twentieth Century," *English Historical Review* 122 (499): 1350–66.

Jepperson, Ronald. L., Alexander Wendt, and Peter J. Katzenstein. 1996. "Norms, Identity, and Culture in National Security." In *The Culture of National Security: Norms and Identity in World Politics*, ed. Peter J. Katzenstein, 33–75. New York: Columbia University Press.

Jessop, Bob. 2017. "The Organic Crisis of the British State: Putting Brexit in Its Place." *Globalizations* 14 (1): 133–41.

Jones, Matthew. 2018. "War and British Identity: A Study of Mass Observers' Perceptions of the Use of British Military Force since 1982." PhD diss., Keele University.

Johnson, Rob. 2019. "UK Defence Policy: The 'New Canada' and 'International by Design." In *The United Kingdom's Defence After Brexit: Britain's Alliances, Coalitions, and Partnerships*, ed. Rob Johnson and Janne Haaland Matlary, 33–57. London: Routledge.

Kampfner, John. 2003. *Blair's Wars*. London: Simon and Schuster.

Kenny, Michael. 2014. *The Politics of English Nationhood*. Oxford: Oxford University Press.

– 2017. "Back to the Populist Future? Understanding Nostalgia in Contemporary Ideological Discourse." *Journal of Political Ideologies* 22 (3): 256–73.

Kenny, Michael, and Nick Pearce. 2018. *Shadows of Empire: The Anglosphere in British Politics*. Cambridge: Polity.

Kertzer Joshua D., and Thomas Zeitzoff. 2017. "A Bottom-Up Theory of Public Opinion about Foreign Policy." *American Journal of Political Science* 61 (3): 543–58.

Keynes, John Maynard. 1945. "Our Overseas Financial Prospects, 13 August 1945." https://srdjanvucetic.files.wordpress.com/2018/09/keynes1945.pdf.

Kinnvall, Catarina, Ian Manners, and Jennifer Mitzen. 2018. "Ontological (in)security in the European Union." *European Security* 27 (3): 249–65.

Klotz, Audie. 2008. "Case Selection." In *Qualitative Methods in International Relations*, ed. Audie Klotz and Deepa Prakash, 43–58. London: Palgrave.

Kolko, Joyce, and Gabriel Kolko. 1972. *The Limits of Power: The World and United States Foreign Policy, 1945–1954*. New York: Harper and Row.

Koschut, Simon, Todd H. Hall, Reinhard Wolf, Ty Solomon, Emma Hutchison, and Roland Bleiker. 2017. "Discourse and Emotions in International Relations." *International Studies Review* 19 (3): 481–508.

Kumar, Krishan. 2003. *The Making of English National Identity*. Cambridge: Cambridge University.

Kurki, Milja. 2008. *Causation in International Relations: Reclaiming Causal Analysis*. Cambridge: Cambridge University Press.

Larsen, Henrik. 1997. *Foreign Policy and Discourse Analysis: France, Britain and Europe*. London: Routledge.

Lawrence, Felicity, Rob Evans, David Pegg, Caelainn Barr and Pamela Duncan. 2019. "How the Right's Radical Thinktanks Reshaped the Conservative Party." *Guardian*, 29 November. https://www.theguardian.com/politics/2019/nov/29/rightwing-thinktank-conservative-boris-johnson-brexit-atlas-network.

Lawson, George. 2012. "The Eternal Divide? History and International Relations." *European Journal of International Relations* 18 (3): 203–26.

Lee, Sabine. 1996. "Staying in the Game: Harold Macmillan and Britain's World Role." In *Harold Macmillan and Britain's World Role*, ed. Richard Aldous and Sabine Lee, 123–48. London: Palgrave Macmillan.

Legrand, T. 2020. "Transgovernmental Anglosphere Security Networks: the Constitutive Reduction of a Shared Identity." In *The Anglosphere: Continuity, Dissonance and Location*, ed. Ben Wellings and Andrew Mycock. Oxford: Oxford University Press.

Leira, Halvard, and Benjamin de Carvalho. 2016. "Construction Time Again: History in Constructivist IR Scholarship." *European Review of International Studies* 3 (3): 99–111.

LeMahieu, D.L. 1988. *A Culture for Democracy: Mass Communication and the Cultivated Mind in Britain between the Wars*. Oxford: Clarendon Press.

Lester, Nick. 2018. "A Fifth of British Troops Are Too Unfit to Fight, Warns Former Armed Forces Chief." *Daily Express*, 25 February. https://www.express.co.uk/news/uk/923677/British-Army-former-Armed-Forces-chief-warns-fifth-troops-too-unfit-action.

Little, Richard. 2008. "History, Theory and Methodological Pluralism in the English School." In *Theorizing International Society: English School Methods*, ed. Cornelia Navari, 78–103. Basingstoke: Macmillan.

Louis, W. Roger. 2006. *Ends of British Imperialism: The Scramble for Empire, Suez and Decolonization*. London: IB Tauris.

Louis W. Roger, and Ronald Robinson. 1994. "The Imperialism of Decolonization." *Journal of Imperial and Commonwealth History* 22 (3): 462–511.

– 2004. "Britain and the Middle East after 1945." In *Diplomacy in the Middle East the International Relations of Regional and Outside Powers*, ed. L. Carl Brown, 21–58. London: IB Tauris.

Ludlow, N. Piers. 2015. "Safeguarding British Identity or Betraying It? The Role of British 'Tradition' in the Parliamentary Great Debate on EC Membership, October 1971." *Journal of Common Market Studies* 53 (1): 18–34.

Mabon, Simon, Mark Garnett, and Robert Smith. 2017. *British Foreign Policy Since 1945*. London: Routledge.

MacDonald, Alistair. 2019. "Sources of Soft Power," British Council Report. https://www.britishcouncil.org/sites/default/files/sources-soft-power-report-perceptions-success.pdf.

Macleod, Alex. 1997. "Great Britain: Still Searching for Status?" In *Role Quests in the Post–Cold War Era: Foreign Policies in Transition*, ed. Philippe G. Le Prestre, 161–86. Montreal and Kingston: McGill-Queen's University Press.

Mangold, Peter. 2001. *Success and Failure in British Foreign Policy: Evaluating the Record, 1900–2000*. London: Palgrave.

Marcussen, Martin, Thomas Risse, Daniela Engelmann-Martin, Hans Joachim Knopf, and Klaus Roscher. 1999."Constructing Europe? The Evolution of French, British and German Nation State Identities." *Journal of European Public Policy* 6 (4): 614–33.

Marsh, Steve. 2019. "Anglo-American Relations and the Past Present: Insights into an (Ongoing) Mythologisation of a Special Relationship." *Journal of Transatlantic Studies* 17 (3): 310–40.

Mattern, Janice Bially. 2005. *Ordering International Politics: Identity, Crisis and Representational Force*. London: Routledge.

MccGwire, Michael. 2006. "Comfort Blanket or Weapon of War: What Is Trident For?," *International Affairs* 82 (4): 639–50.

McClintock, Anne. 1995. *Imperial Leather: Race, Gender, and Sexuality in the Colonial Contest*. New York: Routledge.

McCormack, Theresa. 2011. "From 'Ethical Foreign Policy' to National Security Strategy: Exporting Domestic Incoherence." In *British Foreign Policy: The New Labour Years*, ed. Oliver Daddow and Jamie Gaskarth, 103–22. New York: Springer.

McCourt, David M. 2011. "Rethinking Britain's Role in the World for a New Decade: The Limits of Discursive Therapy and the Promise of Field Theory." *British Journal of Politics and International Relations* 13 (2): 145–64.

– 2013. "Embracing Humanitarian Intervention: Atlanticism and the UK Interventions in Bosnia and Kosovo." *British Journal of Politics and International Relations* 15 (2): 246–62.

– 2014a. *Britain and World Power since 1945: Constructing a Nation's Role in International Politics*. Ann Arbor: University of Michigan Press.

– 2014b. "Has Britain Found Its Role?" *Survival* 56 (2): 159–78.

Martill, Benjamin, and Monika Sus. 2014. "Post-Brexit EU/UK Security Cooperation: NATO, CDSP+, or 'French Connection'?" *British Journal of Politics and International Relations* 20 (4): 846–63.

Mckenzie, Francine. 2006. "In the National Interest: Dominions' Support for

Britain and the Commonwealth after the Second World War." *Journal of Imperial and Commonwealth History* 34 (4): 553–76.

Milward, Alan. 2003. *The Rise and Fall of a National Strategy, 1945–1963*. Vol 1: *The UK and the European Community*. London: Frank Cass.

Mitts, Tamar. 2019. "Terrorism and the Rise of Right-wing Content in Israeli Books." *International Organization* 73 (1): 203–24.

Mitzen, Jennifer. 2006. "Ontological Security in World Politics: State Identity and the Security Dilemma." *European Journal of International Relations* 12, (3): 341–70.

Mondon, Aurélien, and Aaron Winter. 2018. "Whiteness, Populism and the Racialisation of the Working Class in the United Kingdom and the United States." *Identities* 26 (5): 510–28.

Morris, Justin. 2011. "How Great Is Britain? Power, Responsibility and Britain's Future Global Role." *British Journal of Politics and International Relations* 13 (3): 326–47.

Mumford, Densua, and Torsten J. Selck. 2010. "New Labour's Ethical Dimension: Statistical Trends in Tony Blair's Foreign Policy Speeches." *British Journal of Politics and International Relations* 12: 295–312.

Murphy, Philip. 2012. "Britain as a Global Power in the Twentieth Century," in *Britain's Experience of Empire in the Twentieth Century*, ed. Andrew Thompson, 33–75. Oxford: Oxford University Press.

Murray, Donette. 2000. *Kennedy, Macmillan and Nuclear Weapons*. Basingstoke: Macmillan.

Murray, Michelle K. 2019. *The Struggle for Recognition in International Relations, Status, Revisionism, and Rising Powers*. Oxford: Oxford University Press.

NBC News. 1963. "President Kennedy Proclaims Winston Churchill First Honorary Citizen of US." NBC News Archive, https://archives.nbclearn.com/portal/site/k-12/browse/?cuecard=64695.

Namusoke, Eva. 2016. "A Divided Family: Race, the Commonwealth and Brexit." *Round Table* 105 (5): 463–76.

Navari, Cornelia. 2008. "What the Classical English School Was Trying to Explain, and Why Its Members Were Not Interested in Causal Explanation." In *Theorizing International Society: English School Methods*, ed. Cornelia Navari, 39–57. Basingstoke: Macmillan.

Neuendorf, Kimberly A. 2004. "Content Analysis: A Contrast and Complement to Discourse Analysis." *Qualitative Methods: Newsletter of the American Political Science Association Organized Section on Qualitative Methods* 2
(1): 33–6.

Noyes, Dorothy, and Tobias Wille. 2020. Framing paper for the conference
"Exemplarity: Performance, Influence, and Friction in Political Innovation."
The Mershon Center for International Security Studies, Columbus, Ohio,
27–29 February.

Oliver, Tim. 2018. *Understanding Brexit: A Concise Introduction*. Bristol: Policy
Press.

Onslow, Sue. 1997. *Backbench Debate within the Conservative Party and Its
Influence on British Foreign Policy, 1948–57*. New York: St Martin's Press.

O'Toole, Fintan. 2018. *Heroic Failure: Brexit and the Politics of Pain*. London:
Head of Zeus.

Oppermann, Kai, Ryan K. Beasley, and Juliet Kaarbo. 2019. "British Foreign
Policy after Brexit: Losing Europe and Finding a Role." *International Relations* 1–24, https://doi.org/10.1177/0047117819864421.

Paul, Kathleen. 1997. *Whitewashing Britain: Race and Citizenship in the Postwar Era*. Ithaca, NY: Cornell University Press.

Parmar, Inderjeet. 2005. "'I'm Proud of the British Empire': Why Tony Blair
Backs George W. Bush." *Political Quarterly* 76 (2): 218–31.

Parr, Helen. 2006. "Britain, America, East of Suez and the EEC: Finding a Role
in British Foreign Policy, 1964–67." *Contemporary British History* 20 (3):
403–21.

– 2014. "National Interest and the Falklands War." In *British Foreign Policy and
the National Interest*, ed. Timothy Edmunds, Jamie Gaskarth, Robin Porter,
66–82. London: Palgrave Macmillan.

Peden, George C. 2012. "Suez and Britain's Decline as a World Power."
Historical Journal 55 (4): 1073–96.

Peyrefitte, Alain. 1994. *C'était de Gaulle*. Paris: Editions de Fallois-Fayard.

Pierre, Andrew. 1972. *Nuclear Politics*. Oxford: Oxford University Press.

Perkins, Frank. 2003. "A Year in Japan, Post-Hiroshima: Cameron High-
landers as Occupation Force." BBC WW2 People's War Archive. https://www.
bbc.co.uk/history/ww2peopleswar/stories/57/a1143857.shtml.

Porter, Patrick. 2010. "Why Britain Doesn't Do Grand Strategy." *RUSI Journal*
155 (4): 6–12.

– 2018. *Blunder: Britain's War in Iraq*. Oxford: Oxford University Press.

Pythian, Mark. 2007. *The Labour Party, War and International Relations*. London: Routledge.

Raab, Dominic. 2012. "Unleashing the British Underdog." Centre for Policy Studies. https://www.cps.org.uk/research/unleashing-the-british-underdog/.

Ralph, Jason. 2011. "A Difficult Relationship: Britain's 'Doctrine of International Community' and America's 'War on Terror.'" In *British Foreign Policy: The New Labour Years*, ed. Oliver Daddow and Jaime Gaskarth, 123–38. Basingstoke: Palgrave Macmillan.

Rasmi, Adam. 2019. "Only 1% of Brits Cared Much about the EU before the 2016 Brexit Vote." *Quartz*, 10 October. https://qz.com/1725402/only-1-per cent-of-brits-cared-about-the-eu-before-brexit/.

Rees, Wyn. 2001. "Britain's Contribution to Global Order." In *Britain and Defence, 1945–2000: A Policy Re-evaluation*, ed. Stuart Croft, Andrew Dorman, Wyn Rees and Matthew Uttley, 29-48. Harlow: Pearson.

Reifler, Jason, Harold D. Clarke, Thomas J. Scotto, Paul Whiteley, David Sanders, and Marianne C Stewart. 2014. "Prudence, Principle and Minimal Heuristics: British Public Opinion Toward the Use of Military Force in Afghanistan and Libya." *British Journal of Politics and International Relations* 16 (1): 28–55.

Reynolds, David. 2000. *Britannia Overruled: British Policy and World Power in the Twentieth Century*. 2nd ed. London: Routledge.

– 2017. "Britain, the Two World Wars, and the Problem of Narrative." *Historical Journal* 60 (1): 197–231.

Richardson, Louise. 1992. "Avoiding and Incurring Losses: Decision-Making in the Suez Crisis." *International Journal* 47 (2): 370–401.

Rifkind, Malcolm. 2010. "The Future of UK Foreign Policy: Sir Malcolm Rifkind." In *IDEAS reports – special reports*, ed. Nicholas Kitchen. *LSE Research Online*, http://eprints.lse.ac.uk/43554/1/The%20future%20of%20UK%20foreign%20policy_Sir%20Malcolm%20Rifkind(lsero).pdf.

Reuters. 2019. "Britain to Become 'Second Rate' in the World after Brexit: EU's Tusk." 13 November, https://www.reuters.com/article/us-britain-eu-tusk/britain-to-become-second-rate-in-the-world-after-brexit-eus-tusk-idUSKBN1XN2MG.

Ritchie, Nick. 2012. *A Nuclear Weapons-Free World? Britain, Trident and the Challenges Ahead*. Basingstoke: Palgrave Macmillan.

Robbins, Keith. 1998. *Great Britain: Identities, Institutions and the Idea of Britishness*. Harlow: Longmans.

Robinson, Ronald and John Gallagher, with Alice Denny. 1961. *Africa and the Victorians: The Official Mind of Imperialism*. London: Macmillan.

Rogers, Paul. 2006. "Big Boats and Bigger Skimmers: Determining Britain's Role in the Long War." *International Affairs* 82 (4): 651–65.

Røren, Pål. and Paul Beaumont. 2019. "Grading Greatness: Evaluating the Status Performance of the BRICS." *Third World Quarterly* 40 (3): 429–50.

Rossdale, Chris. 2015. "Enclosing Critique: The Limits of Ontological Security." *International Political Sociology* 9 (3): 369–86.

Rubin, Bret. 2010. "The Rise and Fall of British Fascism: Sir Oswald Mosley and the British Union of Fascists," *Intersections* 11 (2): 323–80.

Runnymede Trust and the TIDE Project. 2019. "Teaching Migration, Belonging and Empire in Secondary Schools." University of Liverpool, 3 July. https://www.runnymedetrust.org/uploads/images/TIDE%20&%20%20 Runnymede%20Teaching%20Migration%20report%204.7.19.pdf.

Sanders, David, and David Patrick Houghton. 2017. *Losing an Empire, Finding a Role: British Foreign Policy since 1945*. New York: Macmillan International Higher Education.

Sanders, David, and Geoffrey Edwards. 1994. "Consensus and Diversity in Elite Opinion: The Views of the British Foreign Policy Elite in the early 1990s." *Political Studies* 42: 413–40.

Saunders, Robert A., and Vlad Strukov. 2018. *Popular Geopolitics Plotting an Evolving Interdiscipline*. London: Routledge.

Saunders, Robert. 2018. *Yes to Europe! The 1975 Referendum and Seventies Britain*. Cambridge: Cambridge University Press.

– 2019. "The Myth of Brexit as Imperial Nostalgia." *Prospect Magazine*, 7 January. https://www.prospectmagazine.co.uk/world/the-myth-of-brexit-as-imperial-nostalgia.

Savage, Mike. 2010. *Identities and Social Change in Britain since 1940: The Politics of Method*. Oxford: Oxford University Press.

Schaad, Martin. 1998. "Plan G-A 'Counterblast'? British Policy towards the Messina Countries, 1956." *Contemporary European History* 7 (1): 39–60.

Shonfield, Andrew. 1958. *British Economic Policy Since the War*. London: Penguin

Schenk, Catherine. 2010. *The Decline of Sterling: Managing the Retreat of an International Currency, 1945–1992*. Cambridge: Cambridge University Press.

Schnapper, Pauline. 2011. *British Political Parties and National Identity: A Changing Discourse 1997–2010*. Cambridge: Cambridge Scholars Publishing.

Schneer, Jonathan. 1984. "Hopes Deferred or Shattered: The British Labour Left and the Third Force Movement, 1945–49." *Journal of Modern History* 56 (2): 198–226.

Schofield, Camilla. 2013. *Enoch Powell and the Making of Postcolonial Britain*. Cambridge: Cambridge University Press.

– 2019. "Brexit and Other Special Relationship." In *Embers of Empire in Brexit Britain*, ed. Stuart Ward and Astrid Rasch, 87–100. London: Bloomsbury.

Self, Robert. 2010. *British Foreign and Defence Policy since 1945: Challenges and Dilemmas in a Changing World*. Basingstoke: Palgrave Macmillan.

Sharma, Mihir. "Britain's a Small Country." *Bloomberg Opinion*, 16 January 2019, https://www.bloomberg.com/opinion/articles/2019-01-16/post-brexit-britain-should-get-used-to-being-a-small-country.

Shaw, Tony. 1996. *Eden, Suez and the Mass Media: Propaganda and Persuasion during the Suez Crisis*. London: IB Tauris.

Shilliam, Robbie. 2018. *Race and the Undeserving Poor: From Abolition to Brexit*. Newcastle upon Tyne: Agenda Publishing.

Shifrinson, Joshua R. 2018. *Rising Titans, Falling Giants: How Great Powers Exploit Power Shifts*. Ithaca, NY: Cornell University Press.

Simms, Brendan. 2016. *Britain's Europe: A Thousand Years of Conflict and Cooperation*. London: Penguin UK.

– 2001. *Unfinest Hour: Britain and the Destruction of Bosnia*. London: Allen Lane.

Skey, Michael. 2009. *National Belonging and Everyday Life*. Basingstoke: Palgrave.

– 2010. "'A Sense of Where You Belong in the World': National Belonging, Ontological Security and the Status of the Ethnic Majority in England." *Nations and Nationalism* 16 (4): 715–33.

Slobodian, Quinn. 2018. "Against the Neoliberalism Taboo." *Focaal blog*, 12 January. https://www.focaalblog.com/2018/01/12/quinn-slobodian-against-the-neoliberalism-taboo/.

Smith, Julie. 2017. *The UK's Journeys into and out of the EU: Destinations Unknown*. London: Routledge.

Smith, Evan, and Steven Gray. 2016. "Brexit, Imperial Nostalgia and the 'White Man's World.'" *History and Policy*. http://www.historyandpolicy. org/opinion-articles/articles/brexit-imperial-nostalgia-and-the-white-mans-world.

Smith, Matthew. 2020. "How unique are British attitudes to empire?" YouGov International, 11 March. https://yougov.co.uk/topics/international/articles-reports/2020/03/11/how-unique-are-british-attitudes-empire.

Smith, Simon C., ed. 2008. *Reassessing Suez 1956: New Perspectives on the Crisis and Its Aftermath*. Aldershot: Ashgate.

Spelling, Alex. 2009. "Edward Heath and Anglo–American Relations 1970–1974: A Reappraisal." *Diplomacy and Statecraft* 20 (4): 638–58.

Spiering, Menno. 2014. *A Cultural History of British Euroscepticism*. Basingstoke: Palgrave.

Sprout, Harold, and Margaret Sprout. 1963. "Retreat from World Power: Processes and Consequences of Readjustment." *World Politics* 15, (30): 655–88.

Steele, Brent J. 2008. *Ontological Security in International Relations: Self-identity and the IR State*. London: Routledge.

Stockwell, A.J. 2008. "Suez 1956 and the Moral Disarmament of the British Empire." In *Reassessing Suez 1956: New Perspectives on the Crisis and Its Aftermath*, ed. Simon C. Smith, 227–38. Aldershot: Ashgate Publishing ltd.

Stockwell, Sarah. 2018. *The British End of the British Empire*. Cambridge: Cambridge University Press.

Strange, Susan. 1971. *Sterling and British Policy*. Oxford: Oxford University Press.

Strong, James. 2017. *Public Opinion, Legitimacy and Tony Blair's War in Iraq*. London: Routledge.

– 2018. "Using Role Theory to Analyse British Military Intervention in the Syrian Civil War during David Cameron's Premiership." *British Politics* 12 (1): 42–62.

Suboti , Jelena. 2015. "Narrative, Ontological Security, and Foreign Policy Change." *Foreign Policy Analysis* 12 (4): 610–27.

Subotić, Jelena, and Brent J. Steele. 2018. "Moral Injury in International Relations." *Journal of Global Security Studies* 3 (4): 387–401.

Suzuki, Shogo. 2018. "'World Is Marvelling at Japan!': Japanese Strategies to Cope with 'Decline.'" Paper presented at the 59th Annual Convention of the International Studies Association in San Francisco, California, 4–7 April.

Taylor, Peter J. 2016 [1991]. *Britain and the Cold War: 1945 as Geopolitical Transition*. London: Bloomsbury Academic.

Tate, Simon. 2012. *A Special Relationship? British Foreign Policy in the Era of American Hegemony*. Manchester: University of Manchester Press.

Thackeray, David, and Richard Toye, 2019. "Debating Empire 2.0." In *Embers of Empire in Brexit Britain*, ed. Stuart Ward and Astrid Rasch, 15–24. London: Bloomsbury.

Thatcher, Margaret. 3 1982. "Speech to Conservative Rally at Cheltenham." https://www.margaretthatcher.org/document/104989.

Thomas, Martin, and Richard Toye. 2017. *Arguing about Empire: Imperial Rhetoric in Britain and France, 1882–1956*. Oxford: Oxford University Press.

Thomas, Martin. 2014. *Fight or Flight? Britain, France, and their Roads from Empire*, Oxford: Oxford University Press.

Todd, John. 2016. *The UK's Relationship with Europe: Struggling over Sovereignty*. London: Routledge.

Tomlinson, Jim. 2017. *Managing the Economy, Managing the People: Narratives of Economic Life in Britain from Beveridge to Brexit*. Oxford: Oxford University Press.

Tooze, Adam. 2017. "Logics of Brexit and the Perils of 'Owning the Economy': Engaging with Watkins and Davies." Personal blog post, 7 March. https:// adamtooze.com/2017/03/07/logics-brexit-perils-owning-economy-engaging-watkins-davies/.

Toye, Richard. 2013. "Words of Change: The Rhetoric of Commonwealth, Common Market, and Cold War, 1961–3." In *The Wind of Change: Harold Macmillan and British Decolonization*, ed. Larry Butler and Sarah Stockwell, 140–58. Basingstoke: Palgrave Macmillan.

Towle, Philip. 2009. *Going to War: British Debates from Wilberforce to Blair*. Basingstoke: Palgrave Macmillan.

Travis, Alan. 2011. "Thatcher Went behind Cabinet's Back with Trident Purchase." *Guardian*, 30 December. https://www.theguardian.com/uk/2011/ dec/30/thatcher-cabinet-opposed-trident-purchase.

Tugendhat, Christopher, and William Wallace. 1988. *Options for British Foreign Policy in the 1990s*. London: Routledge/RIIA.

Uttley, Matthew, Benedict Wilkinson, and Armida van Rij. 2019. "A Power for the Future? Global Britain and the Future Character of Conflict." *International Affairs* 95 (4): 801–16.

Valluvan, Sivamohan. 2019. *The Clamour of Nationalism: Race and Nation in Twenty-First-Century Britain*. Manchester: Manchester University Press.

Vernon, James. 2017. *Modern Britain, 1750 to the Present*. Cambridge: Cambridge University Press.

Verrier, Anthony. 1983. *Through the Looking Glass: British Foreign Policy in an Age of Illusions*. London: Jonathan Cape.

Vickers, Rhiannon. 2003. *The Labour Party and the World*. Vol. 1: *The Evolution of Labour's Foreign Policy, 1900–51*. Manchester: Manchester University Press.

– 2011. *The Labour Party and the World*. Vol 2: *The Evolution of Labour's Foreign Policy, 1900–51*. Manchester: Manchester University Press.

Vieira, Marco A. 2018. "'(Re-)imagining the 'Self' of Ontological Security: The Case of Brazil's Ambivalent Postcolonial Subjectivity." *Millennium* 46 (2): 142–64.

Vucetic, Srdjan. 2004. "Identity Is a Joking Matter: Intergroup Humor in Bosnia." *Spaces of Identity* 3 (2): 1–28.

– 2011a. "Genealogy as a Research Tool in International Relations." *Review of International Studies* 37 (3): 1295–312.

– 2011b. *The Anglosphere: A Genealogy of a Racialized Identity in International Relations*. Stanford, CA: Stanford University Press.

– 2011c. "A Racialized Peace? How Britain and the US Made Their Relationship Special." *Foreign Policy Analysis* 7 (3): 403–21.

– 2011d. "What Is So American about the American Empire?" *International Politics* 48 (2–3): 251–70.

– 2016a. "British National Identity and the Anglo-American Special Relationship." *Journal of Transatlantic Studies* 14 (3): 272–92.

– 2016b. "Making It Count Beyond IR." In *Making Identity Count: Towards a National Identity Database*, ed. Ted Hopf and Bentley Allan, 201–18. Oxford: University of Oxford Press.

– 2017a. "Identity and Foreign Policy." *Oxford Research Encyclopedia of Politics*. https://oxfordre.com/politics/view/10.1093/acrefore/9780190228637.001.0001/acrefore-9780190228637-e-435.

– 2017b. "The Global in Canada." *International Journal* 72 (2): 217–29.

– 2017c. "A Nation of Feminist Arms Dealers? Canada and Military Exports," *International Journal* 72 (4): 503–19.

– 2018. "Identity and Foreign Policy." In *Oxford Bibliographies in International*

Relations, ed. Patrick James. New York: Oxford University Press. https://www.oxfordbibliographies.com/view/document/obo-9780199743292/obo-978019 9743292-0250.xml.

– 2019a. "Making Identity Count: UK 1950." *SocArXiv*. https://osf.io/eyd4b/.

– 2019b. "Making Identity Count: UK 1960." *SocArXiv*. https://osf.io/eyd4b/.

– 2019c. "Making Identity Count: UK 1970." *SocArXiv*. https://osf.io/eyd4b/.

– 2020a. "America in "British" History Textbooks." In *Culture Matters: Anglo-American Relations and the Intangibles of "Specialness*," ed. Steve Marsh and Robert M. Hendershot, 41–65. Manchester: Manchester University Press.

– 2020b. "The Anglosphere beyond Security." In *The Anglosphere: Continuity, Dissonance and Location*, ed. Ben Wellings and Andrew Mycock, 77–91. Oxford: Oxford University Press.

Vucetic, Srdjan, and T. Hopf. 2020. "Everyday Nationalism and Making Identity Count." *Nationalities Papers*. https://www.cambridge.org/core /journals/nationalities-papers/firstview.

Vucetic, Srdjan, and Kristen Olver. 2019. "Making Identity Count: UK 1990." *SocArXiv*. https://osf.io/eyd4b/.

Vucetic, Srdjan, and David Orr. 2019. "Making Identity Count: UK 1980." *SocArXiv*. https://osf.io/eyd4b/.

Wallace, William. 1970. "World Status without Tears." In *The Age of Affluence: 1951–1964*, ed. Vernon Bogdanor and Robert Skidelsky, 53–68. New York: Macmillan.

– 1975. *The Foreign Policy Process in Britain*. London: Royal Institute of International Affairs/Allen Unwin.

– 1990. *The Transformation of Western Europe*. London: Royal Institute of International Affairs/Pinter.

– 1991. "Foreign Policy and National Identity in the United Kingdom." *International Affairs* 67 (1): 65–80.

– 2005a. "The Collapse of British Foreign Policy." *International Affairs* 81 (1): 53–68.

– 2005b. *Europe or the Anglosphere? British foreign policy between Atlanticism and European Integration*. London: John Stuart Mill Institute.

Walton, Calder. 2013. *Empire of Secrets: British Intelligence, the Cold War and the Twilight of Empire*. London: HarperPress.

Waltz, Kenneth Neal. 1967. *Foreign Policy and Democratic Politics: The American and British Experience*. New York: Little, Brown and Company.

Ward, Paul. 2004. *Britishness since 1870*. London: Routledge.

Ward, Steven. 2019. "Logics of Stratified Identity Management in World Politics." *International Theory* 11 (2): 211–38.

Ward, Stuart, and Astrid Rasch. 2019. "Introduction: Greater Britain, Global Britain." In *Embers of Empire in Brexit Britain*, ed. Ward and Rasch, 1–14. London: Bloomsbury.

Wearing, David. 2014. "Critical Perspectives on the Concept of the 'National Interest': American Imperialism, British Foreign Policy and the Middle East." In *British Foreign Policy and the National Interest*, ed. Timothy Edmunds, Jamie Gaskarth and Robin Porter, 102–19. Basingstoke: Palgrave Macmillan.

– 2018. *AngloArabia: Why Gulf Wealth Matters to Britain*. London: Polity.

Webster, Wendy. 2005. *Englishness and Empire, 1939–1965*. Oxford: Oxford University Press.

Wellings, Ben. 2019. *English Nationalism, Brexit and the Anglosphere*. Manchester: Manchester University Press.

Wellings, Ben, and Andrew Mycock, eds. 2020. *The Anglosphere: Continuity, Dissonance and Location*. Oxford: Oxford University Press.

Wendt, Alexander. 1999. *Social Theory of International Politics*. Cambridge: Cambridge University Press.

Whitmeyer, Joseph. 2002. "Elites and Popular Nationalism." *British Journal of Sociology* 53 (3): 321–41.

Whittaker, Nick. 2017. "The Island Race: Ontological Security and Critical Geopolitics in British Parliamentary Discourse." *Geopolitics* 23 (4): 1–32.

Whitman, Richard G. 2019. "The UK's European Diplomatic Strategy for Brexit and Beyond." *International Affairs* 95 (2): 383–404.

Wickham-Jones, Mark. 2000. "Labour's Trajectory in Foreign Affairs: The Moral Crusade of a Pivotal Power?" In *New Labour's Foreign Policy: A New Moral Crusade?*, ed. Richard Little and Mark Wickham-Jones, 3–32, Manchester: Manchester University Press.

Willcox, David. R. 2005. *Propaganda, the Press and the Conflict. The Gulf War and Kosovo*. London: Routledge.

Williams, Paul. 2005. *British Foreign Policy under New Labour, 1997–2005*. Basingstoke: Palgrave Macmillan.

Young, Hugo. 1998. *This Blessed Plot: Britain and Europe from Churchill to Blair*. London: Macmillan.

Young, John W. 1989. "'The Parting of Ways'? Britain, the Messina Conference and the Spaak Committee, June-December 1955." In *British Foreign Policy, 1945–56*, ed. Michael Dockrill and John W. Young, 197–224. Basingstoke: Macmillan.

Zarakol, Ay e. 2011. *After Defeat, How the East Learned to Live with the West.* Cambridge: Cambridge University Press.

– 2017. "States and Ontological Security: A Historical Rethinking." *Cooperation and Conflict* 52 (1): 48–68.

Index